TAKEN FOR A RIDE

29/9/09

TAKEN FOR A RIDE

FRANCIS P.M. HYLAND

Gill & Macmillan

Gill & Macmillan Ltd
Hume Avenue, Park West, Dublin 12
with associated companies throughout the world
www.gillmacmillan.ie

© Francis P.M. Hyland 2006

ISBN-13: 978 07171 4016 9
ISBN-10: 0 7171 4016 4

Index compiled by Helen Litton
Typography design by Make Communication
Print origination by Carole Lynch
Printed by Nørhaven Paperback A/S, Denmark

This book is typeset in Minion 10pt on 12.5pt.

The paper used in this book is made from the wood pulp of
managed forests. For every tree felled, at least one tree is
planted, thereby renewing natural resources.

A CIP catalogue record for this book is available
from the British Library.

5 4 3 2 1

If you must play, decide upon three things at the start: the rules of the game, the stakes and the quitting time.

—CHINESE PROVERB

I believe in luck: how else can you explain the success of those you dislike?

—JEAN COCTEAU

CONTENTS

GLOSSARY OF RACING TERMS

Action:	The comportment of a horse in motion.
All Right:	Signal that the winner has weighed-in and the result of the race is official.
Allowance:	A weight concession for young, inexperienced jockeys.
Ante-Post:	Denotes bets struck before the day of the race and settled according to the rule, 'All in, run or not', meaning that if the horse does not run the bet is a loser.
Apprentice:	A young jockey attached to a training stable and entitled to claim an allowance.
Backer:	A person who places a bet on a horse.
Betting Ring:	An area of a racecourse where bookmakers take bets.
Blaze:	A large white marking on a horse's forehead and face.
Boring:	When a horse pushes another in front of it during a race.
Break down:	An injury to the suspensory ligament in the leg.
Breeding:	A horse's pedigree.
Bridle:	Headpiece consisting of a bit, a noseband and reins.
Brood Mare:	A mare breeding at stud.
Bumper:	A race restricted to Amateur riders, now known as Qualified riders.
Colours:	The silk jacket and cap worn by the jockey.
Colt:	An entire male horse under the age of five.
Dam:	The mother of a horse.
Dead One:	A horse that is not 'off', in other words not trying to win the race.

Distance:	Nowadays a margin of over twenty lengths; it originally meant 240 yards.
Doping:	The administering of stimulants or drugs to a horse.
Double:	A bet involving two horses and requiring both to win.
Each Way:	A bet to win and a bet to place.
Enquiry:	An investigation into a race conducted by the stewards.
Entire Horse:	A male horse that has not been gelded.
Even Money:	Betting odds of one-for-one.
Favourite:	The horse that is at the shortest odds in the betting.
Field:	A collective term for all the runners in a race.
Filly:	A female horse under the age of five years.
Fired:	A hot iron applied to a horse's leg as a cure.
Form:	The racing record of a horse.
Furlong:	Imperial measure of 220 yards or one-eighth of a mile.
Gallops:	Exercise courses on a training ground.
Gelding:	A castrated male horse.
Going:	The state of the ground, which can range from firm to heavy.
Guinea:	An old coin used by auctioneers and worth £1.05. The commission was simple to calculate—the buyer paid by the guinea and the vendor was paid by the pound.
Hand:	A measure (4 in.) used to determine a horse's height.
Handicap:	A race in which the horses are set to carry different weights.
Hanging:	When a horse strays from a straight line during a race.
Horse:	A male entire horse aged five years or more.
Irons:	The stirrups.
Jade:	A horse that lacks courage.

Jammy: A sporting term for 'lucky', dating from the mid-nineteenth century.

Judge: An official who lists the order in which the horses finish a race.

Juvenile: A two-year-old colt or filly.

Knacker: One whose trade is to buy animals for slaughter.

Lad: A man, or woman, who looks after a horse.

Lay Horse: A bookmaker taking bets against a particular horse winning a race.

Layer: A person backing a horse at odds-on, although the term is usually used to denote a bookmaker.

Leg: Antiquated term for a bookmaker, in use until the mid-nineteenth century.

Length: About 8 ft: the approximate length of a horse from head to tail.

Maiden: A horse of either sex that has yet to win a race.

Mare: A female horse aged five years or more.

Match: A race between two horses.

Monkey: A slang term for 500.

Multiple bet: A bet involving a number of horses.

National Hunt: General term for jump-racing, which includes steeplechases, hurdles and bumpers.

Newmarket Rules: The Jockey Club Rules of Racing.

Niggle: The movement of a jockey's hands during a race.

Nobbling: The act of interfering with a horse to prevent it from winning.

Nursery: A handicap race confined to horses aged two years.

Objection: Protest lodged by the connections of a defeated horse alleging that rules were broken.

Odds-against: Betting odds greater than even money.

Odds-on: Betting odds less than even money.

Off:	The start of a race.
Outsider:	A horse that is offered at long odds in the betting.
Overweight:	Surplus weight due to rider being too heavy to make correct poundage.
Pacemaker:	A horse that runs to ensure that a race is run at a true pace.
Paddock:	The parade ring area of a racecourse where horses are saddled before a race.
Pari-Mutuel:	The French totalisator system of betting.
Penalty:	An extra weight imposed on a horse for wins.
Pipe-opener:	A gallop to clear a horse's wind.
Place:	Usually refers to a horse that finishes second or third.
Plunger:	An eighteenth-century term for a heavy and reckless gambler.
Point-to-Point:	Races confined to horses that have been regularly hunted.
Pony:	A slang term for twenty-five.
Pundits:	Knowledgable people who give their verdict, usually on radio or television.
Punter:	A person who bets.
Rails:	The white fence that marks out the course.
Retainer:	A fee paid for an option on a jockey's services.
Ringer:	The illegal substitution of one horse in place of another.
School:	To teach a horse to jump.
Show:	A list of betting odds.
Sock:	A short white mark just over a horse's hoof.
Springer:	A horse that is suddenly and unexpectedly in demand in the betting market.
Sprinter:	A horse that runs best at five or six furlongs.
Stake money:	The prize money on offer to the winner and the placed horses.
Stallion:	A horse breeding at stud.

Star:	A small white mark on a horse's forehead.
Starter's Orders:	The runners are ready to race—all bets now stand.
Starting Price:	The odds available at the start of a race used to settle off-course bets.
Stayer:	A horse that runs best at distances over a mile-and-a-half.
Steeplechase:	A race over fences and ditches.
Stewards:	Panel of referees that ensures the Rules of Racing are not broken.
Stipendiary Steward:	A professional advisor to the stewards.
Stocking:	A long white 'sock' extending up a horse's leg.
String:	A term applied to a number of horses.
Tic-tac:	Bookmakers' sign language.
Totalisator:	The mechanical system of pool betting known as the Tote.
Tout:	A person who watches horses in training and sells reports of their work.
Training Owners:	A horse trainer's skill of keeping his owners sweet.
Treble:	A bet involving three horses and requiring all three to win.
Trial:	A private race to determine the merit of a horse.
Under Starter's Orders:	Ready to race, a white flag is raised and all bets stand.
Walkover:	When only one runner takes part in a race.
Warned-off:	Banned from attending a meeting or holding a licence.
Weigh-in:	Procedure by which jockeys are weighed after a race.
Weight cloth:	A pouch carried under the saddle to hold lead weight.
Wing:	The barricades on either side of a jump.
Withers:	A bony lump at the base of a horse's neck; a horse is measured to this point for size.

PART 1
THE CASH COWS

'If there were two birds sitting on a fence,
he would bet you which one would fly first.'

MARK TWAIN

The Evolution of the bookie

Innkeepers were the first people to recognise horse-racing as a spectator sport. Realising that people would turn out to watch horses racing, these innkeepers began to sponsor the running of races close by their establishments as a way of boosting business. At first the sponsorship was merely the provision of a changing room and a meal for the two owners and the stakeholder, but soon it developed into the offer of prize money. The most famous of these innkeepers was William Lynn, reputed to be the best fish chef in the business and owner of the Waterloo Hotel in Liverpool. His main sponsorships were the Grand National and the famous coursing event, the Waterloo Cup, but while these races prospered, Lynn did not. The cost of the sponsorship took its toll. Other hotels, not bearing any of the costs, offered stiff competition to his establishment and a huge loss could be brought about by circumstances completely outside his control, such as bad weather, or an unexpected competing meeting in the vicinity. The sponsorship broke Lynn but proved a lesson for other hoteliers: they protected themselves by offering betting services on the races they sponsored.

Once betting services were available in hotels, inns and clubs throughout the land, a big off-course betting market was established. Prices were offered on an 'all in, run or not' basis and betting on races became a big and profitable industry. Rather than take the risks involved in individual sponsorship, the vintners organised themselves into groups to sponsor races, the most famous being the Grand Metropolitan Handicap and the City and Suburban Handicap, both run at Epsom, the former being sponsored by the London Metropolitan vintners, the latter by the City of London vintners. However, problems soon surfaced for this flourishing business as social problems associated with gambling began to get the attention of Parliament. It soon became clear that ordinary people were losing heavily; betting was causing misery; and families were being evicted from their homes as bookies collected gambling debts. It did not take Parliament long to understand that alcohol and betting did not mix and the trade was drastically changed by a succession of Parliamentary Bills passed between 1853 and 1906. First betting in pubs and hotels was banned, then betting shops were made illegal and finally street betting was prohibited. The eventual result was that the only place where it was legal to place a cash bet was on the racecourse.

'Legs'

Originally, horse races were two-horse affairs called 'matches'. Horse owners competed for their own money, while friends, neighbours and acquaintances joined in by laying side-bets. While some matches were local affairs and passed the time, others were huge events, watched by thousands of people, many of whom travelled long distances to place their bets and bellow at the racing horses. One such match took place on the Curragh in September 1751. This was a two-horse race, contended by *Black and All Black* and *Bajazet*, whose owners had an even £1,000 with each other on the outcome of the race. However, it is estimated that their followers had wagered over £10,000 in side bets! When you consider the sums of money at stake—£1,000 in 1751 is equal to almost €70,000 today—it was inevitable that, sooner or later, someone would attempt to manipulate events to his own advantage.

The early bookmakers were known as 'legs' because of the distances they covered during a day at the races, seeking bets. A leg would tramp round the racecourse, shouting that he wanted to lay, or back, a certain horse according to his fancy. Unlike the modern bookmaker, a leg had no mathematical knowledge of odds and therefore only wanted to lay one horse, which quite often was not the horse the public wanted to back. In order to be more flexible the legs began acting in the role of commission agents, laying horses themselves or on behalf of other legs. With their contacts in racing, legs were able to place money with wealthy gamblers or with other legs, taking a commission for themselves from both backer and layer. Knowing all the other legs personally, a leg would know which one would be likely to be laying a particular horse, so could get a price about any horse in a race.

This arrangement was fine for big punters, but the legs were not in the least bit interested in the ordinary racegoer who wished to bet in modest stakes. The locals and small punters were left out in the cold—until someone had a bright idea: cut out the middleman. Instead of trying to find a leg to take a modest bet, our bright idea man decided to hold all the bets himself and began making a book on each race. Thus was born the bookmaker.

In the 1850s the building of the railway network opened up the hitherto inaccessible countryside to city dwellers and in doing so changed horse-racing completely. First, it created a market for racing as a spectator sport and secondly, it made it easier to transport the horses, enabling the racecourses to attract a better class of horse, which in turn helped draw more spectators. This revolution in racing led to a new type of purpose-built racecourse, the park course.

The traditional natural courses of the time were very like the modern point-to-point: public facilities were virtually non-existent, admission was free (although the wealthy paid an entrance fee for their carriages) and the races were watched from the side of a hill. The course, which was narrow with rough terrain, was marked out by flags. The obstacles were similar to those which would be encountered in the hunting field: banks, brooks, stone walls, ditches, rails, and sometimes even ploughed fields! On some courses not only did races start from different places but the winning posts were in different locations, some a considerable distance apart which meant that only those on horseback could see all the races. Naturally enough, this encouraged spectators to bring their own horses, and a mounted gallery followed the runners as they raced, the runners finding themselves flanked by outriders. In their eagerness to get a close-up of the proceedings, these outriders often got too close to the runners and there were nasty collisions. The jockeys therefore had to be vigilant: watching out for the mounted observers who 'chased' them and also for the spectators on the ground, who seemed to have an equal disregard for their own safety. On more than one recorded occasion jockeys got a bird's-eye view of the shocked, upturned faces of people picnicking under the fence as they sailed over it, clearing the lot by sheer luck. The run-in from the last fence to the winning post often resembled a funnel, with the width of the course decreasing by the yard as those watching encroached in order to see which horse was winning.

This all changed with the arrival of the park courses. These were built beside the railway lines on green field sites and were designed to accommodate racegoers and to collect an admission fee from them.

No more did the spectators become part of the proceedings as a grand stand was provided for the public to view the race in safety and in comfort. The public enclosure had a bar and food stalls, public conveniences, telegraph office and other facilities, all intended to tempt people to pay the entry charge rather than watch the racing from the centre of the course for free. A cheaper outside enclosure was also provided, usually situated at the last fence, and this facilitated the picnickers and day-trippers. Park courses featured an all-grass track, usually about a mile round, which was wider than the natural courses, with the usual sharp turns replaced by sweeping bends. The steeplechase course also comprised an all-grass course, with specially built birch fences placed strategically around the course—no walls, banks or ploughed land to be encountered at all. The face of racing had been changed forever.

A number of the old racecourses were unable to compete with the new venues and were forced to close, for example, the Orchard course at Attanah, because it was isolated, and Maryborough Heath, because the course was too narrow. Others had different kinds of problems. Fairyhouse leased some of its land, therefore could race only on one day in the year, while the Curragh shared its land with local farmers, who had sheep grazing rights, and with the Irish Army. At one time the Army proposed building a military airport there, but it was the sheep that posed the greatest problem for the racecourse: they cropped the grass to such an extent that, in certain conditions, the racing surface became dangerous. The government moved quickly to protect this valuable asset by passing the Curragh of Kildare Act in 1961, which enabled the Turf Club to erect a four-mile fence around the racecourse to deter the sheep.

The racing world was divided into the progressives who rushed to embrace the changes and the traditionalists who lagged behind.

At the Curragh and Bellewstown there was resistance and changes were made reluctantly. However, very soon the entrepreneurs, who had gambled on the combination of cheap train tickets and the provision of betting facilities being the key to a successful race meeting, were thoroughly vindicated. In 1853 the first park course opened in Ireland at Baldoyle, beside the Dublin–Howth Railway line at Sutton, built by the Metropolitan Race Company. In order to provide the public with a betting service, the racecourse organised the legs so they would accept cash bets on all the runners and gave them the run of the enclosure, with the exception of the Club (or Members') section.

In those days the bookmakers mingled with the crowd in the paddock—the area where the horses were saddled before a race—watching and shouting odds, and it was there that most business was done. As the horses left for the start line and the punters headed for the stand to watch the race, the bookmakers moved with them but instead of going up into the stand, they went towards the judge's box, or as near to it as they could get, where they stood around in a circle waiting for the result—hence the term 'betting ring'. From this position they paid out winning bets before returning to the paddock to start betting on the next race. The bookmakers moved around the racecourse in this manner until 1912, when Clonmel racecourse decided to confine them to one area because it had been decided to charge the bookmakers a fee, in addition to the ordinary price of admission. To facilitate this the racecourse allocated each bookmaker a pitch in a designated betting area, from where he took bets and paid out winnings, and barred them from betting outside this area. This innovation was copied immediately by the other courses and is the basis of the modern betting ring.

The Science of Bookmaking
Each bookmaker works on his own behalf, extending the odds against the horses he wishes to lay and reducing the odds of the horses he has already laid. These fluctuations in the prices bring market forces into play: the more money taken on a horse, the shorter its price, which in turn causes the price of those horses that are not supported in the market to drift out. These fluctuations are

referred to as 'shows'. The SP, or Starting Price, is actually the 'show' that is available at the start of the race. It is compiled independently and is the basis on which most off-course bets are settled. However, the SP may not reflect the top price available about each horse in the betting ring, but rather is a reflection of the most common price available; punters who shop around can usually obtain a bigger price about a horse. The reason for this is that the SP cannot be determined by one individual bookmaker, who could display an artificially high price—even if he is prepared to lay it to lose a big sum—in order to affect the returned price. Bookmakers refer to this as the 'knock-out' and it represents an attempt to rig the off-course market by getting a runner returned at an artificially high starting price. During the period of betting the prices against each of the runners will fluctuate as bookmakers do business, lengthening the price of horses to attract business and shortening prices to deter punters, if they are taking too much money on one or two particular horses. Obviously if there is no money for a horse on the course, its price will be lengthened by the racecourse bookies in an attempt to attract bets, but there may be a lot of money for the horse off-course and the extending price threatens to be expensive. To reduce their exposure, the off-course bookmakers will send money back to the course to lower the price available, which in turn will lead to a lower SP and a smaller pay-out for them if the horse should win. This is called 'hedging'. Until the invention of the telephone (called 'the blower' by the bookmakers), it was impossible to hedge directly with the course, which was the link between the two markets.

The bottom line of the racecourse bookmaker's business is to 'make a book' on a race, that is to manipulate the odds against each runner so that they are in his favour rather than in the punters' favour. This is done by mental arithmetic: the bookmaker quickly calculates the odds, estimating the highest price he can offer to attract custom while not making it unprofitable. Each year in Ireland 37 per cent of favourites win. It is a high percentage and basically means that if a bookmaker lays every favourite in a year at 6-to-4, he will make a profit but if he lays every favourite at 2-to-1, he will show a loss. That is how tight the margins are in racecourse bookmaking and there is precious little room for error. A professional bookmaker will couple the odds of two or three horses in his mind, for example, two 3-to-1 chances equals even money and three 5-to-1 chances also means even money. For mere mortals, however, who don't have the bookie's finely tuned mathematical brain, the calculations can be done in simpler way.

An easy example is the tossing of a coin. There are only two possible results: the coin will land either heads-up or tails-up. This means the odds against each possibility is 1-to-1, or even money. To calculate the percentage you add one to the price, in this case evens, which gives you two, divide into 100, which gives an answer of fifty. This means that if a bookmaker lays both the head and the tail at even money, his percentage is 100 per cent, which means he doesn't have an inbuilt profit margin.

Let us turn to a die, which consists of six numbers, each with an equal chance of coming up on a throw. The true odds against any one particular number coming up is, therefore, 5-to-1 (the six numbers minus itself). If a bookmaker priced each number at 5-to-1, that would give him no inbuilt profit margin: add one to the price (5 + 1 = 6), divide 6 into 100 = 16.67 per cent, add up the six percentages of 16.67 and you get 100 per cent. However, if the bookmaker priced all six numbers at 9-to-2 (in other words, 4.5-to-1), then he would be working on a profit margin of 9 per cent (4.5 + 1 equals = 5.5, divide into 100 = 18.18 per cent x 6 = 109.09 per cent). The bookmaker's book is described as being 9.09 per cent 'over round', in other words, the bookmaker has made the odds slightly in his favour. If the bookmaker priced all six numbers at 11-to-2 (5.5-to-1), the punter would have a profit margin of over 7.5 per cent (add 1, divide into 100 = 15.4 per cent per number, add up all six and you get 92.3 per cent). In this case the bookmaker would be said to be betting 'over broke', which no self-respecting bookmaker should ever knowingly do!

A profit margin supposes that the bookmaker will lay each of the six numbers to an equal amount of money, which in practice is almost impossible. Nevertheless there is an inbuilt profit margin for the bookmaker, who only needs the die to be thrown and the backers to bet often enough to make the percentages count. It also supposes that each number has an equal chance of coming up. If, for example, the die has a bias in favour of the number six, enabling it to come up more often than it should, then the bookmaker has no profit margin at all because number six is actually a 5-to-2 chance, but he is laying to punters at 9-to-2! The bookmaker may think that he has a 9 per cent profit margin, but he is actually betting almost 10.5 per cent over broke—and all because the favourite is wrongly priced.

Therefore, the key to pricing an event is to identify the favourite and price it correctly because failure to do so will inevitably lead the bookmaker to bet over broke. In horse races the identification of the favourite is one thing, but another is what price the favourite should be. Unlike a true die, where the odds can be worked out easily, the price of a favourite runner is an opinion— an informed opinion, perhaps, but an opinion nonetheless. Before the race nobody really knows whether the price is value or not: the bookmakers will have an opinion that the price offered is below its true odds, but they cannot be sure, leaving room for a talented punter to get an edge. Pricing a bookmaker's board is never about which horse is going to win the race, it's about what the punters are likely to think is going to win the race. That is foremost in a bookmaker's mind when he prices up odds on a race and he will also be careful not to mark the punters' card as to which horses have no earthly chance of winning.

Horse-racing is the only market left in the world where insider trading is not a criminal offence. Insider trading in the betting market makes it extremely difficult for the market-makers to survive, hence their reliance on 'faces', punters' habits and the riding arrangements. Getting the percentages right can depend on the merest scrap of information, such as the appearance in the Ring of a person known to be connected with a horse or a stable, or even, in some cases, the absence of such people. In such a jittery atmosphere bookmakers are always on the defensive and surprisingly often give credence to rumour in the absence of hard facts. There is very little that escapes the eagle eye of the bookies— a skill honed by years of experience and wariness of the hefty fine the punter will impose if a mistake is made. Bookmakers hate laying a favourite at a wrong price; it ruins the book and invariably results in a loss, so they are inclined to be on edge until they have actually laid their favourite to real money. Bookmakers operate in the knowledge that it is one thing to catch them at a big price, but the horse still has to win! They will not be caught if the horse is beaten and many more gambles fail than are landed, which is why the bookmakers are still around. As one old-time bookmaker commented, when another complained about 'getting caught': 'I wish I was caught on every runner!' This, in brief, is the art of bookmaking and the daily business of the racecourse bookmaker.

Secrets and Spies
In the nineteenth century, as racing grew more popular with the public, many owners resented the fact that people were betting and making large sums on their horses without making any contribution towards the upkeep of their stable. First on their list of people to hate were the bookmakers, who made a living off the horses with no reciprocity. The costs of maintaining a racing stable could not be recovered by stake money, so owners turned to betting to balance the books. They felt they had no obligation whatsoever to the people who turned out to see the race and bet on it and considered bookmakers as 'fair game' and most certainly not entitled to any information about their stable. In order to secure a longer price for themselves about their horses, the owners took considerable steps to keep their arrangements secret, while the bookmakers constantly tried to get the information they required. This was done by paying touts to spy on the stables and to corrupt employees, a tactic that irritated the owners even more. The battle between the owner and the backer had begun.

Ultimately every gambling stable had to learn to live with touts spying on them all the time, monitoring horse movements, recording performances on the gallops and chatting up stable staff in order to squirrel information out of them. In reality, the touts had access only to very basic information that was not important in the normal course of events, but by mixing with the stable lads they could detect if the normal stable routine had been changed in any way, which could provide a clue that something might be planned. But even if a tout did manage to spy on a secret trial and knew the identities of the horses involved, he was missing a vital piece of information: what weight each horse was carrying.

In racing, the weight carried by each horse is very important because every 3 lb of weight is equal to about a length in distance. A horse that beats another at level weights by two lengths is therefore said to be 6 lb superior. Merely seeing one horse beat another on the gallops by two lengths told a tout very little in itself because for all he knew the beaten horse was carrying 12 lb more than the other, which would make it two lengths superior rather than inferior. The problem for the trainer was that the tout might corrupt stable staff by paying for inside information, which would fill in the blanks in his report and give him a lot more to go on. As a result, sensitive information, such as the body weight of jockeys and work riders, was jealously protected lest it help a tout interpret a trial. This was amply illustrated on one occasion at Royal Ascot. One of the big handicap races was won by a horse carrying a feather-weight, in other words, 77 lb. The miniature young jockey was presented to Queen Victoria after the race and, fascinated by the tiny creature standing before her, she asked the obvious question: 'How much do you weigh?' Horrified and ashen-faced, the startled youngster stammered, 'Please your Majesty, my master told me that I must not tell my weight to anyone!'

At the time the big handicap races were enormous betting affairs, with a market up and running months before the race, even before the weights to be carried had been announced. Handicaps involve the allotment of weight to each horse in an attempt to give every runner an equal chance of winning, therefore the better the horse, the more weight it is set to carry. That meant weight was a crucial and sensitive issue, and trainers were always anxious that a horse did not leave a good impression on the handicapper early in its career. Just as the trainers endeavoured to mislead the touts, they also worked to mislead the handicapper and make him believe that their horses were not very good— sometimes blatantly stopping them in races to make the point.

Trainers, broadly speaking, reacted to touts in three different ways. One group refused to accept them at all, spending an inordinate amount of time in a futile attempt to prevent them from doing their business; a second group fled their scrutiny by setting up stables in places so remote the touts could not function in the normal way; while the third group tended to carry on training their horses regardless, as if touts did not exist.

'Honest' John Day was a member of the first group, a tout-hater who tried to run them out of town with threats and violence, to smoke them out of their hiding-places with strategically placed fires and to mislead them by painting over his horses' white markings. His determination to outwit the touts played havoc with his stable routine: he would hold gallops in the dead of night, risking the lives of his horses as well as his staff, and would run a host of pointless trials just to confuse those watching. His efforts were only partially successful, however, because the touts resorted to working in packs to foil him: one pair would draw the trainer onto themselves in order to distract him, while others sneaked into vantage positions they would never dare occupy in normal circumstances. Any information garnered was shared among the pack, which meant the touts worked more efficiently and a twenty-four-hour vigil could easily be maintained on the stable yard, with each tout doing a short stint.

Sombre, cunning, but not bright, 'Honest' John was, of course, anything but honest, although he was a good judge of a horse's ability, a skilful reader of form and a good trainer of owners. An important asset in a gambling stable is a trainer who knows the ability of the horse, but who also has the knack of finding the right race for the coup. 'Training owners' is a racing term for the task of keeping owners 'sweet' so they continue paying the bills, even if the results on the racecourse are disappointing. A repertoire of excuses for poor runs is an essential part of the trainer's armoury. He must never, ever admit that an owner's horse is useless. It can be injured, it can be unlucky, it can have got a bad ride, be in need of more time, or just have come up against better horses, but it is never the horse's ability that is at fault; few owners, after all, are able to stomach being told that their expensive pride and joy is useless.

'Honest' John Day was fortunate that in his physique he resembled his mother rather than his father, an unfashionable country trainer who weighed over 20 stone. A lightweight jockey who could ride at 7 stone, John Day was very successful and rode the winners of sixteen Classic races, including *Elis* in that celebrated St Leger. Always a heavily gambler, 'Honest' John would invoke every trick he could to mislead the bookmakers, but he did not confine his desire to get one over to the bookmakers. Unfortunately for him, he tended to treat his patrons the same way.

Lord George Bentinck, flushed from his success with *Elis* in the St Leger, rewarded 'Honest' John by sending him horses to train now that his riding career was nearing its end. In 1837 Bentinck paid for the building of a stable yard and the laying out of gallops for the new trainer, investing his money in order to reap a rich dividend from the bookies in due course. Lord Bentinck was a plunger—the nickname at the time for very big gamblers—and was constantly plotting betting coups, while his trainer tried to keep some of them for himself. Despite their considerable success, which included a huge betting coup with the top-class *Crucifix*, the relationship between Lord Bentinck and 'Honest' John had its difficult moments, mainly because the gambling owner never really trusted his trainer—and with good reason.

'Honest' John and Lord Bentinck spent a lot of time together planning betting coups, so they knew each other very well. The trainer's success was entirely due to his patron, whose money had built the stable yard and filled the boxes with good horses. On the face of it the pair were close allies, but unfortunately 'Honest' John had a resentful streak in his make-up that ensured he always put his own interests first, or at least what he perceived as his own interests, and occasionally felt compelled to put his patron 'through the wringer' to 'put manners on him'. When it suited him, and for reasons best known to himself, he would make arrangements with a bookmaker to receive payment to prevent a heavily backed runner from his stable from winning. Of course, 'heavily backed' really meant backed to the hilt by Lord Bentinck. The trainer did not do this regularly, but every so often one of Lord Bentinck's gambles would get beaten, the horse would fail to run to up to form, excuses would fly—'They are not machines, you know!'—and the trainer would profit from the defeat, in secret. Who knows if Lord Bentinck suspected his trainer. Secrecy before and after a coup was the hallmark of 'Honest' John Day. No information of any kind was given to his staff—even his wife was told nothing, although she always knew when a coup was planned. The first sign was when her husband left the marital bed for the spare room: he feared that during pillow talk he might let slip the name of the horse!

In 1841 'Honest' John' made a secret arrangement with a book-maker that would prove to be the straw that broke his relationship with Lord George Bentinck. The latter was lining up a big gamble and everything appeared to be normal: the trainer continued his feud with the touts, the secret trials were all positive and a suitable race was selected. Busy in the stable yard and with his battle against the touts, 'Honest' John instructed his son, William Day, to write to Lord Bentinck telling him that the upcoming winner was tried a certainty and all was ready for the coup. He also instructed him to write to the bookmaker, telling him that he could lay Lord Bentinck with confidence because the horse would not win. Unfortunately for 'Honest' John, the hapless eighteen-year-old got the letters and the envelopes mixed up, with the unhappy result that the bookmaker's letter was sent to Lord Bentinck. That was the end of the successful partnership!

The Hermits of Salisbury Plain

One of the most successful betting syndicates in the history of racing involved five gentlemen who became known as the Netheravon Confederacy, or the Hermits of Salisbury Plain. This syndicate went to the opposite extreme from 'Honest' John, running away from touts to the most remote place in England they could find. They set up a stable at Druids' Lodge, in the middle of the great Salisbury Plain, where they installed Irishman Jack Fallon as the trainer. The touts found it difficult to get there, and even when they did they found it almost impossible to find suitable cover to watch the horses unseen. With Fallon, the stable staff and the housekeepers virtual prisoners at the stables, the touts were unable to speak with anyone connected to the yard and therefore failed to get any information to send back to the bookmakers. Once the touts had been sidelined, the syndicate landed a number of huge gambles, notably on *Hackler's Pride* and *Ypsilanti*, which had the bookmakers running for cover. However, the syndicate soon ran into problems with Fallon and the staff, who had made plenty of money but were tired of being cut off from their family and friends, as well as from the bookmakers. But a more immediate problem for the syndicate was the fact that it found it increasingly difficult to 'get on' its bets.

Bookmakers are not really worried about people backing winner after winner if they are betting in fivers, as it marks their card. It is when bets involve thousands that a problem arises. When the syndicate members put down the big money, the bookmakers were in trouble because they knew the bet would probably win, but found it almost impossible to 'lay-off' their liabilities. For one thing, the price was gone because the syndicate was hitting every significant bookmaker in the land, which meant that, to cover their liability, bookmakers would themselves have to bet in amounts of least ten to twenty times larger than the bet they had just taken. Obviously it made good business sense not to take the syndicate's bet in the first place, which is precisely what the bookmakers began to do. The result was that the syndicate could only get on relatively small amounts at the big odds before the price crashed, meaning it was risking a lot more money to win far less. The syndicate members were therefore forced to get other people to bet on their behalf, which was not ideal because information shared got into the public domain more easily, plus the third party would take a large slice of the odds for his own personal bet. It was also difficult to find people the syndicate could trust who had no obvious connection with the stable and who were substantial backers in their own right; bookmakers take particular note of a backer suddenly wanting to put thousands of pounds on a horse trained in a gambling stable when his normal bet is a fiver.

Its betting winnings thus curtailed, the syndicate found it difficult to justify the substantial costs of running a 'prison' for horses and people out in the middle of nowhere, when it could run a normal stable at a fraction of the cost. By this stage touts did not matter because bookmakers refused to take the stable commissions and Jack Fallon and key members of the stable staff were anxious to escape, so the syndicate decided to call it a day and went out of business. The betting syndicate had simply been too successful, winning too much money in too short a time. Perhaps it should have taken lessons from 'Honest' John Day, who helped the book-makers to balance the books by giving them 'dead ones' to lay to the general public, and occasionally to his patron, in return for being allowed to 'get on' when he had a coup ready. In the end somebody must pay, and it certainly won't be the bookmakers— the only one left is the ordinary punter!

Live and Let Live
Tom Cliff took a more rational approach when it came to the spying touts, adopting a policy of live and let live. He tolerated them, on the proviso that they kept their distance and did not approach stable staff, and always kept to the usual stable routine so they could do their job easily. The advantage of this policy was that Cliff could occasionally slip off at an irregular hour with a few horses and do some work unobserved because the touts did not keep a twenty-four-hour watch on his stable. Bookmakers had regular, accurate reports from the stable, which enabled them to price Cliff's horses with confidence, and consequently they were prepared to lay the stable big bets at long odds, even if it meant taking the occasional hit. Cliff was philosophical about setbacks. His definition of bad luck was pulling a horse six times when he might have won only to get beaten when the money was down. These were the qualities that made George Henry Moore of Moore Hall, Co. Mayo, choose Tom Cliff to prepare his horse, *Croagh Patrick*, for a gamble in the Stewards Cup at Goodwood.

Croagh Patrick was being trained at home for Moore, but the cost of running a large house, estate and training stable was sky high and funds were getting low, so a coup was badly needed. It was common knowledge that *Croagh Patrick* was to run at Goodwood and that Moore was short on funds, so the bookmakers were watching closely, knowing that a gamble was in the air. This meant getting a big price would be difficult, if not impossible. Tom Cliff was unperturbed, however. He assured Moore that he would be able to tell him whether *Croagh Patrick* could win the Stewards

Cup and if he felt the horse could, he was confident his price would be large enough to land a tidy sum for a relatively small outlay.

The Irish horse was watched closely once it arrived at Cliff's yard in Hednesford, Staffordshire, because the touts knew that it would have to be tried with *Nutbush*. The latter was the star of Cliff's yard, said to be the fastest ever mare over five furlongs and one of the favourites for the Stewards Cup. Cliff would have to hold a trial between the pair to discover which was the superior at the weights. This was a trial that was not to be missed; consequently the touts were particularly vigilant. Aware of the intense interest in the trial between *Nutbush* and *Croagh Patrick*, Tom Cliff organised a 'secret' trial between the pair, but ensured that news of it leaked out. Touts arrived from all over England to witness this vital pointer to the Goodwood race. Occupying every vantage point in the vicinity, they watched in amazement as the Irish colt ran away from *Nutbush* to win the trial easily.

Doubting the proof of their own eyes, the touts became suspicious about the ease of *Croagh Patrick*'s win. They worried about Cliff's carelessness, how news of the secret trial had leaked out to half the touts in the country and wondered at the lack of security, which had allowed them to watch the trial unmolested. Always suspicious, the touts reached the conclusion Cliff had hoped they would: the trial was a set-up to get better odds about *Nutbush*. They duly reported back to their bookmaker employers that the trial was a hoax, and *Nutbush*'s price shortened while *Croagh Patrick*'s price drifted out to 40-to-1. Moore's agents held their hands and did not step in to back the horse until the eleventh hour, by which time the runners were at the post, the Starter was taking the roll call and the start only minutes away.

The late surge for *Croagh Patrick* caused pandemonium in the Ring as Moore's men backed the horse to win £20,000 for Moore, and no doubt an equal sum for themselves and their pals. The odds tumbled, but the money for the horse still came, forcing the odds lower still until the betting market was turned on its head and *Croagh Patrick* was backed down to favouritism as bookmakers and punters alike rushed to cover their bets. The reason for the chaos in the Ring was the delay to the start of the race: it started three-quarters of an hour late because of a succession of false starts, long delays in getting the field in line again and the jockeys desperately trying to secure an advantage by trying to get off to a flying start. Had the race started on time, no one would have had time to react to the late gamble on *Croagh Patrick*, but the delay gave punters the opportunity to cover their bets by jumping on the bandwagon. Well aware that the late money for *Croagh Patrick* had to mean it was superior to *Nutbush*, the punters rushed to back the Irish horse and were prepared to accept virtually any price.

The outcome was close. *Croagh Patrick* fought off sustained challenges from *Man at Arms* and *Knight of St Patrick* to win the race by a head, landing the massive gamble. The racecourse book-makers were thoroughly cleaned out. The delayed start had cost them dear, as it had the off-course punters who had to take the starting price, which would have been ten times larger if the race had started on time. Tom Cliff had done it again, and he was not finished yet. Three days later, at the same meeting, *Croagh Patrick* turned out again, this time in the Chesterfield Cup, and landed another gamble, confirming the form with *Man at Arms* despite the latter being 9 lb (or three lengths) better off for his head defeat. Cliff had proved that gambles could still be landed and a good price obtained—touts or no touts.

An Irish Stand-Down
On two occasions Irish racecourse bookmakers were provoked into taking strike action after being dreadfully stung by a betting coup. The first occasion took place at the old Kilkenny meeting, which was run over a course at Danesfort on 4 May 1893, when *Master Joe* landed a gamble in the Ormonde Plate.

Master Joe was owned and trained by a leading Curragh trainer named Rice Meredith, who had trained the winner of two Irish Derbies and was about to win the race a third time with *Bowline*. When he turned up on the first day of the Kilkenny meeting *Master Joe*, although a five-year-old, had run only twice, both times unquoted in the betting and both times unplaced. His poor previous form had been over a mile-and-a-half, but as he hailed from a powerful Curragh stable the bookmakers tried to make

Master Joe favourite in a race over a similar distance, with his usual jockey, Edward Malone, in the saddle. There was not a penny for *Master Joe*, but a fortune came for the privately trained *Somnambulist*, who had been beaten out of sight in his previous two races, and it was backed down to favouritism. The gamble was duly landed, with *Somnambulist* beating *Knockmaroon* by a length-and-a-half, with *Master Joe* a well-beaten third some six lengths further back. The inclusion of *Master Joe* in the field had misled the bookmakers on two counts. First, they believed the horse would have public support, coming from a big stable, and secondly, the other runners were priced up at longer odds than would have been the case if *Master Joe* had not been engaged. The bookmakers had therefore concluded that *Master Joe* was entered for the sole purpose of getting a bigger price about *Somnambulist*, a theory that was supported by evidence that persons who would usually back horses from the Meredith stable had deserted *Master Joe* in favour of the winner.

Master Joe was turned out again the following day in a similar type of race. Again the race was over a mile-and-a-half, again it was taking on *Somnambulist* and *Knockmaroon*, who had beaten it easily the previous day. Although 11 lb better off with *Somnambulist*, *Master Joe* was meeting *Knockmaroon* on similar terms and looked to have little chance of overturning the previous day's form. On this second occasion there was no money for *Somnambulist* or *Knockmaroon*, but there was a massive gamble on *Master Joe*, who was backed down to favouritism. In this second race involving the horses, Edward Malone on *Master Joe* merely played with *Somnambulist*, winning cheekily with consummate ease by a length-and-a-half, with *Knockmaroon* and *Noiseless*, a recent winner at Birr, never seen with a winning chance at any stage.

Reeling from having to pay out on two big gambles in as many days, the bookmakers shouted foul and accused trainers Rice Meredith, Michael Dennehy and Larry Ryan of colluding to fix the results. The stewards apparently saw nothing wrong with the running of *Knockmaroon* on the second day, but held an enquiry into the running and riding of *Master Joe* on the first day of the meeting. Dissatisfied with the explanations offered by Meredith and Malone, the Kilkenny stewards referred the matter to the governing body. This was not good enough for the Kilkenny bookmakers, however. They stood down *en masse* and refused pointblank to work on the remaining races, which went ahead without betting. When *Noiseless*, trained by another Curragh trainer, Michael Dennehy—who made no show in *Master Joe*'s race— came out again later in the afternoon and won the St Kieran Plate, the hoots and jeers of the bookmakers were deafening. To a man they believed that this easy victory vindicated their allegation that the trainers had rigged the races to land a gamble.

The stewards of the Irish National Hunt Steeplechase Committee enquired into the Kilkenny running of *Master Joe,* but decided to postpone the enquiry to allow them to examine the bookmakers' ledgers. In the interim Rice Meredith won the Irish Derby with *Bowline,* but five days later, at the resumed enquiry, he and Edward Malone were 'warned off' the Turf.

The only victims of the bookmakers' protest that afternoon were the spectators who had paid for admission. Deprived of an opportunity to bet (Tote betting would not be introduced for another twenty-six years), some of the public moved to the outside enclosure, or the Silver Ring, admission to which was free. The bookmakers in that enclosure bet only in silver coins—wagers too small to be of any use to persons endeavouring to land a betting coup—and had emerged from the two contentious races virtually unscathed. Unaware of the betting coup and the bookmakers' strike in the main Ring, the Silver Ring bookmakers bet away during the afternoon as if nothing had happened. That is, until one particular punter moved outside to have a bet on *Noiseless* in the fourth race, realising that he had no chance of getting his usual bet of £50 on. Deciding to have the smallest of wagers with any individual bookmaker, he tendered a £1 note to the first layer he encountered, only to have the bet rejected. The sight of this big bet caused a stir in the Silver Ring; it was as if a flock of birds were roused by an approaching danger: bookies' runners ran, bookies wiped their boards and a team of runners monitored the 'gambler's' movements and whereabouts. The alarm only subsided when the danger passed, which was when the stranger was seen walking back across the course as he returned to the main en- closure, allowing the flock to settle once again.

Just over eighty-eight years were to pass before the bookmakers stood down again. Like the Kilkenny incident, the strike was prompted by a gamble in the first race, this time at Down Royal, over the Maze course (adjacent to the Maze prison), on Thursday 16 July 1981. Featuring the Ulster Harp Derby, this meeting was the biggest of the year at the venue and always drew a large crowd. It had a strong betting ring and was an ideal place to go for a gamble. Trainer Peter Russell loved a tilt at the Ring and he pencilled in the Gate Handicap Hurdle for *Tilbury*, owned by the well-known punter Charlie (Cathal) Fergus. Backed down to 6-to-4 favourite, *Tilbury* set off with twelve others in pursuit of just £414 in prize money but thousands of pounds in bets. Jockey R. McGlinchey settled *Tilbury* in midfield as *Adirondack*, a horse also owned by Cathal Fergus but trained by J.F. Stewart, made the running. Unquoted in the betting, *Adirondack* may have been in the field specifically to make a pace for *Tilbury*, which would make sense as a false run race often throws up a shock result and connections would be reluctant to ask *Tilbury* to try and make all the running. Bowling along in front, *Adirondack* seemed to be enjoying himself while *Tilbury* had settled nicely and was gradually closing on the leader, the pair being clear of the other runners. Normally a pace- maker will run out of steam early in the straight, but *Adirondack* showed no sign of flagging and the crowd gasped in alarm as McGlinchey began to ride *Tilbury* in an attempt to close the gap. With the whip singing, the jockey did his best to get *Tilbury* into a challenging position, but *Adirondack* never faltered and was still a length-and-a-half in front passing the post. The bookmakers cheered because the gamble had gone astray; the punters moaned about the pacemaker; the red-faced connections looked for some- where to hide.

What happened next depends on whether you are a bookmaker or one of the connections of *Adirondack* or *Tilbury*. Certain facts are beyond dispute, however. As young Gerry McEnhill rode *Adirondack*, his first winner, into the winner's position in the unsaddling enclosure, pandemonium ensued as punters milled around, hurling abuse at the connections of *Tilbury*. Unauthorised persons, most of them the abuse-hurlers, had got into the unsaddling enclosure and were jostling about, jeering and catcalling, while the Stipendiary Steward tried to clear them out. The rules require the winning jockey to go directly to the scales for the weigh-in procedure without touching any person or setting foot in the jockeys' room. At that time the Turf Club provided an official to escort the winning jockey to the scales, to ensure that he was not interfered with or prevented from reaching the weigh-in room, and this official led the way followed by Gerry McEnhill. As the pair weaved in and out through the crowd, a crowd that should not have been there in the first place, they got separated and the jockey found himself in the jockeys' room, having passed the scales without weighing-in.

When the announcement was made that the Clerk of the Scales had lodged an objection to the winner, *Adirondack*, on the grounds that its rider had failed to weigh-in, the bookmakers were furious and instantly suspected foul play. With *Adirondack* facing certain disqualification, the Ring would have to pay out on *Tilbury*, therefore facing huge losses. A delegation was sent to the weigh-in room immediately to protest to the stewards that there had been an organised plot to prevent Gerry McEnhill from weighing-in. In the absence of any proof to back up this allegation, the bookmakers then protested that the Stewards' Secretary had been deliberately distracted and demanded an explanation why the person appointed to take the winning jockey to the scales had failed to do his job. The bookmakers demanded that the stewards use their powers to declare the winner 'all right', deeming that had the rider gone directly to the scales he would have drawn the correct weight. The bookmakers pointed out that this had been done before when Tommy Murphy was unseated from a winner just after passing the post at Leopardstown, broke an ankle and had to be taken to hospital by ambulance. He had obviously been unable to weigh-in, but the stewards had deemed that had he been fit enough to do so, he would have drawn the correct weight and they declared the winner 'all right'. The Down Royal stewards were of the opinion that rules were rules and Gerry McEnhill had not weighed-in properly. They confirmed the disqualification.

When the delegation returned to the Ring an impromptu meeting was held and the bookmakers decided a protest was in order. They collectively agreed to stand down for the remainder of the meeting. There is no doubt that they got the idea from the Leopardstown bookmakers, who had refused to work the first race of the 4 May meeting (just ten weeks earlier) because Terry Rogers moved into a rails pitch when not qualified to do so, according to the pitch rules. Terry worked on the first race on his own before the racecourse manager moved him back to his rightful position, enabling the body of bookmakers to work the remaining five races. That protest was considered a success, a repeat of that action was proposed and it was agreed that no prices be offered for the rest of the day.

The first race to be affected was the Sean Graham race, the second to be run. There was no Tote in operation at the time on the two Northern Irish courses because of the Troubles, which meant the punters had no betting facilities at all. When the expected favourite, *Star Bound*, trained by Dermot Weld and ridden by Wally Swinburn, won the race, the bookmakers felt pleased with themselves. When the same combination won the feature race, the Ulster Harp Derby, with *Dance Bid*, yet another favourite, they were delighted with their protest. The remaining three winners, *Tumble Belle*, *Paddy Bouler* and *Gone Daft* would probably have been favourites, too, so the bookmakers saved themselves a lot of money, in the short term at least, by not working that day.

Despite pleas by the manager of the racecourse to call off the strike, the bookmakers refused, making further threats that they would not work on the second day of the meeting, the following afternoon. Harrassed by an angry crowd of punters who were disgruntled because they had paid for admission but were deprived of a betting service and had missed several winners, the desperate racecourse manager begged the bookmakers to work the following day. He pointed out that they were hurting the race-course and the public who had paid for admission, both of which were innocent of any wrongdoing. He further explained that it was the Turf Club that ran the meeting, not the racecourse, and that it imposed its officials and rules on the racecourse and that he, the course manager, had no say on these matters at all. He was wasting his breath. The bookmakers had a grievance, all of them felt strongly on the issue, they had made a decision and were determined to follow it through. The racecourse manager had no option but to abandon the second day of the meeting.

The Maze bookmakers later regretted their action, however, because the incident so enraged racegoers that attendances at the venue were depressed for many subsequent meetings. In fact, it took almost a decade for the venue's fortunes to recover fully. The villain of the afternoon, *Adirondack*, won next time out at Roscommon the following week. Gerry McEnhill weighed-in correctly on that occasion and finally recorded his first official winner.

The general body of bookmakers learned a few important lessons from the experience of the 'Maze Stand Down'. When the Irish National Bookmakers' Association decided on a bookmakers' strike at Leopardstown in late 1995, the proposed action was advertised extensively so the paying public would know in advance that the bookmakers would not be offering a service. The issue at that time was the introduction of on-course betting shops by the Tote and its partner, Ladbrokes, which attempted to disregard the seniority rights of the existing bookmakers. Although three Leopardstown fixtures in 1995 and one in 1997 were affected, no public hostility was encountered thanks to the pre-emptive PR strike. Experience of these strikes, together with the Tote strike that had occurred back in 1968 when it shut down from 27 July until 4 September, has shown conclusively that such action damages racing and is usually self-defeating.

Tic-tac Signals a Dead Cert

Most people have heard of tic-tac—a signalling code in which the hands are placed on various parts of the face and upper body to denote a number. For example, to show the number one the tic-tac man will place his right hand under his chin, for two the hand is put on the nose, three the cheek, four the top of the head, and so on. It was used as a means of communication between book-makers in one betting ring with those in another, at a time when all racecourses had an outside betting enclosure in addition to the main betting ring. Nowadays an outside betting ring exists only at the Galway and Bellewstown festival meetings, having been killed off by affluence as most people can afford the cost of admission to the main enclosure. Fifty years ago, however, there were many more bookmakers working on the outside than were operating in the main betting ring. The outside enclosure was often referred to as the 'Silver Ring' because all the bets involved coins, rather than notes, with the bookies' clerks recording the bets in the ledger in shillings. In other words, a £1 bet would be recorded as twenty shillings, that is, of course, if the bookmaker was brave or fool-hardy enough to accept such a large wager in an outside enclosure.

Apparently tic-tac was used on the floor of the Melbourne Stock Exchange to signal share price changes quickly and accu-rately. An Australian soldier who had worked on the Exchange fought alongside the Irish in the trenches of the Great War and taught tic-tac to his comrades, which they used as a means of basic communication when the noise of the artillery fire made hearing impossible. Surviving Irish soldiers returned home from the war adept at, but with little use for, tic-tac—for a few years at least.

In 1926 the Irish Free State government decided to legalise off-course betting shops in order to generate revenue from a betting tax; the betting shops had been outlawed over seventy years earlier. When the legislation was passed betting shops opened throughout the State and an old, almost forgotten business re-emerged and had to adjust to modern conditions. The Exchange Telegraph Company telegraphed the results to subscribing bookmakers race by race via the nearest post office. The bookmaker employed a boy on a bicycle to collect the telegram immediately it arrived at the post office and take it to the betting shop as fast as he could. The system worked perfectly until an ex-soldier, who knew the tic-tac, worked out that he could get the result to the betting shop faster than the boy on the bike and saw an opportunity to make money. In those days betting shops did not take particular note of the off-times of races and betting would continue until the result came in, which left the shop open to fraud—as the bookmakers were about to find out.

The ex-soldier organised a number of people to work the 'scam'. One man was positioned in the post office to see the clerk write out the telegram with the result of the race, which would then be given to the bookmaker's boy. As the boy rushed out to his bicycle, the man tic-tac'd the number of the winner to a man down the road, who relayed it to another man further off, who in turn relayed the result to a man waiting at the door of the betting shop. The ex-soldiers were careful not to give the game away by betting on outsiders—they only had a bet if the favourite, the second favourite, or the third favourite won and even then only placed a modest bet on it.

Waiting inside the shop, right by the counter and pretending to be furiously writing out a betting slip, was the man whose job it was to place the winning bet. This man, who was changed as frequently as possible, had three betting slips already written out, each bearing the name of a different horse—usually the favourite and the next two in the betting, or perhaps an Irish-trained horse, which people could be expected to back on patriotic grounds. Each of the three horses was given a code name, being a common surname like Murphy, O'Brien, or Kelly. When the man at the door received the signal telling him the number of the winning horse (provided it was one of the three horses selected), he shouted into the betting shop, 'Is there a Mr Kelly in the shop?' The man by the counter knew immediately which of the three horses had won the race, passed that betting slip to the bookmaker together with the stake, and there was then a comfortable interval before the bicycle boy rushed into the shop with the result.

The gang moved from shop to shop around the country, getting away with small but regular profits for years. Unfortunately for the gang, others observed what was going on and imitators jumped on the bandwagon. When one of these groups went for one big killing rather than regular profits, the bookmakers were finally alerted to the scam. Moving quickly to protect their profits, the bookmakers responded by introducing the timing of bets—the time the bet was accepted was now written on the slip by hand—

and changing their rules to ensure that any bet struck after the off-time of a race was void—win or lose!

Despite the new obstacles to success, the gang did have a fast, accurate communication system that could be put to legitimate use, so they decided to offer a service to on-course bookmakers. The opening of Shelbourne Park Greyhound track in 1928 provided the opportunity for tic-tac men to earn money from their skill because of its inner-city location and six-dog races. There the future tic-tacs could perfect their skill without the expense of travelling around the country and six runner races made it easy to read the signals. Once they had developed the skill for its new purpose, the tic-tacs moved into horse-racing and offered the bookmakers in the Silver Ring a service whereby they would know the prices on offer in the main betting ring. This service was later extended to offer a hedging service at the prices quoted, with the tic-tac man backing the horse on their behalf, by silent signal, with the bookmakers betting in the other enclosure.

'Hedging' is a bookmaker term for laying-off bets by passing on some of the liability to another bookmaker, in other words the bookmaker himself will back a horse with another bookmaker. Obviously hedging is more attractive to a bookmaker when he can back the horse at higher odds than he has laid it, which was possible now that a previously inaccessible market had been opened up by the tic-tac. Outside bookmakers could avail of the bigger market available in the inside enclosure and the variation in prices between the two separate markets. Racegoers were fascinated by the white-gloved men signalling frantically, arms waving amid loud whistles and shouts of 'aye, aye', but it soon became a commonplace sight, with a line of tic-tacs working an unending silent conversation that lasted throughout the day.

As it became the norm, tic-tac men had to address the problem of bookmakers cracking the code and getting to know what each signal meant, and thereby getting the valuable information free of charge by reading other bookmakers' tic-tac. This was overcome by the introduction of a 'twist card'—a list of runners in a different order from that on the racecard, and bearing the special horse numbers that each individual tic-tac man would be using. The tic-tac man would sell his own twist card to his bookmaker clients, which was how he earned his wages. The only people who would know the order in which he was giving his 'show' were those who had purchased his card.

The late Terry Rogers hated the system and used to say, 'Tic-tac means a thief'. Terry was a unique character. On a wet day he would wear a yellow oilskin jacket with the words 'Terry Rogers' or 'Stolen from Terry Rogers' emblazoned on the back. His dislike of tic-tac men was the result of a bad experience, but it did not follow that every tic-tac man was a thief, or a gang-member, or a rogue. Some most definitely were, however, and a wealthy bookmaker like Terry was a prime target for their tricks. Of course, human nature being what it is, tic-tacs sometimes would 'cock the price' of a horse a bookmaker was enquiring about, quoting 16-to-1 when knowing full well that 20-to-1 was on offer, but hoping to 'cop' four points for himself for nothing if the horse won the race. But it must be said that tic-tacs had their own sense of honour and rarely, if ever, reneged on a bet they had struck on behalf of a bookmaker. When one considers the millions of bets struck by tic-tacs down the years, being one man's word against another, the legitimate tic-tac man can be proud of his service.

Within the last fifteen years the tic-tac business has died. Some bookmakers' runners still use tic-tac from time to time, but the last of the old tic-tacs have now retired, their service killed off by the closure of the outside betting rings, their own restrictive practices and, of course, the walkie-talkie. It has survived in Britain, however, where there is a number of different versions in operation, one using six numbers instead of the basic ten, and while similar to Irish tic-tac, the British tic-tacs use different signs.

An amusing story came from a fracas at Clonmel during the National Coursing meeting in the 1970s, when a well-known bookmakers' assistant was charged with a minor breach of the peace. In those days disabilities were not treated with the respect they are accorded nowadays, and the slightly deaf defendant rubbed the judge up the wrong way by continually shouting, 'What did he say?' during the cross-examination of witnesses.

Finally, the defendant's brother took the stand, regaling the court with a version of events that cats would not believe until stopped in his tracks by the judge.

'I've heard enough, I find the defendant guilty and am imposing a fine of a tenner.'

'What's that he said?' came the call from the dock, to which his brother used tic-tac to signal that he had been fined £10, drawing a roar of laughter from the court. Even the judge was amused!

Singing for your Supper!

It would be wrong to think that tic-tac was the only system used to defraud the poor bookmaker, as many different methods were employed successfully down the years. In the days before the legalisation of betting shops, bookmakers ran private offices, generally in an upstairs room, where their clients could bet but persons could not walk in off the street. These offices were exactly the same as a betting shop except that strangers could not gain entry, and it was an intimate atmosphere in which many a pleasant afternoon was passed.

One particular bookmaker ran just such an office over a shop in a busy street, an oasis above the hustle and bustle below, and it proved a nice little earner for him. Then, one summer, it all began to go wrong. The punters were running amuck, backing winners with disturbing frequency, and the bookmaker was losing money hand over fist. A bad run became a spiralling cash leak and the book-maker got suspicious: punters could not suddenly become that good! So he became vigilant. It came to his attention that a lot of these winners were being backed after the advertised off-time of the race, which should not have been an issue because all the punters were locked into the office and had no contact with the outside world. 'But what if there was contact with someone on the outside?' reflected the bookmaker, who then proceeded to watch carefully. It was only then that he became aware of the busker on the street below, busily plying his trade with his poor repertoire and long pauses between tunes. The bookmaker's sleuthing finally turned up the answer: the punters paid the busker and every tune he played represented a number—of a winner, of course. Through his music he told the punters cooped up inside the upstairs office who the winners were. As they say, necessity is the mother of invention!

The Importance of Names

The naming of horses is a business in itself, and one most people take very seriously. Bookmakers have a very simple love of the naming game: it makes life easier for them with the field so clearly differentiated. But not always!

Derby Day at the Curragh in 1951, a time when there was a flourishing outside betting ring in the centre of the course providing a cheap day out at the races for ordinary people who could not afford the 12/6 entry charge to the Grand Stand. Facilities outside were basic: Tote and bookmaker betting and a refreshment tent, but no stand and no racecourse commentary. The outside crowd could get a reasonable view of the race, but only those who managed to get a place along the inside running rail could see the last fifty yards and even then they only had a good view of the horses' behinds. In the absence of a loudspeaker system, the numbers of the winner and placed horses were displayed in a frame, though obviously it took a bit of time for these numbers to be prepared, so it was a while before those outside—bookmakers and people—actually knew the official result of a race.

Fraise de Bois, trained in England by Harry Wragg and ridden by Charlie Smirke, was one of the favourites to win the race. Its name translated as 'Wild Strawberry', but the bookies outside wrongly pronounced it as 'Phrase de Boys'. It was one of them who told me a good story about the finish of that race. The horses had passed the post and the bookmakers, being situated in a slight hollow, had no idea which horses had been concerned in the finish and eagerly sought news from others as they waited for the result to be put up in the frame. People returning from the running rail, who would at least have seen the numbers of the horses as they passed some fifty yards from the post, were asked, 'What's won?' One particular lady looked as if she might be in the know— she wore tweeds and sported a pair of binoculars. She was approached by a couple of bookmakers for news of the result.

'What won Ma'am?' they enquired.

'*Frez de Bwoi*,' she replied authoritatively, eliciting whoops of delight from the two bookmakers.

'A result, a result,' they cried—not recognising the name of the favourite when it was pronounced correctly. After their moments of delight, they were absolutely shattered when the number of the favourite was hoisted in the frame, loudly declaring it the ultimate injustice for a bookmaker to think the winner was a 'skinner', only to discover subsequently that it was a losing race! Obviously the wise William Shakespeare was right: a horse by any other name is just as fast!

Them vs Us
There are about 200 racecourse bookmakers in Ireland, but less than half of them bet regularly throughout the year. A community united by a common sense of persecution and vulnerability, the bookmakers have learned to be vigilant and the tiniest variation in the habits of certain people can be a signal of forthcoming danger. If an alert bookmaker notices something, the last thing he does is inform his fellow bookmakers. At first he will try to use his knowledge for his own benefit, even at the expense of his colleagues, as happened in Navan on a bleak, wet Monday, just before Christmas 1983.

In the second race, a novice-chase, the bookmakers installed a well-bred Menelek mare named *Wee Mite*, who was the even-money favourite despite being trained by an unknown permit-holder and ridden by an amateur jockey who was claiming an allowance because he had ridden very few winners. Joe Donnelly, one of the leading bookmakers in the Ring at the time, was never the first to put up prices, preferring to watch the market for a bit before chalking his board. Standing on the ground watching, Joe recognised a punter going in to back the second favourite, and subsequent winner, *Monanore* at 4-to-1. Initially surprised because he expected that particular punter to be backing *Wee Mite*, it dawned on Joe that *Wee Mite* must not be fancied, so he immediately hopped up on his box and offered 6-to-4 against the even-money favourite, seeking to tap some soft money. Unfortunately for Joe, the other bookmakers knew him too well and his actions aroused suspicion: what was he up to, getting up to bet earlier than usual and seeming overly keen to lay the favourite? It could only mean that the favourite was not fancied. All the bookmakers pushed *Wee Mite* out to 6-to-4; Joe responded by going 7-to-4 and then 2-to-1 to the hoots and jeers of his colleagues. The attendance at the meeting was small, the betting very poor and there was little money for the horse—despite going a big price early, Joe Donnelly got less than £200 in bets on *Wee Mite*. Most of the other bookmakers got nothing, but did lay *Monanore* and were furious that the favourite appeared to be 'dead' and jealous that Donnelly had got the cream, or whatever cream there was to be had.

From the off *Wee Mite* looked a forlorn hope. Slowly away, her inexperienced rider was attempting to ride a waiting race, but found himself well behind the leaders at the halfway point, by which time the observers were already shouting abuse. Slogans like, 'You can give weight but not distance' and 'Not trying a yard' rang out, but when *Wee Mite* began to run on in the straight from a hopeless position, the abuse turned to furious jeering. The exciting finish between the leader, *Monanore*, ridden by Tom Morgan, and the fast-finishing *Virginia Road*, ridden by Michael Cummins, was ignored—all eyes were on *Wee Mite*, who was closing fast on the leading pair. Still three lengths behind on the line, *Wee Mite* had finished like a train and it looked as if she would have won had she been ridden closer to the leaders. Their suspicions confirmed, a crowd of punters, bookmakers, hawkers and bookmakers' staff charged towards the unsaddling enclosure to heap abuse on the head of the unfortunate jockey.

The crowd grew larger as the spectators rushed to see what was going on, so that by the time *Wee Mite* came in almost everyone present on the course that day was gathered round the small winner's enclosure, scrambling for a view, while the ringleaders roared at everyone in sight. All of them, of course, claimed to have backed *Wee Mite*, they had all had been robbed and oozed furious indignation—but the fact was that virtually none of them had backed the horse at all!

For most of the punters, this was all a bit of a lark, but unfortunately there was one idiot present who decided some real action was needed. Jumping the rail, he rushed over to *Wee Mite*, bristling with aggression, and aimed several kicks at the mare. This was too much for Ted Walsh, then the reigning Irish amateur champion rider (although he had not ridden in the race), and he rushed to protect *Wee Mite* from the outraged punter, making the very reasonable point that whatever had transpired, it was not the fault of the horse.

Happy at the chance to humiliate *Wee Mite*'s owner/trainer and rider and creating a diverting fuss, the crowd dispersed, laughing and joking about the fun as each man pronounced the sentence he would impose on the unfortunate jockey if he were a steward. The common verdict was somewhere between a life ban from racing and the death sentence! Having dealt summarily with the connections, a much smaller group turned their attention to Joe Donnelly, who got a terrible ribbing and for years afterwards had to endure the taunts of, 'Remember *Wee Mite*'. Even today, if you mention *Wee Mite* to any Irish bookmaker, he will immediately think of Joe— the memory has not faded in over twenty years.

Knocking

'Knocking' is the racing term for a credit bet that the loser fails to honour and it is part and parcel of betting. Quite rightly, gaming debts are not recoverable at law because they are debts of honour between two people: just as a punter does not have to pay a book- maker, it follows that a bookmaker does not have to honour his bets either. However, while a bookmaker can plead the Gaming Act to extricate himself from a payment owed, he will lose his betting licence if he does so and therefore his business and liveli- hood. Most bookmakers are content to be 'knocked' for a few Euro every year if the defaulter is a good customer and a consistent loser. For example, if a punter can afford to lose, say, €10,000 a year and does so year after year, a bookmaker will treat his bets 'top of the book', in other words, not trading against those bets or hedging them. The bookmaker will not care if the punter runs up a debt he cannot afford to pay because the bookmaker will offer him a settlement at the end of the year at an amount the punter can afford. With the slate wiped clean the punter bets on like before, having too many bets, having impulse bets and bets just to impress his friends, so that by the end of the next year he is guaranteed to owe the bookmaker once again.

On the other hand, the 'knock' the bookmakers resent and will not forgive is where a winning punter dishonours a losing bet. Consistent winners who bet on credit are unwanted by bookmakers on account of the cost factor and the risk that, at some point, a debt will not be paid. Cheques are probably a bookmakers' biggest enemy: not only can they bounce but they can also be stopped. A favourite trick of the conman is to give a bookmaker his personal cheque and bet into it, knowing full well it will not be honoured. A bookmaker will often take a chance with such a cheque on the basis that most cheques are good and there is a possibility of acquiring a good, faithful punter. If the punter wins, the bookmaker won't pay out if the cheque is not honoured. Unfortunately, the con men have cheque fraud down to a fine art. When they back a winner on the basis of a cheque lodged with the bookmaker, they will seek payment by means of the bookmaker's own cheque. They will reason with the bookmaker that if their cheque bounces, then the bookmaker can stop his own cheque and not be out of pocket. If the bookmaker agrees and issues them a cheque, they will immediately seek out one of his colleagues to cash the cheque or let them have bets on the strength of it, so that when it is 'stopped' it is another bookmaker who gets stung.

The first thing a bookmaker will look at when he is given a cheque is the number. A low number indicates that the account has been opened recently, suggesting a high-risk account. However, where the cheque is being issued by a person known to the bookmaker, it will be accepted readily. This was the reason why a man by the name of J. Donnelly travelled to Cork to open a bank account. He opened a current account with a small sum of money and was presented with a chequebook with 'J. Donnelly' printed impressively and authoritatively above the signature. He took his new chequebook to the races. Once satisfied that the well-known Cork bookmaker Joe Donnelly was not in attendance that day, he proceeded to write out a number of cheques with 'cash' as the payee and passed them off as Joe Donnelly's. One by one the cheques were offered to bookmakers with a bet, were accepted without a second glance and the bookmakers paid out the change in cash. Needless to say, every one of the cheques bounced.

It takes a villain to catch a villain, as they say, and bookmakers can be just as villainous as punters when it comes down to money. One enterprising bookie pulled his own fast one on a 'knocker' with an ingenious, but thoroughly illegal move that must have left the cheat scratching his head in puzzlement. The scam was the usual one: a personal cheque was lodged with the bookmaker, bets were struck and winnings were drawn until the credit was exhausted. The punter, of course, was happy in the knowledge that his cheque would not be honoured. When the bookmaker came into this knowledge, in due course, he was livid and determined to salvage some part of the outstanding debt. He bribed a contact in the bank to find out how much money was in the account on which the cheque was drawn (a blatantly illegal act, it must be said), and in this way discovered that it contained a sum about half the value of the cheque that had bounced. The bookmaker re-presented the cheque and then went to the branch of the drawer and lodged enough money to the account to bring its credit up to the value of the cheque. When the cheque hit the account a second time, there was enough money in it to enable the bank to honour the cheque. The bookmaker's tenacity, and villainy, enabled him to collect half his debt!

Taken on Trust

Terry Rogers—for years the public face of Irish bookmaking—was caught out by many scams down the years because he tended to trust people he knew: the bookie's cardinal sin. When the Jackpot began in Ireland in January 1966, punters filled out their selections on a sheet backed with a carbon copy. The Tote clerk stamped the sheet, kept the top copy and gave the punter the carbon copy as a receipt for the bet. The Jackpot requires the punter to nominate the winners of four races, the receipts go into a pool and a successful bet can be worth a lot of money. On one occasion a punter discovered he had the first three winners up in his Jackpot and had one selection running for him in the final leg, so he was anxious to hedge. He approached Terry Rogers, who agreed to purchase a half-share in the bet. The value of the docket was easy to calculate because the Tote announces the amount in the Jackpot Pool and the number of units running on each horse. That enables the bookmaker and the punter to calculate the dividend if a certain horse were to win. Let us assume, for example, that the dividend if the punter's selection won the race was £1,000 and the horse's price was 2-to-1. In those circumstances Terry would offer about £300 for the ticket, which effectively meant he was backing the horse at 100-to-30.

Word got around that Terry would buy shares in Jackpot tickets and before long he was doing a roaring trade. He soon acquired regulars—punters who had an uncanny ability to get the first three winners of the bet up, only to fail to find the winner of the final leg. This continued for some time, until eventually he got lucky and a ticket in which he had purchased a share came up. Terry's assistant went to the Tote to collect the big, juicy cheque, but he was told the bet was a loser and the punter, who was due a half-share of the winnings, had disappeared. Investigation uncovered the scam. Some punters were folding back the carbon copy of the Jackpot sheet, preventing the numbers of the horses appearing on the carbon copy. The Tote clerk never bothered to check the copy, because the bet was as per the original, and returned to the punter the blank copy with the official stamp. After three Jackpot races had been run the backers got an unused Jackpot sheet, tore off the copy, replaced it with the blank, stamped copy and redid the Jackpot, including the winners of the first three legs. There was no more dealing in Jackpot tickets after that!

Poor Terry was even taken for a ride by his pals. A big, hearty Belfast punter used to bet heavily on the racecourse. Although Terry refused to give him credit, he was prepared to accept his substantial bets provided they were backed up with ready cash. The punter got into the habit of going to the Northern Bank in Belfast, withdrawing £25,000 in cash, getting the bank to parcel up the money, whereupon they would put the official Northern Bank stamp on it to guarantee that it was counted out correct. When the punter got to the races he gave the stamped parcel to Terry, enabling him to bet away all day. The profit or loss would be settled after the last race.

After a particularly bad losing run the Belfast punter was broke and could not raise the ready cash to have a bet. Desperate, he devised a daring plan. He got a disreputable stamp-maker to make a fake Northern Bank stamper, purchased a sliced pan of bread, wrapped it up, stamped it like the bank would and headed for the races. Before the first race he handed the parcel to Terry Rogers, as usual. Suspecting nothing, the bookmaker put the parcel of bread in the satchel and the punter proceeded to bet away. After the last race the account was prepared and the punter had won £6,000, so Terry handed him back his parcel and gave him the £6,000 in cash from the bag. Off went the delighted punter, happy to be back in business.

Driving back to Belfast, the punter gave the brown parcel to one of his companions and told him to throw it out the window. Thinking it contained £25,000, the man laughed at the joke. He was dumbstruck when the punter snatched back the parcel and threw it out the window himself. It was only when they got back to Belfast that he told his companion the true story about the discarded 'money'. I don't know if Terry ever found out that he had been conned by this man, but an ink stamp and a loaf of bread got the punter back on track and he never looked back.

What Odds?
Many bookmakers have been caught off-guard, often with painful financial consequences, by the simple question: 'What odds so-and-so?' Anxious to prove that he can price an event, a bookmaker is inclined to quote a price at a moment's notice, without doing any homework at all. Inevitably the bookmaker will quote a false price because the question usually relates to an unlikely outcome. However, that does not necessarily mean it should be a big price.

One particular bookmaker I know, who shall remain nameless to avoid embarrassment, was pontificating about horses on one occasion when the question was posed: 'What odds a horse winning both the Champion Hurdle and the Cheltenham Gold Cup?' With the Champion Hurdle being run over two miles and the Gold Cup a three-and-a-quarter-mile marathon over steeplechase fences, it would require a versatile and sound horse to complete the double, which had never been done at the time, although *Bula* had finished third in the Gold Cup having previously won the Champion Hurdle. The bookmaker quoted 100-to-1 off the top of his head and the clever punter snapped up the odds for a tenner and named *Dawn Run*. The bookmaker was shocked and disappointed that a friend had 'picked him up', but his pride would not let him back down having quoted the price, and so the bet was struck. *Dawn Run* had in fact already won the Champion Hurdle so half the bet was already landed, which meant the true odds were very much shorter than 100-to-1. The horse was now racing over fences and looked threatening in his current form. Sod's law applied: the one time you speak carelessly is the time you get caught out. *Dawn Run* became the first horse to complete that unlikely double, and the bookmaker had to part with £1,000.

Students are bad news for bookmakers because they are intelligent, perpetually broke and always keen to supplement their income. Bookmaker Joe Byrne has a landmark betting shop in Leeson Street, which has been there for years and years. He had a slogan, 'We Bet On Everything', and one day a student tried him out: 'Mr Byrne, I understand that you bet on everything. What odds Blackrock College to win the Leinster Senior Schoolboys' Rugby Cup?' Joe Byrne did not know much about schoolboy rugby, but having ascertained the number of teams in the competition he did a quick calculation and came up with odds of 14-to-1. The young man took the price with £100 to £7—a larger than average bet at the time. Now that £100 was at risk, the bookmaker began following the Cup in the newspapers. He was disconcerted when Blackrock hammered their opponents by thirty points in their first match, so he decided to do some homework—albeit belatedly. Joe quickly realised that he had been far too generous because Blackrock College had won the Cup more times than all the other teams put together! The missing piece of the puzzle was going to cause him £100.

The bookmaking firm Paddy Power loves to promote novelty bets to attract publicity and custom. They ran a very successful bet in the 1980s with the 'Who Shot JR?' conundrum, so when *The*

Simpsons ran a 'Who shot Mr Burns?' storyline, Paddy Power once again saw the chance to make a little ready cash. All the characters were priced, from Homer, the favourite, to the Granny at 200-to-1 and baby Maggie at 500-to-1. Of course, babies don't usually shoot people, but the Simpsons is a cartoon so the company expected the occasional small bet on the unlikely outsider—just for the novelty.

The bet did its job and attracted interest and punters. Bets on the baby at 500-to-1 were particularly popular among the students of Maynooth University, who backed the baby in some numbers in their local Paddy Power betting shop, but only to small stakes. Not one bet was over £2, and several placed a bet on the Granny as well at 200-to-1, helping the throw the betting shop manager off the scent. But humans being what they are, there was one greedy so-and-so. This particular student attempted to put £20 on Maggie as the shooter, exposing the firm to a liability of £10,000 and immediately alerting the manager to contact head office before accepting the bet. Head office enquired whether the shop had taken any other bets on Maggie and was a bit taken aback to be told that the shop had already accepted nearly £80 at 500-to-1. The betting on 'Who shot Mr Burns?' was immediately suspended as the firm investigated whether the information could have leaked out.

This, of course, was in pre-internet days, so the firm had not suspected that the TV-viewing public could have prior access to the Mr Burns storyline. It had not taken into account the fact that it was an American programme, which meant it aired earlier in other jurisdictions. Once the company realised this, a member of staff was asked to ring a friend in the USA. The friend confirmed that the revealing episode had been shown six weeks earlier in America. The scam was painfully simple: one student had learned from a friend in America who had shot Mr Burns, saw the Paddy Power bet and let other students in on the easy money. It was £40,000 worth of easy money, as it happened. Luckily for the firm very few bets on Maggie had been struck in its other shops, so the damage was much lighter than it might have been and the publicity proved to be cheap at the price. For weeks afterwards people were ringing up the company looking for a price on events that had already taken place—just for a laugh!

The Vagaries of the Photo Finish

One of the great mysteries of horse-racing in the 1970s and 1980s was the length of time it took to get the result of a photo finish. In other sports, such as athletics, the top three flashed through the tapes, separated by inches and the merest fractions of a second, but out came the 1-2-3 in less than a minute. Not so in horse-racing, where there was a time lag between the finish and the announcement—it was rather like conducting a frustrating international call with a three-second delay. One wag posited the theory that the delays were due to the photo finish being conducted by use of a Brownie camera! At the races, meanwhile, a flourishing betting market grew up around the photo finish as bookmakers and backers waited up to ten minutes for the result of a race. Steam bets (sometimes called blue bets) held sway in this market, in which those positioned right on the line had a distinct advantage. Steaming is when a person, usually connected with the Ring, rushes in shouting a bet on the horse least likely to have won the race. It is called steaming because no bet is actually being struck—it's a smokescreen. The game is to fool the public into thinking that a bet has been struck and that the photo finish is too close to call with confidence. Another feature of this market was that a bookmaker would only price one of the two horses involved in the photograph: the loser. To the casual onlooker it appeared as if the bookmaker took bets on the horse at all prices out from 2-to-1 to 20-to-1. This charade would extract small sums of money from gullible observers, but there also existed a genuine market in which bookmakers tried to 'save themselves' by offering the punters 'insurance'.

At any given time down the years there was a man who was acclaimed the photo-finish expert. This expert, who was not always a bookmaker, placed himself strategically right on the line, from where he judged the winner in the event of a close finish. Each of these experts flourished for a time, each being dethroned in a similar manner when they eventually got the result of a race wrong. Having backed a loser at odds as low as 1-to-20, the experts' losses were so large that it blew away virtually all the profits they had gained in their reigning period. The losses, which sometimes could not be honoured, tended to shatter the expert's confidence, forcing him to abdicate his position adjacent to the line, at which time a new pretender would step into his place.

The most famous of the non-bookmaker photo-finish experts was 'Major' Michael Vernon, who held sway for many years until almost put out of business by a judge. It happened on one of the Northern Ireland courses when the Major called the winner and backed it at long odds-on, only for the judge to give the race to the other horse. Later, following complaints from the connections of the horse placed second, who had examined the photograph and believed a mistake had been made, the judge re-examined the photo finish strip, accepted that he had erred and corrected the result. This was not much use to the Major, who had lost his money because all bets are settled on the 'winner all right', and it was a hard knock to be cleaned out in such a manner. Certain bookmakers sportingly cancelled the Major's losing bets on the 'winner', but others demanded their pound of flesh and his losses were so great that he never really recovered from this setback.

The Major got his nickname because of his military bearing. He was said to have served with the British Army in Palestine, where he lost an eye in combat, but I don't think he was an Army man at all. It is true that he had one bad eye, however, and he would shut it when viewing a close finish. This, he claimed, was the secret of his success in judging which horse had won the race. The Major landed the longest-priced winning bet ever seen on an Irish race-course, backing a winner at odds of 1000-to-1 at, of all places, a Co. Cork point-to-point. He backed a horse in running, witnessed by several bystanders, when it appeared to have no chance of winning as it toiled in third place. His horse was a distance behind the second-placed horse, which in turn trailed the leader by two fields, but the Major knew there was a tiny chance that the pair in front could fall. One was prone to making jumping errors; the other was a doubtful stayer and tiredness might just cause it to fall. The bookmaker who offered the 1000-to-1 was trying to make a few easy pounds by laying a horse he thought could win only by the unlikeliest freak chance because it was so far behind. The Major did not really expect the horse to win when he speculated a £1 bet, but he did know it was not a 1000-to-1 shot! He took a gamble, had the odds in his favour and luckily for him the bet came up trumps and he was £1,000 to the good.

The problem with these photo-finish experts is that they become so confident in their judgments, they begin to call very close finishes—as if it were up to them and them alone to declare the result. It must be some kind of innate human failing because every single one of them drifted into this mindset sooner or later, and it always finished them. I well remember one day in Killarney when I laid an outsider to a client and decided to stick the bet even though it was a bad loser and I absolutely hated—and still hate to this day—having a losing race when a long-priced horse wins. I remember feeling very frustrated as this loser was prominent all the way and I was very apprehensive when it passed the post upsides another horse. I knew it was very close, but was relieved and delighted when the photo-finish expert of the time backed the other horse, at 20-to-1 ON with the bookie beside me. 'That's enough,' I said, 'the outsider is beat,' as it duly was by a short head. However, I later had a look at the photograph of the finish, which is put on display after a race, and was amazed to see just how close a finish it had been. I wondered how this expert could risk £1,000 to win a miserly £50 on a finish that must surely have been too close to call when judged by the naked eye. A fortnight later that particular expert came to grief at the Phoenix Park when he called a finish that was too close to call, and that was the end of him.

In the 1980s one greedy bookmaker decided to bet on photo finishes on the basis of 'dead heat, you lose'. Basically, the book-maker was laying the horse to win by a short head or more, but the hidden skinner in his favour was the dead heat. One afternoon at Punchestown the judge declared a dead heat and the punters who had backed one of the horses in the photo-finish market expected to lose half their stake to the bookie and draw the full odds to the other half of their stake. That meant a punter with £1,000 to win £100 (odds of 10-to-1 ON) on one of the horses would lose £500, but would get the full odds to the other £500, thereby getting back £550 of his original bet of £1,000 and taking an overall loss of £450. However, when the punters attempted to draw this proportion of their winnings, some bookmakers refused to pay them anything because they were betting 'dead heat, you lose'. The bookmakers claimed they always bet 'dead heat, you lose' as a matter of course, even though they had no sign up to indicate this; the punters were most unhappy. The incident caused such confusion and ill-will that the Racing Board immediately introduced rules to cover photo finish betting, which had not been officially recognised until then. The new rule stated that bookmakers could no longer bet 'dead heat, you lose'. They could either bet on the photo, settling all bets on the winner under the usual rules, or they could bet on the distance, which would bring the dead heat into play, provided that the contingency had been priced up.

Even before the new, fast photo-finish equipment was installed the whole photo-finish betting market at the race meetings was tottering because one clever punter had arrived on the scene armed with a piece of equipment of his own: a small video camera. Proving that a camera was surer than the naked eye, this punter was soon cleaning out the bookies and fewer and fewer were willing to bet on the photo finish in light of this threat. In its heyday, however, the photo finish was a big market, all bets were free of tax and everyone could have an opinion because they all had seen the finish—or had they? I recall one painful day at Navan racecourse, Proudstown Park—surely the coldest spot in Ireland—when there was a big rush to get the 1-to-2 being offered by a bookmaker in the betting on a photo finish. A crowd had panicked in its eagerness to get on before the price disappeared, bookmakers were being knocked down in the rush to buy money and I followed the herd. I put £100 on to win £50, or, to use the lingo of the Ring, had 'two fifties' on the horse that the whole track seemed to want to back. Needless to say, the short head went the other way. I had lost my century, but it served me right: I had not even seen the finish!

One day a new punter entered the photo finish market, betting late and with great success—but he only ever bet at the Curragh. Not only was he getting the result of the race right, he was also able to gauge the correct distance and back the winning distance from the choice offered, such as short head, head, neck or half-a-length. Bookmakers wondered at his uncanny ability and wanted to know more about this punter, although they did not think foul play was afoot. It was strange that a punter with an obvious talent for interpreting tight finishes had never attempted to try his skill at courses other than the Curragh. Anxious to know who they were dealing with, the bookies monitored his movements during the day and were amazed to discover that he did not watch the finish at all. Instead of going up to the finishing line, he always watched the races from the betting ring. It was soon discovered that he was getting a signal from another man, apparently the person who was watching the finish and forming the opinion of the result. However, surveillance of the second man proved that he did no such thing. He never bothered to position himself on the line at all, preferring to loiter at the back of the judges' box, high up in the stand. A little more sleuthing in this area led the bookies to discover a hole in the wall of the judges' box, allowing the second man to eavesdrop on what was being said inside. Listening to the deliberations inside the box, he would hear the winner and distance being agreed and while this information was being conveyed to the weigh-in room and the PA announcer, the eavesdropper signalled the result to our punter, who got in with his bet just before the result was announced. Another little coup had been exposed and the loophole that had facilitated it was closed—literally! The perpetrators had lost their winning streak simply because they never thought the bookies would become suspicious of their incredible run of success.

How to Win a Small Fortune: start with a big one
Too many people come into racecourse bookmaking with a lot of money but little experience of the business. The betting ring is full of people adept at separating a man from his money, by fair means or foul, with schemes that seem very plausible to the unsuspecting. In the old days, before computerised tickets became the norm, a bookmaker had to watch his tickets just as closely as his cash because another bookmaker's ticket was as good as cash to the disreputable bookie, who would slip it to an unsuspecting client. Punters rarely checked the name on the ticket before the race, habitually slipping it into the top pocket of their jackets. A problem arose if the horse won and the bookmaker whose name

was on the ticket was not at the meeting and the punter could not remember where he had the bet. This trick was invariably employed on the last race, giving the culprit an opportunity to escape before the punter began to look for his bookmaker.

A particularly horrible variation of this stroke was played frequently on bookmakers working at the races for the first time. An established bookmaker would never give a ticket to a person associated with another bookmaker, but a new bookie would be unfamiliar with the faces and the strokes. On his first day, a person associated with another bookie would have a bet (on the second-last or last race), proffer cash and get a ticket. A likely bet would be £3-to-£2 the favourite, in other words £2 at 6-to-4. The backer would give the ticket to another bookmaker working in the Ring, who would later slip that ticket to a punter that was having, say, £200 at 6-to-4 the same horse. The situation now was that the punter who had backed the favourite to win £500 with one book-maker actually had a different bookmaker's ticket, which was worth only £5 if the favourite won. If it got beaten, nobody was any wiser except the crooks, who had turned £2 into £200 with no liability at all. However, if the favourite won, the punter approached the bookmaker whose name was on his ticket, claim-ing £500, blissfully unaware that he had struck his bet with a different bookmaker. The bookmaker he approached would protest that the bet was only £2, therefore the punter was only entitled to £5, and one hell of a 'barney' would result. As the row blazed the rogue bookmaker would depart the scene with the argument between the punter and the debutante bookmaker ringing in his ears.

Another nasty trick played on novice bookmakers by hangers-on was the 'dead one' trick. A person familiar, but not really known, to the bookmaker would approach the bookmaker in the middle of the betting, claiming he had information that the favourite would not win. Asking the bookmaker to lay the horse on his behalf to 'loose a monkey' (£500), the hanger-on would not put the money into the bag, although he was liable for that amount if the horse did, by some chance, win. Again, if the horse gets beaten, there is no trouble—the bookmaker is a big winner having stood the horse for more money than he had originally intended, while the hanger-on gets the stake money on his monkey. It is a very different matter if the horse wins, which it often will do because it is not 'dead' at all, merely not fancied by the hanger-on. In that situation the bookmaker has a bigger loss on his hands than he expected, which will be exacerbated when the hanger-on knocks him for the monkey!

The problem with bookmaking is that almost everyone who has an interest in betting believes he would be a successful bookmaker, if he only had enough money. Down the years there was a regular entry into the business by people who had come into money and wanted to fulfil a dream. In virtually all cases the late-starting bookmaker lost his money and had to bail out of the business. Bookmaking is a young man's business. It is fiercely competitive and in those pre-computer days required a fine mathematical brain and a clear understanding of odds—something most people find very difficult to master.

One elderly man, we shall call him Gerry Smith, came into racing after retiring from his day job. He bought a betting shop in Bray and also turned out as a racecourse bookmaker. He started out in the mid-1970s, when trainer Vincent O'Brien and jockey Lester Piggott were winning all before them at the Curragh. A horse trained by O'Brien and ridden by Piggott was invariably an odds-on shot, but our ambitious bookmaker chalked up a generous even money against one of their hotpots in a two-year-old race. Upon seeing this, one of his colleagues immediately warned him to be careful because the horse in question was one of Vincent O'Brien's, to which Gerry optimistically replied, 'Vincent O'Brien's horses have four legs and a tail just like any other horse', and continued to offer, and lay, the price to punters. Predictably enough, ignoring his colleague's advice in this instance cost poor old Gerry a fortune.

Shortly after this incident, the secretary of the Bookmakers' Association noticed Gerry's death in the obituaries and hurried out to the church in Bray with a wreath. It was in the middle of the busy racing season, so he knew none of his colleagues would be able to attend the funeral and he felt someone ought to make an appearance on the bookies' behalf. Just as he expected, not a single bookmaker turned up, apart from himself. He approached the grieving widow, Mrs Smith, and offered his condolences, 'Very sorry to hear of Gerry's death,' he said with sincere regret, 'he will be badly missed in the betting ring.' He gave her the wreath from the bookmakers, repeated these sentiments to the rest of the Smith family and went home, pleased that Gerry's death had not been completely ignored. Imagine, then, his shock the following Saturday when he saw Gerry, large as life, betting away as usual in the Ring!

Billy Heffernan's short-lived career

The shortest betting-shop career must surely be that of Billy Heffernan's outfit in Clonmel, Co. Tipperary. Heffernan started trading in the days of the 20 per cent tax, which the punters had to pay every time they had a bet. Unlike some other bookies, Billy refused to evade the tax, and his honesty was to be his undoing. It also must be said that the shop's location was not the best either, but the combination of a bad location and the charging of betting tax ensured it remained open for only one week, during which time it did not take a bet of any description! That was enough for Billy Heffernan, who promptly returned to the pub business, which has loyal and devoted punters, regardless of tax!

The on-course equivalent of Billy Heffernan was James Simpson from Killenaule, who hit Irish racecourses in the mid-1980s in Galway's outside enclosure, but decided to pack the business in after the Tramore meeting—just three weeks later. Known for his cheery good humour and Stetson hat, Simpson owned the Punters' Paradise betting shop and the racehorse *James Rose*. The Punters' Paradise was aptly named because his punters never stopped winning, which meant that this Garden of Eden soon became a wilderness. Simpson's diversion into racecourse book-making was short and sweet: he didn't enjoy a single winning day before packing it in, being one of those unfortunate, but rare, bookmakers who seem to attract winning punters and get shunned by losing ones. Nevertheless, he is one of the few bookmakers to be genuinely missed by the punters.

And finally there was Reg, who returned to Ireland from

Australia with a few bob in the 1970s and decided to give
bookmaking a fling. Bookmakers operate under a pecking order
known as 'seniority', which broadly means that those who are
there the longest have the best pitches. As he was just starting out
in the business, Reg had to take his place at the end of the line; I
remember betting beside him at the Phoenix Park. In those days,
the new bookmakers were accommodated on a line outside the
betting ring proper, which was situated right in front of the gents'
toilet. Reg was not happy with his pitch, loudly accusing his fellow
bookies of deliberately putting him out in the 's***house' (insert
a crude Aussie term for public convenience!). Reg moaned about
his cruel misfortune all day long—so much so that it became a
sort of trademark.

Poor Reg, who was a big man, caught a terrible wasting disease,
went to skin and bone within weeks and was dead within a few
months. I remember his funeral well: we were standing in the
cemetery during the interment when suddenly there was the
unmistakable sound of stifled giggles all around me. Perplexed, I
looked around for the cause of this grave disrespect, and saw that
the guilty parties were bookmakers. They had noticed that Reg
was being buried right next to the cemetery's public conveniences!

PART 2
THE CHARACTERS

'Depend on the rabbit's foot if you will, but remember, it didn't work for the rabbit.'

R.E. SHAY

In racing parlance the term 'character' can mean one of three things: the person under discussion is either a rogue, a maverick, or famous. If applied to a rogue, it means the person is a plausible rogue, even a lovable rogue—but a rogue nonetheless! That rogue may even be a villain by normal standards, but through familiarity his personality has made an impression and his acquaintances routinely forgive and forget his dark side. That is, of course, until they are caught up in one of his scams!

It reminds me of the old story about the snake and the swan. The snake was trapped on an island without food and was desperate to escape. It asked a swan to give it a lift across the water to the mainland. The swan, afraid of the snake, refused at first, but then relented when the snake pleaded for mercy, pointing out that it would make no sense for him to hurt his rescuer. The swan duly carried the snake across the water to safety, whereupon the snake bit the swan with its poisoned tongue. As the swan lay dying, it asked the snake why it had done this. The snake replied, 'It's my nature'. The same applies to some of the characters of racing—it is in their nature to pull a stroke, even if it is at the expense of their friends and patrons. Money is sometimes, but by no means always, the root cause because most 'characters' would prefer to win €100 by pulling off a coup than win €1,000 by fair means. It is also likely that the 'characters' in this generation are doomed to die, like those of past generations, penniless and forgotten.

If the 'character' is not a rogue, then he will be an eccentric or one who does his business differently from everyone else, in other words, a maverick. Like rogues, mavericks generally do not prosper and are forgotten almost as quickly. However, when there is a bout of nostalgia and their name crops up, they are usually remembered because of some amusing story in which they played a starring role. That leaves us with the famous—nothing need be said about them!

RAS PRINCE MONOLULU (c.1885–1965)

In the first half of the last century there was a tipster named Peter McKay who referred to himself rather grandly as Ras Prince Monolulu, even though he was not a prince of any description.

Conspicuous and ubiquitous, Monolulu claimed to be 'in the know' and sold his information to racegoers for a few pence. Dressed up in a pearly jacket, baggy trousers, an ostrich-feathered head-dress and armed with an umbrella, whatever the weather, Monolulu would position himself at the entrance to the race-course, where he would wave a piece of paper he claimed was a telegram from a training centre with a 'dead cert' for that day. All the while he shouted his slogan: 'I gotta horse'. Those who paid him sixpence were given the name of that 'certain winner' and earnestly urged not to divulge it to anyone, lest the name got back to the bookies and they hammered down the price. Monolulu almost certainly gave different horses to different folk. He classified people into groups, such as old, middle-aged and young, and each group got the name of a different horse. One of the tips was sure to win, guaranteeing Monolulu after-race gratuities from delighted clients.

Monolulu was a typical racing character: a plausible rogue who got more than his fair share of publicity down the years, wrote an autobiography (published in 1950) that succeeded in revealing little about his real self, then died penniless and forgotten. The subject of thousands of photographs taken by both amateurs and professionals, he was an interesting sideshow for the infrequent racegoer and the tourist, but regulars did not give him a second glance—he was just another racecourse 'face' seeking to eek out a living selling 'tips' to unsuspecting mugs. When he disappeared from his usual pitch he was barely missed and immediately forgotten. Today it is a different matter, however. Monolulu has become part of the nostalgia market and his grubby, pearly jacket, fit only for the bin when he died, somehow survived and is now worth more money than the skint tipster ever had when he was alive. People who would run a mile from him were he alive today now describe him affectionately as part of a long tradition of characters who have brought colour and excitement to the sport of racing; who is a true example of how all men are equal on, and under, the Turf.

CAPTAIN DENIS O'KELLY (c.1728–1787)

One of the most astute purchases of a horse took place in 1769 when Captain Denis O'Kelly purchased the racehorse *Eclipse* after he had backed it to win a race by a distance. His celebrated bet was struck on the basis of '*Eclipse* first, the rest nowhere', which, according to the rules in force at the time, meant that the horse had to beat every other horse by a distance, i.e. 240 yards! In those days there were two judges: the judge and the distance judge. It was the job of the former to declare the result and of the latter to declare those horses that were unplaced. The distance judge sat in a chair down the course at the distance post, twenty yards beyond the furlong pole. When the winner passed the winning post the judge would give the distance judge a signal and any horse that had not already passed the distance judge would be declared unplaced, no matter if it went on to finish second or third in the race, and all the stake money was paid to the winner. On the occasion of O'Kelly's bet, *Eclipse* passed the judge before any of his opponents had passed the distance judge. *Eclipse* was declared the winner, all the other runners were distanced by the distance judge and were not eligible to be awarded second or third place, which was exactly the outcome that O'Kelly had bet on.

O'Kelly came from humble origins. Born into an impoverished Irish family, he had no education to speak of and as soon as he was old enough left home, seeking his fortune in London. Forced to take on menial and odd jobs to survive, O'Kelly was a 'chancer' and a fearless gambler, but then, he had nothing to lose. He ran in and out of money and served a jail sentence for debt before his luck turned. A sequence of winning bets enabled him to amass a tidy sum of money, which he put to good use. With his eye firmly on the future, Denis O'Kelly purchased a commission in the Army, funding his new lifestyle by successful betting. His innovative bet on *Eclipse* changed his life forever and set him on the road to a fortune. Never beaten on the racecourse, *Eclipse* retired to stud, where he was destined to become one of the greatest stallions of all time.

Foaled in 1764, the year of a spectacular eclipse of the sun, *Eclipse* won eighteen races in his unbeaten career at places like Winchester, Canterbury, Lewes, Ascot, Salisbury, Newmarket,

Guildford, Nottingham, York and Lincoln. O'Kelly purchased the large Clay Hill Stud Farm at Epsom, installed *Eclipse* as the resident stallion and kept fifty brood mares. He charged mare-owners fifty guineas for *Eclipse*'s services, which earned him a steady income for the rest of his life. Although *Eclipse* never became the champion sire, he did finish runner-up in the list of leading stallions eleven times and his progeny won 862 races and £158,047 in prize money. *Eclipse* begot three winners of the Derby, two of them—*Young Eclipse* and *Sergeant*—for the then Colonel O'Kelly and one winner of the Oaks. Incidentally, *Sergeant* became the first Derby winner to go to stud in Ireland, taking up duties at the Castletown House Stud, Leixlip, in 1790.

The purchase of *Eclipse* allowed Denis O'Kelly to live out his life in splendid style, sharing his time between his stud at Epsom, an estate in North London and a town house in Piccadilly, and the great horse that had made it all possible survived him by two years. All this came about from a betting coup when O'Kelly landed a bet nobody else believed could be pulled off!

JAMES CARR-BOYLE, FIFTH EARL OF GLASGOW (1792–1869)

This well-known owner raced horses on a large scale for over fifty years, yet despite his willingness to get rid of the bad ones as quickly as possible and bearing in mind the amount of money he ploughed into the sport, he met with little success on the Turf. During his lifetime his 'white, crimson sleeves & cap' colours were generally regarded as being unlucky, with his only Classic success coming towards the end of his life when *General Peel* won the 1864 Two Thousand Guineas. Lord Glasgow was equanimous about his reputation as an unlucky man, responding philosophically, 'that nobody with an income of a quarter-of-a-million pounds a year could ever be called unlucky!'

Famous for his reluctance to name his horses, Lord Glasgow had no sentimental attachment to his horses at all, despite keeping them in the lap of luxury, no expense spared—as long as they reached a certain standard. He had no time at all for slow horses, which were liable to be shot on the spot, but sometimes he would give a frustrating type of horse one last chance to save itself. In the latter case, before a race he would make a public declaration that if a certain horse of his did not win, it would be shot immediately after passing the post, a statement that encouraged the ghouls to come to the races in force. They would gather around the gun-man, who was waiting just beyond the finishing line, ready to shoot the horse if it was beaten. Surprisingly, more often than not the ghouls were disappointed. It was uncanny the number of times the threatened horse would win, or would run so well that it earned a reprieve. As a result, the sight of Lord Glasgow's man with a gun actually encouraged backers to back the horse that was under the death sentence, knowing that it was a certain trier and was running for its life—literally!

JOHN GUBBINS (1840–1906)

The inheritor of a sizeable sum from a wealthy uncle, John Gubbins accepted his good fortune with an easy come, easy go attitude, investing almost the entire amount on the outcome of a horse-race. Luckily for him the horse, *Whisper Low*, won the race. Even when he had acquired great wealth, he never lost his love of bringing off a betting coup. Fortunate to have the brilliant Henry Eyre Linde as his trainer, Gubbins successfully clobbered the bookmakers when the 'Linde-jumpers' were supreme and was one of the few plungers to make racing pay consistently. Gubbins bred and owned two winners of the Derby, *Galtee More* and *Ard Patrick*, and one winner of the Irish Derby, *Blairfinde*, and was lucky in everything except the Grand National. He never managed to win that important race and had the misfortune to see his horse *Cyrus* finish second, beaten a head by his cast-off, *Seaman*, which he had sold a few weeks before the race. He owned two beaten Grand National favourites: the beauti-ful mare *Zitella* and the ill-fated *Usna*, who looked sure to win until breaking a shoulder half-a-mile from the finishing line. Based at Bruree, Co. Limerick, the obese John Gubbins was a decent rider in his youth and a keen follower of hounds, but high living had made him not only fat but also a martyr to gout in his middle age. The local rumour mill credited him as being the real father of Éamon de Valera, although the latter's lanky frame, which he kept into old age, presented no suggestion that the rumour might be true.

RICHARD 'DICK' DUGGAN (1875–1935)

One of the largest public funerals ever seen in Dublin was that of Dick Duggan, bookmaker, director of the Irish Hospital Sweepstakes Company and a prominent owner of racehorses, who died on 4 November 1935 at his residence, Wilton House, on the Merrion Road. Born in Dublin, Duggan was working as a commercial traveller when he caught the racing bug and began making a book in his spare time. After a while he found bookmaking more lucrative, albeit more risky, than a permanent job, though not secure enough to give up work completely. Displaying the kind of astuteness that would make him a winner, he employed a deputy to do his job for him while he worked as a bookmaker at the races. The subterfuge was exposed, however, when his growing prominence in the betting ring led to his photograph appearing in a newspaper. He was subsequently sacked. Forced to swop a regular income for the glorious uncertainty of racing, Dick Duggan never looked back and went on to become one of the leading bookmakers in Ireland. As well as his on-course business, Duggan operated a large credit SP business from plush offices at 38 St Stephen's Green, Dublin, had his own distinctive telephone number, 5555, and a telegraphic address, Dulcet Dublin.

Although Duggan was comfortably-off as a bookmaker, it was his association with the Irish Hospitals Sweepstake Company that made his fortune. Fortunate indeed to be an ally of Joe McGrath, who persuaded the Irish government to give him a Sweepstake licence in 1930, Dick Duggan became a director of the company. It proved to be a licence to print money and made its promoters a fortune, but its operation is only now being critically examined. For many years the Irish Hospitals Sweepstakes was lauded for the employment it generated and for the financial assistance it provided to Irish hospitals, enabling it to operate in relative secrecy. However, recent exposures indicate that only a trivial amount of money was actually passed on to the hospitals, that the company involved itself in bribery and corruption of officials, especially in the United States, and that Dick Duggan's policy of buying shares in tickets drawn by subscribers was grossly unfair, to say the least.

The Sweep operated by drawing a ticket out of a drum. A runner in a forthcoming big race was allotted to that ticket, and the size of the winnings was decided by the final placing of that horse. First prize went to the holder of the ticket that drew the winning horse, second prize to the holder that drew the second and so on, but the holders had no idea how much or how little they had won until after the race. Appreciating this uncertainty, Duggan was in a position to get the names and addresses of the persons who had drawn horses and, being a bookmaker, he understood the odds and started the practice of officially contacting winners, suggesting they hedge against the risk of bagging only a small prize by selling a share in the ticket. However, it has since been alleged that the offer was made too quickly after the draw, that an interested party persuaded the ticket-holder that it was in his interest to sell a share and that the price offered was way below the market value. These allegations may or may not be true, but there is no doubt that it was company policy to trade in the tickets—with the odds very much in the company's favour. Emilio Scala, the Battersea Café owner who won an incredible £354,724 in 1931, did not receive that amount at all because he was persuaded by the Sweepstake Company to sell it a share in the ticket for a consideration.

The company would point out that if the horse failed to reach a place, the winnings would be tiny, therefore selling a share made good fiscal sense. The official nature of the approach was quite wrong, however, and the Sweep should not have been wheeling and dealing in shares of tickets in secret—a fact the company eventually conceded. When it withdrew from this market, a number of independent professionals, notably the bookmaker Terry Rogers, competed in an open-market bidding for shares in winning tickets.

In the 1920s Mrs Gillespie, known as the 'Blue Lady' became the first female on-course bookmaker in Ireland, taking cash from her pitch in the betting ring just like the men. She worked the Metropolitan meetings (i.e. those close to Dublin), but she did not prosper and was eventually saved from extinction only by the intervention of Dick Duggan, who put up the cash to keep her in business. Unfortunately, it was a case of postponing the inevitable.

Sharks rarely show mercy, particularly when a rich man is paying the bills, and Mrs Gillespie was a target for every 'toucher' on the racecourse. Her losses mounted, the rich man pulled the plug and the only lady bookmaker of the time disappeared into the mists of legend.

HORACE J. PINK (FIRST HALF TWENTIETH CENTURY)

In 1936 an unknown Australian professional jockey named Horace Pink arrived in the Emerald Isle to try his luck after a poor spell back home. The poor fellow's Irish career lasted just six weeks and consisted of only four rides, all included among the also-rans, yet there is a bar named in his honour at the Curragh racecourse— the Horace Pink Bar. How on earth did such an abject failure achieve such lofty status?

Pink's first mount in Ireland was at Baldoyle on 19 August on a no-hoper named *Miss Mufsie*, trained by Senator Jim Parkinson. Then followed two rides at the Phoenix Park on horses trained by John Staunton, a Great War veteran who had trained in Ireland only for a couple of seasons. Then came the infamous day at the Curragh—Wednesday, 16 September 1936. As racegoers gazed at the unfamiliar figure of Pink, standing in the parade ring in his black and white halved silks, awaiting his riding instructions, little did anyone know—least of all himself—that he had reached the end of his brief Irish career.

He was to ride a two-year-old named *Another Greek*, trained by Staunton. It was the horse's first race, but its form on the home gallops indicated it should be good enough to win an average Curragh maiden race. As Pink watched his mount being led round the parade ring, clad in a light blanket, he must have been reflecting on the effect that his first Irish winner could have on his career. A bombshell awaited poor Horace, however. Unexpectedly, he received new riding instructions: not to win on any account. The gamble was off because someone other than the connections had got in first and taken the price. All the big odds offered against *Another Greek* had been taken by outsiders, leaving those who owned the horse with the miserly 3-to-1 now on offer. Miffed that their price had been taken and determined to punish those who stole the market, the connections abandoned the intended gamble, deciding instead to give the horse an easy introduction to racing by not trying to win.

Startled by the unexpected instruction not to win and disappointed that his opportunity to ride a winner had been wrested from him, Pink was nonetheless well aware that in Ireland a jockey was expected to ride to instructions—no exceptions. Failure to do so would mean instant dismissal, but he fretted over how he was to get beaten on a fancied horse, a horse whose performance was now of interest to a great many people. Nobody is particularly interested in a seeming no-hoper, but a fancied horse is another matter altogether. It meant the jockey had to stop the horse while being seen to be doing his very best to win. Daunted by the task, wary of the stewards and downright afraid of an irate Mr Staunton, Pink may have reflected that in his native land the stewards would give a jockey a six-month suspension if he failed to ensure that his mount achieved its best possible placing. Unfamiliar with Irish conditions, the fear of a long suspension must have weighed heavily on his mind as he pondered the best way to give *Another Greek* an easy race.

He could have got left at the start, he could have been slowly away, but in his anxiety Pink messed things up and found himself in a prominent position, full of running with just two furlongs to race. In a quandary, he had two bleak choices before him: win, in which case he would have to face the furious connections and an uncertain future as a jockey; or lose and hand in his licence to the stewards before they took it off him. Pulling a horse in full view of the public is not tolerated in Ireland, not even on a two-year-old first time out! Of the two, the first option was the better one, but the flummoxed Pink was too scared to face a furious employer. That's when he did the entirely unexpected. He jumped off his horse, risking life and limb in the process. When he gingerly rose to his feet after his unseemly exit from the saddle, it dawned on him that this hasty third option might not have been so clever after all. His employers would still be furious that he had failed miserably to carry out a simple instruction. *Another Greek*'s ability had been exposed and the stewards were certain to inquire into his fall—they always did. Not wanting to face the music, the faint-hearted Horace Pink ducked under the inside rail, disappeared across the Curragh plain and was never seen or heard of again. At least, not until the Horace Pink Bar opened at the Curragh some sixty years later!

THE HONOURABLE DOROTHY PAGET (1905–1960)
One of the great characters of her time was the Honourable Dorothy Paget, whose oversized, unfashionable figure and drab overcoat, which she called the 'speckled hen', hid her enormous fortune and her youthful skills on a horse. Eccentric, reclusive and deeply suspicious of men, Dorothy was a granddaughter of the American multi-millionaire W.C. Whitney, inheriting that family's love of horses and racing together with a large slice of its fortune. Her 'blue with yellow hoop' colours were dominant on the Turf for over a quarter of a century, both in Ireland and England, but she was impossible to train for and fought continually with her successive trainers. Only Charlie Rogers, whom she called 'Romeo', could handle her, so he remained her Irish trainer and manager throughout her life. Although she owned the Ballymacoll Stud in Dunboyne, Co. Meath, she never visited the place in her lifetime, but knew it intimately by means of photographs sent regularly to her in England.

Dorothy Paget's first love was motor racing. She was reputed to have spent £20,000 a year in the 1920s on that craze before dramatically switching to horse racing in 1931, at which time she bought extensively and expensively at the various autumn horse sales. A recognised judge of a horse and once very keen on hunting, she had been breeding hunters and show horses for several years and had won many prizes for her stock, but now racing became her passion. Her love of racing was spiced by her love of betting and she entered into an arrangement with William Hill, the famous bookmaker, whereby she could place bets on races that already had been run.

This unusual arrangement was down to Miss Paget's ridiculous nocturnal lifestyle: she slept by day, rose in the evening and had her main meal after midnight. Her habit was to rise, read the

Sporting Life, pick out her selections (which had already run and won or lost) and before dinner phone Hill personally with her bets. When Charlie Rogers sent over one of her horses to run at places like Folkestone, William Hill knew that just before midnight Miss Paget would be calling to put on something in the region of £20,000! Sometimes they won, sometimes they lost, but they were always a short price—nevertheless, when one of them did win, Hill had to sweat for several hours before he knew exactly what it was going to cost him. Luckily for him, Paget's integrity was impeachable. There was never a chance she might have a bet knowing the result, and she always paid up her losses promptly. A story is told of the day when the great jockey Gordon Richards, recently knighted, won the Derby on *Pinza*, thus ending a voodoo that had seen him fail to win the race, despite thirty years' dominance in the saddle. That Saturday evening in June Miss Paget rose as usual, studied the form and decided on her selections, one of which was *Pinza*. Before she had telephoned William Hill with her bets, one of her many secretaries forgot herself in her excitement and told Miss Paget the great news about Sir Gordon winning the Derby at long last! Shocked and disappointed by the revelation, Miss Paget rebuked her, 'Why did you tell me that? *Pinza* was my nap of the day and now I can't back it.'

JAMES CONNOLLY QUINN (*c.*1918–*c.*1988)
A man named James Connolly Quinn was cock o' the walk in Belfast at the end of the Second World War. A dapper man in his mid-twenties, he had made a fortune smuggling, black marketeering and doping greyhounds before diversifying into legitimate business by setting up as a bookmaker. Working at the Belfast greyhound tracks and the two Northern racecourses, the Maze and Downpatrick, Connolly Quinn acquired a reputation for being able to get money on horses or dogs at a fair price, which meant he was constantly in demand to do commissions on behalf of others. A gangster he may have been, but he had integrity, did the job well and his services were the preferred option for owners and trainers going for a gamble in the North. Well-known in both horse and greyhound racing circles, Connolly Quinn was awash

with cash and ensconced in a pleasant house on the Malone Road, a prosperous area in Belfast. Reputed to have been the first person in Ireland to pay £1,000 for a greyhound, he had lots of dogs and a few horses in training, but, like most villains, his horses and dogs did not race in his name.

Jimmy Rooney trained Connolly Quinn's horses, the best of which was *Mount Mills*, a moderate handicap hurdler but good enough to win four races. The previous year Connolly Quinn had purchased a horse named *Carmeen* and sent it to be trained by W.A. Parks. *Carmeen* did not run for eighteen months until, out of the blue, it appeared among the entries for a novice hurdle at Haydock Park on 1 December 1949. Meanwhile, *Mount Mills* finished third at Naas on 19 November 1949, but sometime during the next eleven days *Mount Mills* and *Carmeen* somehow got 'mixed up'. *Carmeen* would probably have been good enough to win that race anyway, but Connolly Quinn wanted to be sure. An experienced jumper of hurdles, *Mount Mills* was ineligible to run in a novice race and its jumping would have been much too slick for the inexperienced opposition, making it a 'good thing'. Anxious to back a certainty rather than a horse with a fair chance, Connolly Quinn arranged for *Mount Mills* to go to Haydock Park in place of *Carmeen*.

Mount Mills travelled to England under the care of its regular rider, Johnny Mescall, the stable's young apprentice, who was told that he was riding the horse in its race. Unfortunately, as it turned out, Connolly Quinn and Jimmy Rooney got cold feet, changed their mind about Mescall and jocked him off in favour of the vastly more experienced Bobby O'Ryan. A fellow Irishman, Bobby O'Ryan had won the Champion Hurdle on Dorothy Paget's *Distel* and had ridden *Mount Mills* previously, notably when winning at Baldoyle in 1946. Brooding over being jocked off, Mescall could think only of revenge. He had risked his licence by bringing the wrong horse to the meeting, had been promised the ride, but Jimmy Rooney had reneged on the deal.

There were no betting shops in Britain at the time, so Connolly Quinn got Victor Chandler to back the horse for him. Chandler placed most of the money with the legal off-course credit bookmakers, but it flooded back to the course and caused *Carmeen*'s price to tumble from 10-to-1 down to 13-to-8 favourite. Chandler had not expected the bookmakers to dump the money into the on-course market in such a manner: *Carmeen* had no worthwhile form, had been off the course for eighteen months and was trained by a virtually unknown Irish trainer. Smelling danger, the bookmakers made the right call because *Carmeen* ran out an easy winner by two lengths. As Connolly Quinn and Jimmy Rooney celebrated in the winner's enclosure, rumours were already starting to circulate that a ringer might be involved; Johnny Mescall had been talking.

Unaware of the rumours but following good practice when using a ringer, Jimmy Rooney attempted to get the horse away from Haydock Park as quickly as possible before anybody asked to examine it. He was delayed because Johnny Mescall had not loaded the horse and was nowhere to be found. As Rooney was loading the horse himself, Connolly Quinn arrived in the stable yard, panting. Between gasps he advised the trainer to get out of there immediately because Mescall had spilt the beans and the stewards would be looking for the horse. Instead of heading for Liverpool and the ferry back to Ireland, they headed to a rural area to dump the horse, fearing the police might be waiting for them at Liverpool. Stopping at the first farm he could find, Connolly Quinn asked the farmer to keep the horse for him for six months, paying him well over the going rate for the privilege. The farmer agreed readily, took the money and *Mount Mills* was released into a field where nobody would ever think of looking for it. Having safely stashed the horse, Connolly Quinn and Jimmy Rooney headed back to Ireland.

Upon arriving back in Dublin, the owner and trainer headed for home, unaware that their jockey was making a beeline for the offices of the Turf Club, the governing body of Irish racing, which at the time were located at 9 Hume Street, Dublin, just off St Stephen's Green. Johnny Mescall was singing like a canary, the stewards were very interested and they decided to employ a man to complete a professional investigation. They called in Andy O'Connor, 'the man in the green volure' as he dubbed himself when he wrote a series of articles about his experiences for a Sunday newspaper many years later. The Turf Club knew O'Connor from the time he worked as a bodyguard for Percy Reynolds, a member of the Club and a prominent owner of racehorses, who was the Chairman of CIÉ (Córas Iompar Éireann, the newly nationalised bus and train company). Reynolds went racing regularly and O'Connor was with him all the time, so he became well-known in racing circles by association. The government had provided Reynolds with a bodyguard because some twenty years previously, during the struggle for Irish independence, Frank Brook, Chairman of the Dublin & South Eastern Railway Company and a steward of the Turf Club, had been shot dead in the company boardroom at Westland Row. The perpetrator was never caught, but it was assumed Mr Brook was killed because he was the head of the railway company and not for his racing activities. At the time the nationalised transport company was formed, the IRA was active and the government feared an attack might be directed at CIÉ, with Percy Reynolds being the likely target. Andy O'Connor was charged with the safety of Mr Reynolds and did his job well.

By now the coup and the suspected ringer was headline news and the police, the press and Andy O'Connor were all looking for *Mount Mills*. They descended *en masse* upon Jimmy Rooney's stable near Drogheda, in Co. Louth. Rooney could not produce *Mount Mills*, which was supposed to be in training there, nor could he tell them where the horse was. Meanwhile, Connolly Quinn was lying low in Belfast and had a more immediate problem to contend with: Victor Chandler reported that the bookmakers were refusing to pay out on *Carmeen*. With an official enquiry investigating the identity of the winner, bookmakers had every right to withhold payment until it was confirmed that it was the horse it was purported to be. This setback was followed by more bad news. The Cheshire farmer who was keeping *Mount Mills* telephoned Connolly Quinn in a panic and insisted he remove the horse from his land within twenty-four hours, or else he would call in the police. Alerted by the publicity, the farmer had put two and two together and realised that the horse in question was grazing in his field and he did not want to be involved.

Left with no other choice, Connolly Quinn rushed to Liverpool, hired a horsebox and collected *Mount Mills* from the farm. Knowing that proving the charge of running a ringer would be difficult to do if the horse could not be found, he took the unfortunate horse straight to a knacker's yard and agreed to pay the knacker £3 to destroy it. In those days a horse was humanely destroyed with a hammer and chisel, the hammer being used to drive the chisel into the horse's temple, leading to instant death. As the knacker prepared the horse, he remarked that he could see nothing wrong with it, to which Connolly Quinn replied, 'I am paying you to kill the horse and dispose of it, not to examine it.' The knacker stood back and refused to kill the animal, arguing that if there was nothing wrong with the horse, then killing it would be tantamount to murder. No financial incentive would change his mind. The knacker told Connolly Quinn that he would have to do the job himself, but warned that it would bring him bad luck. Exasperated, Connolly Quinn took the hammer and chisel, asked to be shown how it was done and set about killing the horse himself. The knacker again pleaded with him not to kill the horse: 'If you do, you will never have a day's luck in your life.' Unmoved, Connolly Quinn put the chisel to *Mount Mills'* head and swung the hammer. The horse dropped to the ground, spraying blood from its nostrils all over Connolly Quinn's expensive, immaculate suit. The stewards would never have their evidence!

Thanks to Johnny Mescall's enthusiastic co-operation, Andy O'Connor was hot on the heels of the perpetrators. He knew that a ringer had run in the place of Carmeen, and that *Mount Mills* was that ringer, and he assembled a dossier of evidence. This was enough to seal the fate of the conspirators, Messrs Parks, Rooney and Quinn, without having to produce *Mount Mills* for inspection. The stewards warned the three men off the course, which barred them from entering a licenced stable and from going racing. In return for his co-operation, Johnny Mescall escaped punishment for his minor part in the affair, but his career suffered nonetheless because racing people disliked a 'rat' and were wary of him ever after. In later years Mescall blamed Connolly Quinn for ruining his career: Connolly Quinn blamed Johnny Mescall for ruining his life.

To his dying day Connolly Quinn maintained that his murder of *Mount Mills* had turned him from a top dog to a 'beaten docket', just like those that lay on the floor of a betting shop at the end of the day. Warned off the Turf and thus deprived of his livelihood, Connolly Quinn went back to his roots and started doping greyhounds again. He met an American man who was an expert on drugs and doping, and from him learned the art of doping an animal with a tiny syringe. In this manner a horse could be doped, quickly and effectively, by an innocent-looking pat on its neck, in full view of everyone, and the deed not noticed by anyone. As an up-to-date expert on doping, Connolly Quinn's services were once again in demand, but just as he was establishing himself in his new career he was stopped in his tracks, when he was caught doping a dog. Banned from all greyhound tracks as well, his needling career was brought to an abrupt end but worse was to follow when the police charged him with the offence of doping a greyhound. Connolly Quinn responded by trying to bribe the jury, was caught and ended up in gaol. On his release he began to drink heavily—although he was never seen drunk in public. His well-appointed house was sold, his wealthy friends shunned him and the hangers-on deserted him.

His lot improved when his warning off was eventually lifted, at which time he got a job working as a bookmakers' assistant and was never out of work again. As a former bookmaker, Connolly Quinn knew the job well, his legitimate services were in constant demand but his nature would never leave him. Employment enabled him to earn a living and to regain his self-respect, but he still had no compunction about climbing a fence and unscrewing a lock if a 'climber' was needed to get at a dog. Connolly Quinn audaciously 'nobbled' the top-class greyhound *Not Flashing* right under the nose of its owner. *Not Flashing* lined up for the semifinal of the English Greyhound Derby, but was sensationally and controversially disqualified for fighting and its place in the race given to a dog owned by the Duke of Edinburgh. The decision was roundly condemned in Belfast as biased. Doggy people there would never believe that *Not Flashing* had been fighting, preferring to put its disqualification down to the desirability of having a Royal greyhound in the final.

Not Flashing was 3-to-1 ON to win a big stake at Celtic Park and its owner feared an attempt might be made to dope the dog, so he guarded it twenty-four hours a day. Hired to do just that, Connolly Quinn kept a close watch, waiting for his opportunity. The dog was kennelled in a building located in the garden of the owner's house, a lookout was always on duty and the owner had set up a camp bed inside the kennel, where he slept next to the dog for several nights before the race. In spite of all this caution, the wily Connolly Quinn discovered a small gap in the security measures. Each morning the owner emerged from the kennel and slipped into his house for a quick breakfast, without waiting for the sentry to arrive. For that short space of time the dog was unattended, and this was when Connolly Quinn struck. Over the fence he went, screwed off the lock, doped the dog and made his escape before the owner had finished his bacon and eggs.

Ever on the lookout for new ideas to stop horses or dogs, now that he was getting too old to climb fences, Connolly Quinn took a keen interest in a tiny torch with a long, bright beam that came on the market in the late 1970s. He purchased one and took it to Fairyhouse, declaring that he would stop an odds-on shot running that day. As his bookmaker friends laid the horse in the Ring, Connolly Quinn strolled down to the penultimate fence, where cars used to park in a small adjacent enclosure. Loitering among the cars, Connolly Quinn watched the favourite approach the fence in the lead, turned on his torch and directed the beam towards the horse's eye. The favourite did jump out to the right at the fence, losing a couple of lengths, and was subsequently beaten in a close finish, enabling Connolly Quinn to boast that he had done it again. He claimed that the favourite had faltered when the light hit its eye, causing it to jump to the right, losing valuable ground and ultimately the race. Perhaps the little torch was decisive that day, perhaps it wasn't, in any event the torch method of stopping horses was abandoned because of its unreliability and the very real possibility of getting caught.

An insurance scam was rife in Ireland around this time and a small trainer, who later became well known, introduced one of his bookmaker clients to the scam. He urged the bookmaker to take a chance with a highly strung horse that a leading stable was selling off, the trainer not having the time to devote to it. Available at a knock-down price of £5,000, the bookmaker was advised to purchase the horse and to insure it for £25,000. If the horse proved to be no good, then its leg would be broken and the bookmaker could claim the insurance. The bookmaker was guaranteed either a good horse for £5,000 or a £15,000 profit (his trainer's commission was £5,000)—a certain winning bet. It was an offer that could not be refused, and it wasn't!

At first all went well. The horse ran reasonably well in a bumper at Gowran Park only to flop in a maiden hurdle at Navan a couple of weeks later. It was displaying signs that it was not in love with the game and the problem got progressively worse. Having run abominably in another maiden hurdle at Navan, it was clear that the horse had become a rogue, being almost impossible to coax out of its stable, and when it did emerge it was unmanageable on the gallops. The trainer telephoned the bookmaker: the horse was useless, it was not worth persevering; it was time to break its leg. The bookmaker told his trainer to do what he had to do, and he would make a claim from the insurance company and pay the trainer his commission. Pleased with his £15,000 profit, the bookmaker met Connolly Quinn completely by chance in the street later that morning and told him all about the stroke. Connolly Quinn made no comment on the matter, they spoke for a few more minutes about other things, then went their separate ways.

Unknown to the bookmaker, Connolly Quinn headed straight for his house and told the bookmaker's wife what her husband intended to do with his horse. He begged her not to allow the horse to be killed, or 'murdered' as he called it, and related the story of *Mount Mills*. Connolly Quinn confessed he rued the day he murdered *Mount Mills*, that he regretted ignoring the knacker's warning that it would bring bad luck and how those words came back to haunt him every day of his life. He told her that within three years he had lost his lovely house and every penny he had, was incarcerated in prison and that the incident destroyed his life. He did not want to see her husband end up the same way and pleaded with her not to allow it happen. The bookmaker's wife had no idea what was going on with the horse, but she was appalled at the prospect of it being killed in cold blood and she too believed that it would be an unlucky thing to do. She immediately telephoned the trainer to protest, threatening to report him if he killed the horse. She succeeded in stopping the execution. Her husband could not believe his ears when he came home to a tirade of abuse from his wife. How she could send £25,000 down the Swanee on the say-so of Connolly Quinn and destroy a scam that would make his horse ownership much less expensive over the next few years? Not being in the least superstitious himself, he did not believe in bad luck and was devastated by Connolly Quinn's unwanted intervention. He sought him out to give him a tongue-lashing for ruining his carefully laid plans, but his ire had no effect on Connolly Quinn, who was entirely unrepentant: 'I have saved you from certain ruin. You should be thankful.'

Patrick J. 'Paddy' Prendergast (1909–1980)

Known to racing insiders as 'Darkie' because of his sallow complexion, Paddy Prendergast left Ireland for England, where he rode as a professional jockey on the small jumping courses until the outbreak of the Second World War in 1939. Jump-racing was suspended, so Paddy volunteered to join the Royal Air Force, but the numerous injuries he had sustained in jumping falls, including a broken neck, made him unsuitable for service. He returned with his family to Ireland. Out of work and broke, Paddy had no idea what he was going to do until a chance meeting in a bar with Mr J. Bradley, in 1941, gave him his break. Bradley suggested that Paddy take up training and offered to give him a horse or two to train. It was an offer that could not be resisted. As Paddy had neither money or yard, he was helped out by Michael Connolly, who was licenced to train on the Curragh and who lent Paddy a couple of boxes in his yard.

Now that he had a stable of sorts, Paddy bought *Spratstown* from Willie Ashe and within weeks landed a big gamble at Naas, when turning over the Bob Fetherstonhaugh-trained odds-on shot *Monk's Mistake* in the Mallow Plate. This win inspired Paddy to buy another horse for Mr Bradley, through Bertie Kerr, picking up *Rao Raja* from the Roderick More O'Ferrall stable for twenty-two guineas. Then *Spratstown* landed another gamble when winning at the Limerick Christmas meeting, but thereafter things began to go wrong. *Rao Raja* fell and was injured in his first race, which was over hurdles, and *Spratstown* was unable to keep on winning now that he had to compete in better class races and the stewards took an interest in the arrangements between Prendergast and Connolly. Rule nineteen of the Turf Club required that every trainer who wished to train horses on the Curragh had to apply every November for a special licence to do so. Furthermore, a Curragh trainer had to obtain permission from the Club before bringing any new horses on to the training grounds. Michael Connolly was fined a fiver and Paddy Prendergast a tenner for breaches of this rule, forcing Paddy to hand both horses over to Connolly to be trained. Meanwhile, Paddy went about getting his own yard and on 12 March 1943 was officially given permission to train horses on the Curragh. Paddy laid out a horse named *Pelorus* for his next gamble, he chose the Mallow Plate at Naas, which he had won with *Spratstown* two years before, and duly landed another spectacular coup, helping himself to lots of bookmakers' money.

Paddy survived those difficult years during the war by landing a number of betting coups, which kept him in business and brought him to the attention of influential owners. A charming man, Paddy succeeded in retaining his owners throughout their careers on the Turf. When the war was over, a succession of fast two-year-olds established his reputation and one of these, *Port Blanc*, provided him with his first winner in England. He dominated the Phoenix Stakes, commonly known as the Fifteen Hundred, winning the race six times in a row between 1950 and 1956. He could train older horses as well, winning both the Irish Derby and the Irish Oaks in 1952. In 1963 he became the first Irish-based trainer to head the list of trainers in England, retaining the title for the next two years—a feat only three men, all England-based, had managed before him.

(A little aside, if I may. In the early 1950s my grandfather came up from the country for the Phoenix Park races. Arriving by train at the Kingsbridge terminus, he went to catch a taxi for the short trip up to the course and was invited to share one with three other gentlemen, which he did. None of the four knew each other, but all were keen racing men and during the journey they discussed the various races. One of the four ventured a piece of information he had heard to the effect that Prendergast fancied his horse in one of the races and had said that it would win. That titbit drew a firm response from another: 'I'm Prendergast and it won't!' Not even the top trainers were familiar to racegoers at the time and none of the three realised that it was Paddy Prendergast himself who was sharing their taxi!)

In a big yard the trainer must work closely with the stable jockey to determine a horse's level in order to separate the better class of horse from the dross. The trainer will concentrate on the better horses, leaving his assistant to take charge of the lesser lights. In 1952 Paddy Prendergast had hopes of winning a big race with a useful but injury-plagued three-year-old colt named *Blue Chariot*. Injury had ruled *Blue Chariot* out of the Irish Two Thousand Guineas, but the horse was fancied to win a weak-looking Irish Derby, in which there were no English-trained runners because of an outbreak of foot-and-mouth disease there. The trainer decided he would not use his stable jockey on this occasion, instead booking the best big race jockey of the time to ride *Blue Chariot*, Charlie Smirke, with the stable jockey 'Corky' Mullane switching to the stable's second-string, *Thirteen of Diamonds*. *Blue Chariot* opened favourite, but began to drift in the betting when money came for *Thirteen of Diamonds*. Backed from 20-to-1 to half those odds, although apparently unfancied by its trainer, *Thirteen of Diamonds* swept past the pacemaker approaching the straight, surged clear and was never caught. The uneasy favourite was never going well on the hard ground, broke down in running and could not race afterwards. The source of the inspired gamble was revealed when a delighted Mullane confirmed that he had always thought *Thirteen of Diamonds* was the superior horse and had fully expected *Blue Chariot* to break down. Paddy Prendergast was not amused. Whether or not the jockey had expressed this view before the race, I do not know. He may have done so and the trainer simply dismissed it, or he could have wilfully withheld the information from Prendergast. Assuming the former scenario was the correct one, 'Corky' Mullane had done nothing wrong, except to make a fool of his boss in front of his owners and the public, an action which cost him his job and, ultimately, his career.

Paddy was dying when his charge *Nikoli*, unbeaten winner of the Irish Two Thousand Guineas, started favourite for the Derby, one of the few big races that the great trainer had never won. The dramatic end to a great career, wished for by many ordinary people in Ireland and in England, was not to be. *Nikoli's* temperament got the better of him and he ran poorly, finishing a disappointing eighth. By the time *Nikoli* flopped again in the Irish Derby, Paddy Prendergast was dead. Nikoli had been the last of his seventeen Irish Classic winners, which included four Irish Derby winners, *Dark Warrior, Thirteen of Diamonds, Ragusa* and *Meadow Court*. He had also trained winners of four of the five English Classic races; the Derby eluded him, although *Meadow Court* did finish runner-up to the exceptional *Sea Bird II*. He had won the Irish Trainers' Championship seven times, headed the list of trainers with the most winners in a season six times and left two sons, Kevin and Paddy Jnr, training in their own right on the Curragh.

Vincent O'Brien (1917–)

Michael Vincent O'Brien, the son of a trainer, began training on his own account in 1944 at Churchtown, Co. Cork, and immediately planned his first big gamble by trying to land both legs of the Irish Autumn Double of that year. The Autumn Double involved the two big flat handicaps run at the Curragh, the Irish Cambridgeshire and the Irish Cesarewitch, over distances of one mile and two miles respectively. Vincent's father, Dan O'Brien, had won both races, the former with *Solford* in 1938 and the latter with *Astrometer* three years later, and now his son planned to do the same, in the one year, with *Drybob* and *Good Days*. Although both horses were rank outsiders in the betting, Vincent convinced the champion jockey of the time, Morny Wing, to ride both horses. His decision to book the best jockey he could find was vindicated when Wing had to use all his skill to force a dead heat on *Drybob*. Although the divide reduced the SP of 20-to-1, backers of *Drybob* still got paid 10-to-1 for their money, which was a very satisfactory return. Vincent had to contend with a change of venue for the Irish Cesarewitch, the second leg of the double, which was transferred from the Curragh to the Phoenix Park that year, but all went well. On this occasion Wing had things a bit easier on *Good Days*, but only a bit, getting the horse up to win by a neck to record a staggering 199-to-1 double.

While these races were on the flat, Vincent was predominately a jumping trainer at the time and by the time the 1949 Irish Cesarewitch came round, his yard contained several high-class National Hunt horses, *Hatton's Grace, Cottage Rake, Knock Hard, Royal Tan* and *Castledermot*—horses that were to dominate jump-racing during the next few years. Having won the previous two runnings of the Irish Cesarewitch with *Cottage Rake* and *Hot Spring*, Vincent lined up three runners in search of his hat trick, *Cottage Rake*, already the winner of two Cheltenham Gold Cups, the Champion Hurdle winner *Hatton's Grace* and the young *Knock Hard*, a bumper winner for Willie O'Grady earlier in the year, which Vincent had been campaigning on the flat. Even with this master of his profession, things did go wrong occasionally and this was one of those rare occasions. The stable had gone for a big coup with *Knock Hard*, owned by Moya Keogh, whose husband Harry was a really big gambler, and there was so much money for the horse that it was backed down to a ridiculously short price of even money, bearing in mind that it was running in a competitive twenty-four-runner handicap. With all the money coming for *Knock Hard*, Vincent's other two runners drifted ominously in the market despite having worthwhile form on the flat. *Hatton's Grace*, with the brilliant champion jockey Martin Molony aboard, had won that year's Irish Lincoln, while *Cottage Rake* had won the Irish Cesarewitch two years previously.

To Vincent's embarrassment, Martin Molony gave *Hatton's Grace* an inspired ride to beat the gambled-on *Knock Hard* into second place, the pair going right away from the others. It was another big winner for the stable but the result was a reverse from the betting point of view, although Vincent tried to play it down by implying that the stable had not backed *Knock Hard*. Everybody knew that it had, though, and that the maestro had been caught out by his second string—even if pride would not allow him to admit it openly. Over the next half-a-dozen years the stable went from strength to strength, taking Cheltenham and Aintree by storm, winning the Cheltenham Gold Cup three times with *Cottage Rake* and once with *Knock Hard*; the Champion Hurdle three times with *Hatton's Grace* and an unprecedented three Grand Nationals in succession with *Early Mist* (1953), *Royal Tan* (1954) and *Quare Times* (1955). *Early Mist* and *Royal Tan* were owned by the well-known character Joe 'Mincemeat' Griffin, who threw celebration parties in the Adelphi Hotel that were still being talked about thirty years later, by which time poor Mincemeat Joe was long since flat broke. All this time Vincent's flat horses were also making a mark. *Chamier* had provided him with the first of his twenty-seven Irish Classic winners in 1953, while his departure from training jumpers to concentrate entirely on the flat coincided with his first real champion flat horse, *Ballymoss*. Owned by John McShain, *Ballymoss* gave Vincent his first English Classic success with the 1957 St Leger—the first Irish-trained horse to do so. *Ballymoss*, who was unlucky to come up against the brilliant but unsound *Crepello* in the Derby, won the Irish Derby and there were excuses for his flops in the Great Voltigeur Stakes (York) and the Champion Stakes (Newmarket). However, the following year the four-year-old was established as a true champion, winning the Coronation Cup (Epsom), Eclipse Stakes (Sandown Park), King George VI & Queen Elizabeth Stakes (Ascot) and the Prix de L'Arc de Triomphe (Longchamp), a feat that has not been matched before or since. *Ballymoss* ended the season having won record stakes on the British Turf.

Down the years O'Brien, like most top trainers, had his fair share of 'talking horses', the most sensational of which were *Storm Bird* and *Try My Best*. The *Try My Best* saga was the talk of the early months of 1978, when the twenty-seven-year-old millionaire Patrick Gallagher, Managing Director of the building firm Gallagher Group, purchased a quarter share in the colt for an enormous £750,000. *Try My Best* was the unbeaten winner of three races as a two-year-old in 1977, including the prestigious Dewhurst Stakes, and his jockey, Lester Piggott, claimed that he was easily the best juvenile seen out that year. Robert Sangster, in whose colours it ran, thought *Try My Best* was something exceptional even before it ran and Vincent O'Brien predicted that it might develop into another *Nijinsky*, the brilliant winner of the Triple Crown. *Try My Best* was actually the property of a syndicate headed by Sangster, but included Simon Fraser, Danny Schwartz, John Magnier and Vincent himself. Racegoers were incredulous because just over a year earlier Patrick Gallagher had sold his horse *Godswalk* to Robert Sangster and his pals for something over £300,000. *Godswalk* had just finished a successful two-year-old career, in which it won five races and was rated the second-best juvenile both in Ireland and in England. Now he was paying over twice that sum for a quarter share in the leading Irish two-year-old of the following year. In financial terms it did not make sense because *Try My Best* would have to win the Derby for Patrick Gallagher to get a profit on his investment.

Try My Best was already a 3-to-1 ante-post favourite for the Derby, when winning its introductory race at the Phoenix Park at odds of 4-to-1 ON and then embarked of its first real test—the Two Thousand Guineas. Vague rumours were circulating that all was not right with *Try My Best*, some said that the colt had gone wrong in its wind and it was an uneasy favourite, drifting out to even money on the day. Punters were wary of the horse, all the hype seemed to be tempting fate and there was also a nagging feeling that Robert Sangster would not part with a quarter share if *Try My Best* was as good a horse as it was being hailed in the press. The bubble burst spectacularly at Newmarket, *Try My Best* never really got into a challenging position and when Lester Piggott tried to push him up to the leaders with three furlongs to run, the colt hung left, found absolutely nothing under pressure and dropped steadily back through the field, finishing a dismal last of the nineteen runners. The three million pound horse had sensationally flopped! *Try My Best* never ran again. A routine dope test proved negative and the stable later reported that a virus was the cause, although that virus could never be identified.

Patrick Gallagher cut his losses, selling his quarter share back to the syndicate of Sangster, Fraser, Schwartz, Magnier and O'Brien stating that, 'I took the businessman's approach. You go into something hoping that it will come off for you. If it doesn't, then it may be best to get out and invest in another venture.' Hard-nosed inhabitants of the betting rings believed that Patrick Gallagher had been naïve, to say the least, rushing in to buy at the top of the market, paying over the odds and then having to cut his losses at the first setback. He surfaced again in 1981 when his company, Track Investments, bought the loss-making Phoenix Park Racecourse for £2.5 million in partnership with Vincent O'Brien, John Magnier and Robert Sangster and spent over £1 million refurbishing the course and building a new sunken parade ring. In April 1982 all work on the racecourse had to stop when the Gallagher Group crashed with debts of over £30 million. Few racegoers were surprised: racehorses, a loss-making racecourse, a big estate in Co. Kildare and a Rolls Royce gobble up a lot of money.

Vincent O'Brien, who retired in 1994, won the Derby with *Larkspur*, *Sir Ivor*, *Nijinsky*, *Riberto*, *The Minstrel* and *Golden Fleece* but the one that got away surely left an indelible mark on his heart. *El Gran Señor* displayed sheer brilliance when decisively beating a top-class field in the Two Thousand Guineas, tempting Vincent to express his opinion that he might be better than his outstanding charge, *Nijinsky*, winner of the Triple Crown in 1970. Then it was reported that a group of American breeders had offered an amazing $80 million for *El Gran Señor*, provided he won the Derby, and the horse started a hot, odds-on favourite to do so. When *El Gran Señor*, ridden by stable jockey Pat Eddery, cruised into the lead two out, it looked all over—the £228,000 prize money and the $80 million secure. He had cruised up to *Secreto* as if that horse was standing still and the latter was all out. Confidently, Eddery looked back at Christy Roche, as if to gloat about *El Gran Señor*'s superiority and brilliance and the backers of the favourite roared their approval. Suddenly and unexpectedly it all went wrong.

Eddery seemed to be riding a cheeky race, aiming to win without pushing his mount to the limit, but it allowed *Secreto* to come back at him under strong driving from its rider, Christy Roche. Now *El Gran Señor* was involved in a scrap, with *Secreto* staying on stoutly, and lacked the courage to deal with it. With *Secreto* getting back up, the spectators waited for *El Gran Señor* to sprint clear, but he could not do so—the brilliant burst of speed was gone. As *El Gran Señor* began hanging away from the rail, slightly hampering *Secreto* in the process, the two horses crossed the line inseparable to the naked eye. Vincent's emotions were in turmoil as they awaited the result of the photo finish; this Derby meant so much to him. *El Gran Señor* was possibly the best horse he had ever trained, the prestige of winning yet another Derby and the $80 million that was now in the balance weighed heavily on his mind, but on the other hand *Secreto* was trained by his son, David. Recognised by everyone as the trainer of the future, twenty-eight-year-old David trained nearby, but completely independently of his father, at Rahinaghmore, Cashel, where he had sixty-five horses under his care. Although only training for four years, he had already won an Irish and a French Derby with *Assert* and now he was inches away from winning the greatest Derby of them all.

The short head went David's way: *Secreto* won the Derby and the $80 million deal went up in smoke. Pat Eddery, in the shock of his disappointment, lodged an objection, although it was obvious that it was he who had caused the interference. His objection was quickly dismissed, and when he had cooled down he said he had never been travelling so easily in a race before and lost: 'I thought I had a stone in hand.' The young trainer had triumphed over his legendary father, but no good was to come of it. Four years later he got out of the business, apparently unable to stand the pressure.

Vincent soldiered on for another ten years before retiring, by which time he had equalled Michael Dawson's Irish training record of thirteen titles, had won a record twenty-seven Irish Classics, was champion trainer in England twice and *Nijinsky* had retained the honour of being the best horse the Maestro ever trained.

PADDY SLEATOR (1910–1986)

The legendary jumping trainer Patrick Joseph Sleator, who began training at Grange Con, Co. Wicklow, in 1928, landed little gambles all his life, but of course in those days prize money was so poor the only way racing could be made pay was through successful betting.

'Little and often' was Paddy's motto, but this genius with horses had to employ all manner of tricks to mislead bookmakers and the public—who were always inclined to back a Sleator-trained horse—in order to get a decent price. Sleator trained his first winner when *Slaney Boy*, owned by Captain T.J. Wilson, won a handicap steeplechase at the Meath Hunt meeting over the Boyerstown course at Navan. Paddy himself rode the horse to victory, recording the first win of his riding career, during which he was three times the top amateur rider in Ireland.

On one occasion the trainer ran a number of horses at a meeting but intended to land a big gamble with one of them, a horse making its racecourse debut in the last race. Having won two of the early races, Sleator pretended he was going home early, but before he left he instructed the jockey riding his runner in the last race to give the horse a quiet race. 'It's his first run, settle him at the back of the field, don't give him a hard race or hit him because, with the experience under his belt, he will win next week.' Having given the instructions, Paddy went to his car and drove off.

Once the boss was off the scene, the jockey confidently told all his pals not to back the horse because it was getting a quiet run. The jockey's pals told their pals, who in turn told other people, so that by the time the race was lining up, the news that the Sleator horse was not fancied had permeated down to the betting ring. The odds offered against the Sleator horse drifted out ominously, until suddenly all hell broke loose as Sleator's men stepped in to back it. Meanwhile at the start the horse was walking round, its jockey oblivious that his mount was now the hot favourite. Suddenly, out from behind a bush stepped Paddy Sleator, with new instructions for the jockey: 'There's been a change of plan, jump off in front, make all the running and win.' The horse and jockey duly did so, giving the bookmakers a roasting. Also caught were the invisible middlemen, those who never owned a horse in their lives nor paid a training bill but managed to be in on every betting coup by befriending jockeys. As I said, Paddy Sleator was a genius and the bookmakers never knew what he would do next.

Between 1961 and 1967, Sleator operated a second stable, in England, bending the rules in order to do so. His English base was

Guy's Cliffe, Warwick, but as far as the authorities and the public was concerned this was the licensed yard of Arthur Thomas. It was Thomas who was officially the trainer of the Sleator horses but actually he had nothing whatever to do with the Irish horses. All the Irish horses were contained in a separate yard under the care of Sleator's staff, who had no contact at all with Thomas, receiving their instructions from the man himself over the telephone. The few horses that Thomas trained were not allowed go near a Sleator horse and Bobby Beasley, Sleator's retained jockey, was under strict instructions not to tell Thomas anything. Having been prepared at Grange Con by Paddy himself, the horses were sent over to Guy's Cliffe shortly before they were due to race and everything was done in secret. Within weeks of this unusual arrangement coming into existence, every bookmaker and punter was talking about the unknown trainer, A.J. Thomas, who was landing gambles with ex-Sleator-trained horses. The English trainers had noticed Thomas, too, and were suspicious that rules were being broken, but they had no proof.

For a while Arthur Thomas revelled in the limelight, but soon he began to feel duped as it became evident that he knew nothing about what was going on. His post-race comments about his future plans for a horse invariably turned out to be completely wrong, making him a standing joke with the press and a target of resentment for his fellow trainers. Although he was training a lot of winners, including big races with *Scottish Memories* (Mackeson Gold Cup) and *Black Ice* (*Daily Express* Triumph Hurdle), Arthur Thomas was unhappy that he was being kept in the dark and had an increasingly uneasy relationship with Paddy Sleator and Bobby Beasley. The stewards were also unhappy about the arrangement between the two trainers and were looking at it closely to see if it involved a breach of the rules.

What Sleator was doing was not strictly against the rules of racing, which state that the trainer is responsible for the horses under his care, but the problem for the authorities was: who was the trainer? Ostensibly Arthur Thomas was training the horses, but all the talk, and much of the available evidence, indicated that Paddy Sleator was the person in charge. Sleator was not licenced and lived outside the jurisdiction of the governing bodies, which meant he could do as he pleased without fear of a penalty. As the authorities dilly-dallied on taking action, the Sleator/Thomas relationship continued its successful run, but the resentment among the other trainers was building, particularly as the partnership had now become public knowledge. For some reason the stewards did not hold an official enquiry into Arthur Thomas' position at his stable, instead deciding to address the whole business by subterfuge. They kept a close watch on Thomas, until one day a stipendiary steward witnessed him giving money to an amateur rider and reported him. The incident, which occurred in full view of everyone in the weigh-room, led to Thomas being hauled before the stewards and charged with making an illegal payment to an amateur rider. Despite his pleas that he was merely giving the rider legitimate travelling expenses, Arthur Thomas lost his licence and was informed that it would be restored only when all the Sleator horses left Guy's Cliffe.

Sleator's successful Irish career continued undisturbed by the events across the Irish Sea, except that Bobby Beasley remained in England, to ride for Derek Ancil, so Bobby Coonan replaced him as stable jockey at Grange Con. The new Sleator/Coonan partnership got off to the best possible start by winning the Galway Plate with *Royal Day* and led to Coonan becoming the leading jump jockey in Ireland six times in succession 1967–1972. Nine years later, in 1976, the partnership had their last big winner when O'Leary was successful in the same race. O'Leary's victory in the Kerry National at Listowel, Liam O'Donnell up, later in the year proved to be the last of the great trainer's long list of major jumping races.

Throughout his career Paddy Sleator was renowned for his ability to place his horses to maximum advantage, an important but rare skill, and was still among the top trainers in Ireland when he decided to retire, although only in his mid-sixties. He handed over control of the Grange Con stable to Bobby Coonan, but despite a flying start, notably with *Levanka*, the new arrangements did not work out. Sleator had retired too early; he constantly interfered in the running of the yard and Coonan soon had enough. After twenty years of restless retirement, Paddy Sleator died in June 1996.

SEAN P. GRAHAM (1936–1986)

Few bookmakers had an impact on the betting ring like Sean Graham, the Belfast bookie, who arrived on the racecourses of the South in the late 1960s. Hampered initially by a law that barred bookmakers resident in Northern Ireland from betting in the Republic, Sean Graham was freed by Charles Haughey, the government minister who amended the legislation. Once the way had been cleared, he arrived on the rails like a tornado.

Prior to the agreement that allowed bookmakers to sell their seniority rights, the Ring was full of old, tired men, with a couple of notable exceptions. Sale of seniority enabled them to sell out and brought into racecourse bookmaking a new breed and Sean Graham led the first wave of invaders. First up with the prices, Sean's familiar cry, 'let them in and let them out' rang out as he pleaded with the onlookers to allow access to his joint. Hustle, bustle and noise ruffled the calm as punters battled to have a bet with Sean—betting on the rails would never be the same again!

Sean was the first racecourse bookmaker to go into sponsorship in a big way. He became an ubiquitous sponsor of races, big and small, on a range of courses in Ireland and Britain, some of which he did not have a pitch. The *Sean Graham Racing Annual* became a regular Christmas treat for racing fans and he also supported the *Formbook* and other racing publications almost as a matter of course. He and Brenda, his wife, owned a number of racehorses, including the Irish Grand National winner *Tartan Ace*, and his constant support and promotion of Irish racing earned him everyone's respect. Poor Sean died young in 1986, but the Graham name lives on through his sons, Brian, Ronan, Garrett and Simon, who are carrying on the business on behalf of their mother.

DES FOX (d.1990)

Dungannon bookmaker Des Fox began his career in 1975 as a small bookmaker at the end of the line. In the 1980s he suddenly and unexpectedly emerged as one of the biggest layers in the Irish

Ring. Always betting to his opinion, if Des did not fancy a horse he would take money on it until the cows came home, paying up with a smile if he was subsequently proved wrong. Too big for the end of the line, Des soon began to purchase positions on the rails, where the biggest bookmakers bet, and seemed destined for the very top of the bookmaking profession. Moving from a bad pitch to a good one is similar to moving a shop in Dublin from a quiet *cul de sac* to Grafton Street—business boomed and he was taking money that his erstwhile colleagues at the end of the line could only dream about.

Des purchased a pitch at Roscommon races from a small, old-time bookmaker named Paddy 'Titch' Martin for a couple of thosand pounds, which was more than a fair price for the position. The first day Des bet in this new pitch the results were good for bookmakers and when Errol Golding, Des' right-hand man, arrived back at Shelbourne Park Greyhound Stadium to work for his brother at the dogs, Titch could not resist commenting, 'I suppose Des got his money back on the pitch today?'—correctly assuming that Des had recovered the purchase price in one day's racing. But poor Titch was left ruing that he had not asked a higher price when Errol replied mischievously, 'No Titch, we got it back on the first race.'

Des Fox lived in Northern Ireland at the height of the Troubles, and it goes without saying that a bookmaker was at a particular risk from the various armed gangs. Robbed in his own home at gunpoint and mugged successfully in a car park, Des was no pushover when cornered outside, successfully resisting a number of other attempts—on one occasion escaping by driving his car through a stone wall, admittedly an old weak one! One of the most audacious robberies took place at the dogs. Before the races began, a forward-thinking gang cut a hole in the galvanised fence, just behind the place where Des Fox's satchel hung from his cash tray. The gang then replaced the piece into the fence, holding it in place with sticky tape and hoping nobody would notice. That evening, when everyone was watching a race, the gang returned, removed the piece, took Des' satchel out through the hole and made off with it and its contents!

Des' battle with thieves was to end in tragedy, however. One morning in late September 1990, on a back road leading to the Curragh, a gang waited for Des Fox's car at an old bridge, where approaching cars had to almost come to a stop in order to negotiate the turn. As Des slowed right down, an armed gang jumped out from behind a wall and attempted to pull him out of the car. Thinking quickly, Des put the car into reverse and sped backwards up the road, but the gang shot out the front tyres and the Mercedes skidded into the ditch. Racing up the road after the car, one of the gang opened the front passenger door and fired a single shot into the driver's leg in order to keep him quiet. Meanwhile, his comrades forced open the boot, removed its contents and made off with the cash. Although the gang had not intended to kill Des, the bullet fired into his leg had struck an artery and he bled to death in minutes.

Many bookmakers took that road to the Curragh and I well remember one reporting to me that he thought Des had died on the way to the races. He saw Des' car, surrounded by police, with the betting bag lying on the road behind the car and the front wheel punctured. The consensus was that Des must have suffered a heart attack when attempting to change the wheel. The true, terrible facts emerged later. Des rarely travelled to the races alone, but he was alone the day the fatal attack came. Nobody will ever know how much money was taken.

Although a substantial reward was offered for information leading to the capture of his murderers, nobody was ever caught. A family was deprived of its father, employees were put out of work and bookmaking lost a star and now the ill-gotten gains have long since been spent by the murderers. It was a sad end to an illustrious career.

Mick O'Toole (1931–)

Mick O'Toole was the most flamboyant trainer of his era, a man whose happy-go-lucky lifestyle, abilities with a golf club and way with horses made him a great trainer of owners. He would regularly purchase the most expensive horse at the important Bloodstock Sales, even though he had no owner for it, banking on the publicity generated to encourage wealthy businessmen to ring up looking for a share. Unlike most gamblers, Mick freely admits to winning and losing a few fortunes down the years with his tilts at the betting ring. His particular delight—to bring off a gamble with a bit of style—has cost him a few bob, as has his love of the Cheltenham Festival. Mick has 'done his brains' punting there too many times to remember, on one occasion losing so much money it took him a full year to recover. He just got carried away with the occasion. As he describes it: 'The trouble with backing at places like Cheltenham is that the atmosphere overtakes you. It's like a disease and even people like me, who should know better, start behaving like mug punters, chasing losses, increasing bets and the bookies are only too happy to give me all the credit I want.'

O'Toole's most famous bet is the £1,000 he put on *Davy Lad*, a horse he trained, with the late Sean Graham, to win the 1977 Cheltenham Gold Cup at odds of 50-to-1. The horse duly obliged, netting Mick and his many pals one of those elusive fortunes— although some of it he was destined to lose back to the bookies. A butcher by trade, Mick O'Toole started out training greyhounds in a small way, gradually expanding the business as he was given charge of more dogs. Many winners later, including a successful raid on the Greyhound Oaks at the old Harringay track in London, Mick diversified into horses, following in the footsteps of his uncle, the well-known 'Rasher' Byrne. The 'Rasher' was training in Castleknock, just outside Dublin's Phoenix Park, and Mick took a yard in the same area, although he was still predominantly a dog trainer at this time, having two horses and twenty-four greyhounds under his care. Mick started his new career as he was to continue it—with a gamble.

He purchased a filly named *Lintola* out of Sid Dale's yard and sent her back across the Irish Sea to contest a sprint handicap at Edinburgh in 1966, backing her from 10-to-1 to 6-to-1. Ridden by his uncle's useful apprentice John Murtagh (not related to the present jockey of the same name), *Lintola* ran on gamely to win the race in a four-way photo finish. M.A. O'Toole had trained the first of his 800-odd winners. Mick soon got out of dogs to concentrate on the horses and moved to a yard at Maddenstown, on the Curragh, not far from where the legendary trainer Senator Jim

Parkinson used to live. Three years later, in 1969, Mick trained his first big winner when *St Sebastian*, again ridden by Murtagh, won the Irish Cesarewitch in 1969 and the following year they won the Irish Cambridgeshire with *Mighty Quin*. Having trained the Royal Ascot winners *Balios* and *Faliraki*, Mick O'Toole was established on the flat but he was also making his name over the sticks, with horses like *Our Albert* (Galway Plate), *Chinrullah* (Sweeps Hurdle), *Kilkilwell* (Leopardstown Chase) and *Bustinetto*, the champion four-year-old hurdler.

Down the years Mick has trained winners on the flat, over hurdles and over fences, at Royal Ascot and at Cheltenham, at the Curragh and on the beach at Laytown in Co. Meath. Easily the best horse he ever trained was *Dickens Hill*, runner-up in two Derbies and winner of the Irish Two Thousand Guineas and the Eclipse Stakes in 1979. In that same year Mick won the Arkle Challenge Trophy at Cheltenham with *Chinrullah* and was honoured with the Trainer of the Year award. At the peak of his training career in the late 1970s, Mick had over 100 horses in his care and retained leading jockeys, such as Pat Eddery, Tony Murray and Dessie Hughes.

Over the Christmas holidays in 1980, Mick invited Mike Dillon of Ladbrokes to breakfast at Maddenstown on the morning of the big Sweeps Hurdle race. This was actually the last time the race was run at the Leopardstown Christmas meeting, as it moved to its present date, in January, the following year. Over breakfast, Mick asked Dillon to quote a price about *Carrig Willy* to win that race and was offered 40-to-1. Mick took the odds to £1,600 and stood to win £64,000 if *Carrig Willy* won the race. One can only imagine the mental and emotional state of each man during the four minutes it took to run the race. It was a very exciting four minutes. At first the well-backed English challenger, *Starfen*, looked likely to win, only to take a crashing fall at the second last hurdle, leaving the favourite, *Daring Run*, to fight out the finish with *Corrib Chieftain* and *Connaught Ranger*. Each of these flattered in turn before being passed by *Carrig Willy*, whose strong late run got it home by a head. Delighted at winning yet another fortune, O'Toole commented wryly, 'Bacon and eggs don't come cheap on the Curragh.' The following day's papers described

Dillon's breakfast as the most expensive ever eaten, but Ladbrokes cannot have been too disappointed: *Carrig Willy* started a 33-to-1 chance and would have been a big winner in every one of the firm's 1,400 betting shops.

Mick O'Toole retired from training at the end of the last century when he was sixty-seven years of age, still young enough to enjoy his hobbies of golf and travelling. He did not complain, as most retiring trainers seem to do, that uncaring owners had forced him out by not paying their bills and he makes a point of not knocking the game that gave him so much fun. He still goes racing, looks younger than ever and continues to cause palpitations among the bookies and looks like he hasn't a care in the world; but then, Mick O'Toole always looked as if he hadn't a care in the world!

DERMOT WELD (1948–)

When Charlie Weld announced, in 1972, that he was handing over the reins of his training stable to his son and erstwhile assistant, Dermot, the bookmakers paid little attention. Charlie Weld began training at Castleknock, Co. Dublin, moving to Rosewell House in 1955, where he trained a relatively large string of horses and got his fair share of winners, none of which was of a particularly high quality, the best being the Ascot winner *Wily Trout*. Charlie Weld never topped the list of winning trainers and never trained a Classic winner, but he did train *Decies* to win the National Stakes in 1969 as a two-year-old. *Decies* was a decent juvenile, but was unfortunate to have been foaled in the same year as the great *Nijinsky*, finishing second to that horse in both the Railway and the Beresford Stakes. In the latter race *Nijinsky* had to battle to win by three-quarters of a length, a performance that enabled *Decies*' owner, James Flahavan, to cash in by selling the horse to Nelson Bunker Hunt for 110,000 guineas. Transferred to the Newmarket stable of Bernard Van Cutsem, *Decies* returned to Ireland to compete in the Irish Two Thousand Guineas, in which it scrambled home by a short head. Charlie Weld also trained a couple of decent jumpers, winning the Galway Plate with *Highfield Lad* and the Galway Hurdle with *Ticonderoga*, the latter also being successful in the valuable Amateur Handicap, with Dermot in the saddle.

When Dermot qualified as the youngest veterinary surgeon in the world in 1971, Charlie encouraged his son to take control of the training stable, leaving himself free to pursue his farming and breeding interests at the newly acquired Pipers Hill Stud. Although the twenty-three-year-old Dermot Weld, the new master of Rosewell House training stable, was well-known in racing, having been Champion Amateur rider three times in Ireland, he was regarded as very inexperienced. Everyone knew that Mr D.K. Weld was a very good amateur rider, but that did not automatically mean he would be a good trainer. In fact, he was far more experienced than anybody realised, having spent his student summers working with horses and vets in America. Dermot's love of travel—which he would put to good use with his horses later in life—led to his riding big winners in France, America and South Africa, which was very unusual at the time. Young, ambitious and anxious to expand the Rosewell House stable, Dermot needed to land some nice bets to raise the necessary capital because prize money was small and the Celtic Tiger boom was many years off. Right from the very start of his new career Dermot Weld was successful and his betting was no exception—the bookies were about to be hit for six!

Dermot's first betting coup involved a delicate, nervous, but nice three-year-old filly named *Klairlone*, which had not raced at two years. Convinced she was a bit special, although she had never ran in a race, Dermot mapped out a gamble with the filly, but as he did not have a retained stable jockey finding a suitable rider was not easy. J.V. Smith had been booked to ride the stable runners at the Phoenix Park on Saturday, 25 March 1972, where he provided D.K. Weld with his first winner as a trainer with *Dark Blue*, following up later with another on *Master Albert*, giving Dermot a double. *Klairlone* was due to make her racecourse debut in the last race that afternoon, in the Ardee maiden, and Dermot decided to put up her work rider, who knew the filly well, rather than the established jockey. Jimmy Phillips, the senior fast work rider at Rosewell for several years, took the mount and *Klairlone* ran really well to finish a close-up fourth.

Dermot was confident that *Klairlone* would easily win a maiden race and earmarked the Glengariff Maiden at the same venue the following Saturday. Concerned about the possibility of *Klairlone*'s reacting negatively to an unknown rider, Dermot Weld decided to give the ride to Jimmy Phillips again, although Phillips had never ridden a winner in public and the stable money would be down. Any misgivings Weld may have had were set aside by the certainty that the bookmakers would be generous in pricing *Klairlone*, confident that if the filly was going to win a top jockey would have been engaged. *Korotrin* was installed favourite, trained by John Bryce-Smith and ridden by 'Buster' Parnell, but it drifted out to 100-to-30 as a deluge of money for *Klairlone* set the bookies' dusters into furious action and the filly's price into a nose dive, settling at 7-to-2 second favourite at the off. Jimmy Phillips' first and only win was as easy as it was memorable. *Klairlone* strolled home to win by five lengths and Dermot Weld had landed his first betting coup. What a certainty *Klairlone* was! Next time out, again at the Phoenix Park, J.V. Smith was given the ride and the filly won the Mulcahy Stakes, well and truly turning over the Vincent O'Brien hot pot *Cambrienne*, owned by the sponsor of the race, John A. Mulcahy. *Klairlone*, ridden by Willie Carson, was an unlucky third to *Pidget* and *Arkadina* in the Irish One Thousand Guineas, having had to weave her way through the field.

Young Dermot Weld continued to plague the bookmakers all year, winning a remarkable eighty races in his first season as a trainer—the highest total of winners in Ireland for forty-six years, which put him on top of the winning trainers' table. Goodness knows how much the bookmakers had to fork out as Weld made his way to the top of the training profession. His first Royal Ascot winner came in 1973 with *Klairvimy*, and the following year he trained 102 winners in Ireland—the highest total since Jim Parkinson's record 134 in 1923. He won big English races with *Red Alert*, *Highest Trump*, *Hot Spark* and *Steel Heart*. In 1977 Dermot trained a record 106 flat-race winners in Ireland and was now firmly established at the top of his profession. The quality soon appeared to complement the quantity. *Blue Wind* won both the Epsom and Irish Oaks in 1981, the first horse to do so and further Classic success followed with *Prince's Polly*, *Flash of Steel*, *Trusted Partner* and *Vintage Crop*, together with a sensational Irish

Derby/Irish Oaks double in 1996 with *Zagreb* and *Dance Design.*

Dermot Weld is one of the most adventurous trainers of all time, sending runners all round the world seeking success, and he has trained winners on all four continents, and not just winners, but the winners of the biggest races in the racing world. The most famous of his globetrotters is *Vintage Crop*, whose lad was David Phillips, a nephew of Jimmy, which was sent halfway across the world for a pioneering and ultimately successful tilt at the Melbourne Cup in 1993. This success was rightly acclaimed as a wonderful feat of training, but in my opinion it was not Dermot's greatest achievement as a trainer. *Vintage Crop* won a handicap, albeit a really big handicap, but his perspicacity in targeting the Belmont Stakes with *Go and Go* in 1990 was incredible. With *Go and Go*, Dermot took on the Americans in one of their biggest races, one of the legs of the US Triple Crown and a race that was run on dirt—and beat them! *Go and Go* remains the only European-trained winner of an American classic race. Dermot also won the Prix de l'Abbaye twice, France's top sprint race, with *Committed* and other big races in Germany, Hong Kong and Italy, including the Italian Derby with *In A Tiff* (1992).

Although primarily a flat-race trainer, Dermot has always had a few quality jumping horses in training during the winter, which has enabled him to emulate his father by winning the Galway Plate and the Galway Hurdle and to outdo him by winning both races more than once. Successful in the Plate with *Kiichi*, *General Idea* and *Ansar*, Dermot has won the Hurdle with *Spanner*, *Strathline* and *Ansar*. Other top jumpers trained by D.K. Weld include *Allen's Mistake*, *Archive Footage*, *Fortune and Fame* and *Rare Holiday*, winner of the Triumph Hurdle at the 1990 Cheltenham Festival.

Many records are likely to be broken by Dermot Weld over the next few years. In 2004 *Vinnie Roe* chalked up a piece of history, racing through the driving rain to record a fourth successive win in the Irish St Leger. *Vinnie Roe* became the first horse to win the same Group 1 race in Europe four times since the Pattern system was established in 1971, equalling the record of *Marsyas*, winner of the Prix du Cadran, the French equivalent of the Ascot Gold Cup, from 1944 to 1947. Phil Bull, the founder of Timeform and a great judge of horses, described Marsyas as 'a phenomenon among racehorses'. Dermot Weld is one of only two trainers to have sent out the winners of more than 2,000 races in Ireland. He smashed Jim Parkinson's Irish record of 2,577 winners and notched up his 3000th winner in Ireland when *Clearing the Water* won at the 2005 Galway Festival.

Dermot Weld has enjoyed a long, distinguished and successful career, receiving so many awards down the years that few stick in the memory. One award that he will never forget, however, and of which he is particularly proud is not a racing award at all, but the coveted Charter Day Medal awarded to him in 2002 by his *alma mater*, University College Dublin.

BARNEY CURLEY (1940–)

Fortunately for the bookmaking fraternity, very few people use their brains to beat the system when going for a gamble, preferring instead to pull a stroke and grab the headlines. Every punter loves to hear the bookies' cry, but the brainiest betting coups are simple and involve no breaking of the rules of racing or betting, thereby forcing the bookies to pay up, albeit through gritted teeth. Barney Curley is an expert at the clever betting coup and has been living it up on the bookmakers' money for years and years as a result, yet he never has a good word to say about them.

Unfortunately, the *Yellow Sam* coup, landed by Barney and friends back in 1975, gave him a taste of their blood and an appetite for more. Some of the proceeds from the *Yellow Sam* betting coup were invested in Midleton Park, a Georgian mansion on nearly 400 acres near Mullingar, Co. Westmeath, which was once owned by the Boyd-Rochfort family and was the birthplace of Captain Sir Cecil Boyd-Rochfort, the famous Newmarket trainer. The 'Celtic Tiger' was unheard of in the Ireland of the early 1980s, money was tight and large properties like Midleton Park were expensive to maintain and difficult to sell. Barney had decided to sell, but became impatient with the lack of interest and decided to raffle the property instead.

In order to circumvent Ireland's strict anti-lottery laws, Barney formed a club and made the raffle a game of skill rather than one of chance by asking each subscriber to answer an easy question. The scheme might have worked save for the publicity the draw attracted, forcing the Gardaí to take a case against him in the courts. Barney was convicted for running an illegal lottery and given a three-month jail sentence, which he appealed. The draw took place on 7 February 1984 and was a big success. Barney was reported to have netted over £1 million from the receipts—about four times the property's value on the open market. Later, Barney scored another victory when his jail sentence was set aside on appeal and replaced by the Probation Act.

In the spring of that year Barney tore into the Irish racecourse bookmakers, landing three huge gambles with horses that he trained himself under permit, which allows a person to train only for his wife and children. All three horses were owned by Maureen, Barney's wife, and ridden by the up-and-coming amateur rider Willie Mullins. The first strike was on Saturday, 3 March 1984 when *I'm Incommunicado* was backed at all odds from 20-to-1 down to 5-to-2 in a bumper at Naas and duly obliged. The bookmakers knew Barney well by this time, but doubted his ability to train a horse to win first time out, despite the services of a decent jockey, so they were willing to take him on. They paid the price.

Three weeks later, Barney was back at Naas, this time with another debutant named *The Tariahs*. Doubting that Barney could do it again, but fearful that he might try to, the bookmakers willingly took his bets but chalked up a more cautious 6-to-1 this time, only for the price to be snapped up and forced down to 7-to-4 favourite. Again, Barney was successful as *The Tariahs* won the race. A month later, on Easter Tuesday, 24 April 1984, Barney attempted to go for a hat-trick of big coups with *The Hacienderos* at Fairyhouse. This was a much bigger meeting than Naas, with a much larger attendance, more bookmakers and a stronger market, but Barney's men found it difficult to get the money on as bookmakers refused to accept larger wagers. They had been hit hard twice and in a very short period, and the survival instinct came into play with the realisation that Barney was too good for them. They were right, of course. *The Hacienderos* took the race, and it was then Barney realised that Ireland was too small for his business and removed himself to Newmarket, from where he has ever since been waging a battle, more or less successful, with both the bookmakers and the stewards.

The son of a Northern Irish greyhound trainer and a brother of Cathal, a member of the Irish Greyhound Board, Barney Curley has done tremendous work for many charities down the years. But he has not neglected his other activities, such as training racehorses, organising gambles, thinking up unusual bets that bookmakers do not know how to price, as well as lambasting the bookies for not being brave enough to take his bets in full and protesting against racing's shortcomings. It is all part of his psychological warfare with the bookmakers. His war of words with the big three bookmaking firms, Ladbrokes, William Hill and Corals, led him to start the Punters' Association, which championed the rights of punters, but it collapsed. He ran a huge raffle for the Great Ormond Street Children's Hospital in London, and when it failed to raise the sum of money expected, Barney stumped up £350,000 of his own cash to make up the shortfall. He later began raising money for an African charity as well, but amid all this activity he still had time to pop back to Ireland to help himself to some Irish bookies' money, entering horses at the famous Galway races and successfully collecting yet again. It is not all take though. Barney willingly comes over to Ireland, at his own expense, to enliven some of those Cheltenham Previews, which have become so popular, rather than take money from the benefiting charities. A regular at the Friends of Irish Racing's (successor of the Racing Club of Ireland) Preview, the original of the species, Barney was heckled by Paddy Keogh, owner of that fine racemare *Grabel*, who demanded to know when *The Third Curate* (a horse trained by Barney) would win again. Barney caused great mirth in the Submarine Bar in Crumlin when he replied, 'Paddy, when you pay its keep for a year I will tell you!'

TERRY DOLAN (1949–)

Terry Dolan was a boarder in Blackrock College at the same time as Edward O'Grady, whose father, Willie, was the former Irish Champion Jockey and who was then training near Thurles. Terry's uncle, Hugo Dolan, owned three pubs in Dublin, including the famous Scotch House on Burgh Quay and he had also owned a string of decent racehorses down the years, which led to young Terry becoming keenly interested in racing. This shared interest ensured that Terry Dolan and Edward O'Grady were close friends and they kept up with the racing news through the *Sporting Chronicle*, which Ciaran Kennelly, one of the day boys who later became the Irish handicapper, brought in to them. Athletic in his youth, Terry was the Irish Schoolboy Hurdles champion and played rugby for the College but signs of a misspent youth may be detected from his ability at the game of snooker, at which he reigned supreme at school. Later he became a leading figure in the Irish Snooker Association and was responsible for running the Irish Snooker Championship in its inaugural years.

In January 1967, while in his final year at Blackrock, Uncle Hugo told Terry that his horse *Cushendawn* would win at Navan the following Saturday. Cooped up in the Castle House of the College, this was the incentive Terry needed to get a day away, so he asked Edward O'Grady to 'bunk out' with him to the races. The pair slipped out of the College, got a bus into town and then 'thumbed' their way to Navan, being lucky enough to get picked up by a race-goer who sportingly agreed to give them a lift back again after the races. While on the bus heading into town, the two boys discussed backing *Cushendawn,* but an immediate problem presented itself—they had only shillings between them, far too little money to have on a 'good thing'.

Edward O'Grady had the solution. He telephoned his uncle, the legendary point-to-point rider and trainer P.P. Hogan, and explained his dilemma. P.P. told him not to worry, 'Go up to the bookmaker Bill Quinlan and have £100 on for me and back the horse to win £100 each for you and your friend and put the bets down to my account.' Edward approached Quinlan the moment he priced his board. Quinlan had installed *Vulpine*, subsequent winner of the Irish Grand National, as hot favourite, and Raymond Guest's *Firm Favourite*, from the powerful stable of Dan Moore and ridden by Tommy Carberry, as the second favourite, with *Cushendawn*, trained by Charlie Weld and ridden by Peter

Russell, priced at 16-to-1. Quinlan recognised Edward, whom he referred to as 'Young O'Grady' and accepted the bets, £1,600 to £100 for P.P. and £100 to £6 each for Edward and Terry.

Suddenly, all hell broke loose as *Cushendawn*'s price began to tumble. It seemed the whole track wanted to back the horse and at the off its SP was only 4-to-1! *Cushendawn* beat *Firm Favourite by* a neck in a photo finish, to the delight of the two boys, whose only interest now was food. Boarders in those days were perpetually starving, so back they went to Quinlan to get paid so that they could head to a restaurant for a hearty and well-deserved meal. Eventually they got paid. First they had to wait for the 'winner all right', then they had to listen as Quinlan moaned about how much he had lost on the race and finally a fatherly lecture on gambling. It was well worth it when the bookmaker handed each of them their £100 winnings, five big red £20 notes were put into their hands—it was a small fortune at the time! The boys arrived back in Blackrock College, their absence having gone unnoticed, laden with cakes that they carefully stored in their lockers. News gradually got round to the other boys that there were cakes loose in the school and Edward and Terry were the most popular boys in the place for the next few days.

Great trees from little acorns grow, and both Terry Dolan and Edward O'Grady were destined to land a number of huge betting coups over the next few years. On leaving Blackrock College, Edward went to study veterinary science, a study that had to be abandoned after the death of his father, whereupon he went home to take over the training stable. Terry went to Bolton Street and emerged as an expert on roofs, which became his business, and he prospered and was able to get into horses, becoming the first Irish owner with Martin Pipe (the great English trainer of winners), sending him a horse named *Sound Argument*. Terry used to ride in charity races, but had an ambition to ride in bumpers as a fully fledged amateur rider, which looked likely to be unfulfilled until a chance meeting with Martin Mulligan, a jockey who had just set up as a trainer in Glencairn. Terry was roofing Mulligan's house in Ballyogan when he discovered that Martin had been riding for the Durkans, builders for whom Terry did work, and they became friends. On hearing of Terry's ambition, Martin suggested he buy a cheap, unregistered mare owned by a builder named Fanning, from Roundwood, whose tiny son Joe, incidentally, is currently a successful jockey in England. Terry named the mare *Miss Breta VI* after his wife, Breta, who, like so many people in Ireland, also has racing connections: her grand-father, Jerry Mulcair of Rathkeale, Co. Limerick, was the breeder of the 1912 Grand National winner, *Jerry M.*

Miss Breta VI turned out to be a hard puller and therefore an unsuitable ride for an inexperienced amateur rider, and she ran away with Terry on several occasions. She was a useful mare on her day, however, and Willie Mullins rode her to victory in a bumper at Clonmel, but afterwards she was seriously injured at Downpatrick and was almost destroyed. The racecourse vet wanted to put her down and *as she was* well insured, Terry was happy for him to do so, but Breta Dolan refused to allow it, standing by the mare's head to protect it from the vet's humane killer. *Miss Breta VI* was taken home and rewarded Breta Dolan's kindness by breeding four winners. One of her offspring was *Asolas*, named after a faith-healing group, who came to Tramore in January 1991 with four duck eggs and an 'r' before her name—four unplaced runs and a 'refused to race'. The latter incident was due to a wart: when a jockey stood up in the saddle on *Asolas*, the girth rubbed against the wart and caused the horse pain, making her whip round in distress.

The horse was trained by Tony Mullins, who reported that *Asolas* was a nippy horse that would be suited by the tight turns of Tramore—just the type to land a gamble for Terry and his pals. Of course, to get a price about a horse you have to take on a horse with a bit of form and the form horse in this bumper was *Skinaway*, trained by Tony's father Paddy Mullins, who had been second in a Leopardstown bumper and was now dropping down in class. With a strong odds-on favourite in the field, *Asolas* was freely priced at 12-to-1. Tom Mullins rode *Skinaway* and his brother Willie was aboard *Asolas*, who was backed at all prices down to 4-to-1, forcing the favourite to drift out to 6-to-4, where he received renewed support from ordinary punters, and started a 5-to-4 shot.

Willie Mullins sent *Asolas* into the lead, racing down the hill, while Tom went after him on *Skinaway*, the pair going clear. The leader, full of running, stayed on stoutly, and the favourite came under pressure and was well-beaten in the finish, albeit only two lengths behind the winner, *Asolas*. Although *Skinaway* was clearly run on its merits the punters were not amused, nor were the bookmakers, who were hit particularly badly; David Power was said to have lost a six-figure sum. With Tony Mullins's gamble beating his father's hotpot, tongues were bound to wag and Paddy Mullins, who does not back horses, was embarrassed by the sarcastic comments from some members of the public. Mrs Mullins was mortified, rebuking her son, 'Tony, you'll have us all killed!'

Terry Dolan and his friends reckoned that there was another gamble to be landed with *Asolas*, which took place the following year, at Hereford, on the Saturday before the Cheltenham Festival meeting. The horse was sent over to an unknown trainer named I.R. Jones, who trained on the England–Wales border. People from various coursing clubs were organised to hit every betting shop from Donegal to Kinsale, and Terry Dolan went about getting a jockey for the horse. He asked Kieran Gaule, a young claiming jockey who had ridden *Asolas* on the training gallops and knew the horse, to come to England to ride it in a trial gallop. Nothing was said about riding the horse in a race. Terry met young Gaule at Busarus in Dublin, drove him to the airport, put him on a plane to Birmingham, where he would be met by the jockey Tom Morgan. Gaule told Dolan that he had never been in Dublin before, let alone England, but he must have been surprised when he ended up at Hereford races. Meanwhile, Terry and his friends took the ferry to England in the car and drove straight to Hereford, where in the middle of the night they visited the racecourse. There they loosened the first frame of each hurdle, the one nearest the running rail, so that it would be easily knocked aside, before disappearing into the night. Upon being told he was riding in a race, Kieran Gaule was instructed to inform anyone who asked that *Asolas* was mad, nobody else could ride her, which is why he has been brought over for the ride. Only Terry Dolan showed up at the course, the others spent their time backing the horse each way in every betting shop they could find in the area. The owners knew that there was no point trying to back the horse on the course—Hereford's market was notoriously weak and, anyway, only six racecourse bookmakers priced up their boards on the race.

Kieran Gaule did as he was instructed. On hearing of the 'mad' horse, the other jockeys told him to keep clear of them and everybody was happy to let *Asolas* jump off in front, where it could do no harm to the other runners. Bowling along in front, with the hurdles falling flat in front of them, *Asolas* quickly established a commanding lead. All alone in front, the young jockey wondered where the others had got to and, after jumping the second-last, looked round to see where they were. In doing so, he stood up in the saddle, the girth irritated the wart, the pain caused the horse to veer into the running rail and in doing so struck itself with its shoe, inflicting a serious cut on its leg. Remaining in the saddle, Gaule did his best to keep his mount going, it hobbled over the last only to be caught in the dying strides by Adrian Maguire, a jockey who never gives up. A massive coup had been foiled, although not completely lost because *Asolas* had been backed each way and the bookies had to pay out on the place.

Bookies squealed at the losses they might have sustained and the attempted coup became headline news. Mr Jones was none too pleased as he has known nothing about it and yet was being besieged by the press, who were, as he put it, 'Making me out to be a villain.' It was yet another coup to have been doomed by an unknown factor—this time a little wart!

DAVID HYLAND (1956–)

Wine-tasting is a job that would appeal to most of us—sampling the best wines money can by and getting paid for it. Few of us would give up such a job but David Hyland did—to go bookmaking. Such is the appeal of a career on the Turf! Starting out with T.P. Reynolds, that big man from Roscommon, David Hyland came to prominence just over a decade ago when he began to take on Nic Stassen, who was having difficulty getting his bets on at the market price. Born in Belgium, Stassen spent the Second World

War in a concentration camp and survived, coming to Ireland on his release, penniless but alive. He set up the Liga Baby Food business, made money and acquired a love of racing. Stassen liked to keep a number of cheaply bought horses in training with Joseph M. Canty in Kildare, which usually paid their way but only due to his successful gambles. He loved to bet on his horses when he thought they had a winning chance, but rarely gambled on other people's and was regarded by bookmakers as being as hot as mustard—hence the reluctance to take him on until David Hyland did so. Nic Stassen was a shrewd punter, landing some hefty bets with horses such as *Sweet Nasha* and *Euphoric*, and he got much the better of the exchanges with David Hyland. Not that David was worried—unlike most other bookmakers, he seems happy to accommodate consistent winners. Another feature of David's business is his willingness to let the ordinary punter on after the price has gone, having been taken by the shrewdies, a service that is popular and appreciated by regular racegoers, even if the downside is waiting in a long queue after the last race to collect winnings.

Just what a handful Nic Stassen could be, and how he refused to give any bookmaker even the slightest edge, was amply demonstrated in what occurred at Leopardstown in August 1994. *Sweet Nasha* was running in a handicap, the bookmakers were wary, David Hyland did not care, but his runner, Greg Loughran, nevertheless kept an eye on Stassen's movements. As the owner of *Sweet Nasha* headed from the parade ring into the betting ring to back his horse, David was waiting for him. Stassen began backing his horse heavily with any bookmaker who would lay him a large bet but never came near David Hyland, the man who would usually take the biggest chunk of his bet. At the off, David unexpectedly found that *Sweet Nasha* was a big winner on the book, Stassen had made his point that he did not depend on any one bookmaker and David Hyland, as only he can, proceeded to cheer *Sweet Nasha* to victory. *Sweet Nasha* made the running from the start, but was tackled in the closing stages by Kevin Manning on *Al Mohaajir*. She held on in a thrilling finish to win by a short head. David's delight was shortlived! A stewards' enquiry followed, the placings of the first two were reversed and *Sweet Nasha* was relegated to second place. Stassen did not leave David out when landing two enormous gambles with a horse named Euphoric, at Roscommon and again at Gowran Park the following October. On both occasions David laid Stassen a huge bet and on both occasions was stuck with a bumper payout, leaving him to reflect that he was the unluckiest person in the world.

David Hyland is still offering value to the ordinary punter, provided he bets in stakes of €20 or more, and is still taking on the big-hitters, although probably not as recklessly as he has done in the past. To some extent, David has been tamed by the downturn in the on-course betting market, the high cost of his contribution to racing through the turnover charge and unfair competition from Betting Exchanges, who are betting away without paying anything at all towards the running of racing.

NOEL FURLONG (1939–)

Those of you who are observant may have noticed the name 'Furlong Carpets' emblazoned across the sides of large lorries on the country's roads. That is the business of Noel Furlong who, when he is so inclined, is one of the biggest punters in the Irish betting ring today. A ferocious gambler all his life, Noel ran away to sea when he was fifteen, later settling in Belfast where he became known as 'Dublin Noel'. A great doggie man, Noel only bet when he believed he was on a winner and attempted to have as much money on the selection as the bookies would take. When he did put his money down, he could not get enough money down and he was his own man, always. In the early 1990s Noel pulled off a series of gambles with *Destriero* and *The Illiad*, both trained by Andy Geraghty, and had *The Illiad* been successful in the 1991 Champion Hurdle, he would have won the most money ever won in a single gamble.

The Illiad won the valuable Ladbroke Handicap Hurdle at Leopardstown, netting Noel £1 million, and he went for broke at the Cheltenham Festival, doubling *Destriero* and *The Illiad* to win their respective races. When the former landed the first leg of the double, winning the first race of the meeting, the Trafalgar House

Supreme Novices Hurdle at odds of 6-to-1, Noel had half a million rolling on to *The Illiad* to win the Smurfit Champion Hurdle an hour-and-a-quarter later. Standing to win a tantalising £4 million, Noel had a nerve-jangling wait for the feature race, but his bet went down like a lead balloon when *The Illiad* made a blunder at the halfway point, never recovered from the setback and finished well behind. Although he must have been bitterly disappointed, he was playing with the bookies money so could afford to be lighthearted about it, saying afterwards that he was very pleased he gave the big British bookmakers a fright they would not easily forget.

Noel Furlong has plenty of money, bets for fun and gets his kicks by going for a big touch in a big race, enjoying himself whether he wins or loses. The reason I include Noel here is not for his gung-ho tilts at the Ring, which could be termed reckless gambles rather than shrewd betting coups, but because of the ingenuity that enabled him to get a monster bet on *Destriero* in a bumper at Leopardstown. It was sheer class and a very intelligent betting coup.

Destriero was well-known to the bookmakers as a good horse and Noel Furlong's massive gambles were legendary. Consequently, bookmakers were not particularly anxious to take big bets on the horse when it took part in a maiden hurdle at Leopardstown on St Stephen's Day 1990. Aware that the racecourse bookmakers would keep the price short, Noel knew his best chance of getting a bit of value was to give the impression that he was not going to back it at all. He decided to back *Destriero* with one of the large off-course bookmaking chains, but feared the firm might not take the bet if he tried to take a fixed price. Instead, he offered the firm a bet of £50,000 on the SP favourite in the second race at Leopardstown. The bet was accepted, Noel was on and he would not have to back the horse at Leopardstown with the racecourse bookmakers, which might mean, with a bit of luck, that *Destriero* would start at odds of even money rather than the expected odds-on.

The on-course bookmakers installed *Destriero* the odds-on favourite at 4-to-5, with *Randaka* at 5-to-2 and *Circus Dance* and *Wolver Sovereign* priced at 5-to-1. A deluge of money for *Circus Dance*, trained by Con Collins, forced its price down to 2-to-1, while *Destriero*, with no Furlong money coming for it, drifted out to 2-to-1. The bookmaking chain had a man on the course ready to hedge some of Furlong's bet, but he was unable to do so because he could not be sure which horse would actually start favourite. As *Destriero* drifted out further to 9-to-4, Noel Furlong had to intervene and back his horse because, as things stood, his £50,000 was now on *Circus Dance*, it being the favourite. His intervention did the trick: his money forced the price of *Destriero* back in to 2-to-1 favourite, which was the price at which it was returned, while *Circus Dance* drifted out to 9-to-4.

Destriero dominated the race, staying in the first three throughout, pulled its way to the front in the straight and raced clear to win unchallenged by twelve lengths. As the race had been been won by the favourite, the off-course bookmaking chain had to pay out £100,000 to Noel, who was particularly pleased because he had been forced to have more money on the horse than he actually intended. It was a brilliant coup, thought up by a man with an astute gambling brain.

MICHAEL FUTTER (1946–)

Michael Futter is one of those individuals who never tires of taking money from bookmakers, while they continue to take him on because they believe he has too many bets to make gambling pay. So far the bookies have been wrong, and Mike Futter is a winner despite doing everything conventional wisdom says a successful punter should not do. A basic rule of backing is that the more bets a person has the less likely he is to come out a winner. The rationale of this rule is that the bookmakers have a profit margin that will gobble up any winnings if it is applied again and again. However, when a person who knows the form inside out, understands horses and goes racing regularly, it is not much fun having no bet at all. In fact, it can be uniquely frustrating to miss winner after winner while waiting for the 'dead cert' to come. Mike Futter loves going racing, but he wants to enjoy his sport so he is prepared to bet more often than the average betting pro, even if it does mean backing more losers and not making as much money from betting as he could do with a little more patience. In all other respects he is a formidable professional who does his homework, remembers what he saw and knows that there is always another day. He is well aware of the dangers of chasing losses, so he has a rule that when he goes £20,000 behind, that's it: no more bets on that day! Occasionally Mike breaks the rules—after all, they are his rules and they are there to be broken!

When studying the race programme, Mike spends 80 per cent of his time working on the first race because he believes it is usually the least competitive race of the day and he feels more confident when he is playing with the bookies' money. He will pocket 10 per cent of the first-race winnings and bet away with the other 90 per cent, hoping to play it up into big money. Although Mike strongly advises punters never to chase their losses, he does not always practice what he preaches, but then, he is 'jammy'.

One day at Downpatrick, Mike found himself losing £65,000 with two races to go and chased. He was in the middle of a roll, having won at thirteen meetings that year, which was an excuse but no justification for what he did next. Not only did he set aside his own rule of stopping when his losses reached £20,000, he proceeded to break the most important rule in the book of successful punting by backing two horses in one race. Incredibly, Mike put £35,000 on an odds-on favourite to try to win back £20,000 of his losses, and he also backed another horse to finish second to the favourite, placing £10,000 at 6-to-4. The race proved one thing: Mike Futter has the heart of a lion, because both bets looked likely to be lost and one can only imagine his inner turmoil as he watched a loss of £105,000 materialising before his eyes. He never showed any emotion as the doomsday scenario was played out, but when the race changed dramatically and both bets came up, the steely, professional straight face disappeared and his voice bellowed in relief. Although still £20,000 behind he felt he was winning and, never a man to flinch when on a winning streak, now had the confidence to try to turn the tables on those bookmakers who had him on the run an hour earlier. Backing an odds-on favourite trained by Christy Roche in the last race, which won easily, Mike Futter walked out the gate £10,000 to the good, watched by shell-shocked bookmakers who were scratching their heads in disbelief. Explaining his rash actions, Mike calmly said he was determined to win because there was no way he wanted to be stuck on unlucky thirteen! Even the coolest, most knowledgable and bravest punter cannot get away from that old superstition.

Born in Blackpool, Mike Futter came into the Bingo business via Hollywood, where he worked for a time and played on a cricket team with the actor Montgomery Clift. During the Troubles, when everybody was getting out of the province, Mike went in, setting up a Bingo hall in Belfast. Nowadays, his company runs seven Bingo halls in Northern Ireland and three in Dublin. Mike's racing career began in the point-to-point field, where his encyclopaedic knowledge of the horses he saw running enabled him to win £30,000 a year from his betting. All point-to-point races are run over three miles and there are no handicaps, which ensures the form is consistent and the state of the going is the only complicating factor. Newspapers do not publish form guides for point-to-point races, so most punters and many bookmakers are betting completely in the dark (the trainers of the horses are not even printed on the race card), a fact that presents an ideal opportunity for a man like Mike Futter to use his knowledge and back horses that are overpriced. As the bookmakers find it difficult to recognise the form horse, they often price it much too generously, but as the average punter does not know it either, the lack of support causes its price to drift out even further. This is how Mike gets the odds in his favour—and those who get the odds in their favour will win regularly! He also believes that two lengths is nothing in a three-mile race and will not back a horse unless it has more than this in hand over its rivals.

The bushy grey head of Mike Futter is now familiar to racing fans because of *Monty's Pass*, winner of the 2003 Grand National. The horse is owned by a syndicate, of which Mike is a member, and he backed it to win the big Aintree handicap at odds as high as 66-to-1, winning over £1 million. It was a dream come true and as Mike shared the moment with millions of television viewers, he appeared a real hero—a man who could beat the bookies regularly and well. Most bookmakers think Mike is simply 'jammy', that he has got away with it so far and one day the wheel will come off as he chases his losses and they will clean him out. While the book-makers wait for that day to come, Mike Futter continues to drain off some of their money, enjoying himself enormously while he does so.

MICHAEL NAGHTEN (1962–)

The well-known racecourse bookmaker Michael Naghten is one of a new breed of bookmaker who bets exclusively on an opinion. Recognised and respected as an outstanding judge of racing form, Michael will back a horse if he feels he is not getting value by laying the other horses in the race. Despite the popular belief, racecourse bookmaking is a tough business, with very few book-ies making more than wages from their toil and many falling by the wayside prematurely. Consequently, bookmakers and their assistants tend to advise their sons to stay well away from the business on the grounds that it is very risky and the surface glamour hides the reality of long, unsocial working hours, erratic earnings and frustrating, time-consuming car journeys. Michael's father, Thomas, popularly known as 'Tilly', had been in racing all his life, notably working for Terry Rogers before setting up as a bookmaker in his own right with Frankie Saul, starting at the Dundalk dogs and later expanding on to Irish racecourses. Tilly kept his four sons away from racing, insisting that each took his education seriously and learned a proper trade. Michael always yearned to come into racing, but was blocked by his father, who only relented after his son qualified as a plumber.

Forsaking the water pipes for the betting ring, Michael Naghten started out clerking for bookmakers Paul and Albert Sharpe, and Edward Flood, learning his new trade before branching out him-self as a bookmaker. The first place that he actually 'stood up' under his own name was at a pony meeting at Trim, then he grad-uated to point-to-points and from there to the racecourses. Now he works at most of the Irish meetings, as well as at York and Cheltenham in England, and is one of the leading bookmakers in the Irish Ring.

I asked Michael for some simple advice for people who might wish to bring off a betting coup, or simply want guidance in their punting habits. His first point was that he is not at all superstitious and does not believe in luck, believing luck means having the odds on your side. He advises those planning a coup to keep clear of racecourses with a weak betting market, which is obvious, but also to rule out big bets on horses running on sharp tracks, like Kilbeggan, Bellewstown and Killarney, where horses often do not act round the tight turns. Steeplechases should be given a miss also and never, ever back a newcomer in any kind of race. Betting on a horse running for the first time or one facing hurdles or fences for the first time should be resisted. It is much cheaper to just watch it run, win or lose.

J.P. McManus (1951–)

J.P. McManus, bookmaker, gambler and major owner of jumping horses, is an odds expert who can see instantly when the book-makers have priced up a race incorrectly and has supreme con-fidence in his own judgement. Through shrewd gambling, involv-ing horses, cards, backgammon, stock markets and money markets, he has accumulated a vast fortune that allows him to indulge in his passion for horses at his Martinstown Stud in Co. Limerick. Liberal in his support for trainers—there are very few good jump-ing trainers that do not train at least one horse for him—J.P. has a vast string, mainly with Christy Roche on the Curragh and with Jonjo O'Neill at Jackdaw's Castle in England, and is also the proud owner of a private plane and a helicopter. J.P. advises gamblers to never, ever chase losses. When things start going against you, stop betting: a gambler under pressure becomes desperate and his judgment becomes suspect. J.P. is one of the few gamblers who is really feared in the betting ring, with bookmakers refusing to bet him, directly or indirectly. I remember a young up-and-coming bookmaker being approached by one of the senior layers and told that he could not have any more bets with him. Shocked, the young bookmaker stammered, 'Why? What have I done?' The senior layer replied, 'You are betting McManus, which means that I am indi-rectly betting McManus and I don't want to take his bets!'

Most bookmakers will take on a big gambler eagerly when he backs his own horses, for ownership moves the heart rather than the head and an owner will put more money on, and take a shorter price, in the belief that all his geese are swans. Not J.P.! The bookmakers did not want to take him on even when he was backing his own horses, fearing his ice-cool judgment and unsentimental approach. However, it seems that J.P. is just as sentimental as any other owner, which can be seen by his desire to give every horse he owns, whether it be good or bad, a nice retirement out at grass in his Martinstown Stud.

PART 3
THE COUPS

'In most betting shops you will see three windows marked "Bet Here", but only one window with the legend "Pay Out".'

JEFFREY BERNARD

The Devil, as they say, is in the detail and it is the tiniest details that can alert the observant man to a betting coup. Human nature being what it is, winning and losing, the thrill of chance, the skill of informed guesswork, these are not enough for the average gambler. No, if we're being honest, we all want that dead cert, we all want to stand in the crowd, smiling in our secret knowledge that something is afoot that makes our 'bet' no gamble at all—or rather, makes it a gamble of the sweetest kind. Horse-racing and betting coups go hand in hand: where one exists, so too does the other. Some people might see this as a bad thing, as an indictment of the sport, but that attitude is a little too serious. It is the coups that provide the sport with its greatest fun and best anecdotes and, of course, one must always remember: there's no such thing as a 'dead cert'! The organisation of a betting coup is a major undertaking because it must be done in secrecy. The more people who know about it, the more likely that news of the coup will leak out prematurely, alerting the bookies and slashing the odds. The art of assessing the ability of the horse on the gallops rather than on the racecourse is rare, even among trainers, and the skill of selecting the right race for it is rarer still. It is one thing to catch the bookies, the horse still has to win and for this reason hundreds of betting coups fail every year. Everybody knows how important it is to keep quiet before a betting coup, but it is just as important to keep quiet after the coup, whether or not it has been successful. Most people have no problem hushing up a failed coup, but few can resist telling the world when they have pulled off a brilliant, successful gamble—it is part of the fun of a coup! The problem is that once everyone knows how it was done, it will be impossible to pull off such a coup again; and the majority of gamblers want to go to the well again, and again and again.

The First Betting Coup (early eighteenth century)

The first races were two-horse affairs known as 'matches' and were basically challenges between two owners to find out whose horse was the best. When a challenge was accepted, the two owners appointed a third party to act as the stakeholder, with responsibility for holding the stake, for ensuring the riders weighed out with the correct weight and that the race was started fairly. He then had to judge which horse had won the match, to supervise the weighing-in procedure of the winning rider and to declare a winner and to pay the stake to the winning owner. Racing has not really changed too much in the intervening years, except that today there are multi-runner races and the stakeholder is Horse Racing Ireland.

In the early days cheating was not an option because matches were made among a small, wealthy group of people who had reputations to keep, and those involved in making side bets were all friends or neighbours of the two horse owners. There was little incentive to bend the rules and incur the wrath of one's friends and neighbours and risk being shunned by society. That didn't mean there was no scope for invention, however, and the first betting coup is the proof: audacious and ingenious, it was won fair and square and every loser was content to accept that his money was lost fair and square.

One day a proud horse-owner was boasting about the speed of his prize possession when an unusual challenge was thrown down. A local man challenged the horse to a race—against his pig. When the laughter had subsided, it became clear that the owner of the pig was not joking. He boldly claimed that his pig was faster than the horse and he was prepared to put his money where his mouth was. The owner of the pig just had two stipulations: first, the race must be over sixty yards and secondly, he needed a few weeks to get his pig in shape. The horse-owner eagerly accepted the challenge and the conditions, a match was arranged and each owner put up a stake of £100. A stakeholder was appointed and the race was on.

Little else was discussed in the weeks leading up to the day of the race. The pundits had a field day. These 'experts'—who confidently predict the outcome before a race and afterwards are able to tell you earnestly and eloquently why they were wrong—were adamant that the horse would win. They offered a variety of reasons why the pig's attempt was doomed: it would not be fast enough; the pig would slit its own throat if it ran too fast; it would tread on its ears and do a somersault; no man would be able to make a pig run in a straight line up a course! The betting was hot and heavy, with the pig offered at odds up to 10-to-1, a price the owner of the pig had no hesitation accepting. He told his friends to 'help themselves', but most declined. Surely a horse can beat a pig? Surely?

The owner of the pig set about training his animal to run fast and straight up the course. He did this by moving the pig's sty to a field, with the door facing a sixty-yard grass track. At feeding time he placed the pig's trough outside the door of the sty, each day placing it a little further up the course, until it was sixty yards away. Anyone familiar with feeding a pig will know that when the animal hears the food bucket rattling outside it squeals wildly, and when the door is finally opened it races to the bucket in its eagerness to eat. Through the Pavlovian conditioning the pig soon understood that the trough was sixty yards down the track, and when the sty door was opened its only aim was to get to it as fast as possible.

On the day of the race the pig was left hungrier than usual as he waited in his 'trap', grunting, with his owner, armed with a bucket, standing by, ready to open the door when the Starter dropped the white handkerchief. Meanwhile, the supremely fit horse and jockey lined up beside the 'trap', awaiting the signal to start. The pig-owner rattled the bucket and the pig began to squeal; the horse danced nervously and pawed the earth, disconcerted by the noise, the jockey attempting to settle it down by stroking its neck and whispering soothing words. When the handkerchief dropped, the 'trap' was opened and the pig screamed out like a thing possessed, blazing a trail for the trough. The jockey roused the horse with a cut of his stick but, slightly off-balanced and bewildered by the experience, the horse took a few moments to get into its stride, and then quickly went in hot pursuit. The pig ran straight towards the trough with the horse, now in full cry, closing up with every long stride. Spectators held their breath, it was going to be close, but the post came just in time for the pig, whose snout was in the trough an instant before the horse's head had reached the finishing line. The impossible had happened: the pig had won and the owner of the pig had landed a spectacular coup and had landed it fair and square.

Afterwards, the 'after-dinner speakers' performed the inquest. 'He pigged it,' one declared; 'A dirty pig,' exclaimed another—they were talking about the horse, mind you, and all were unanimous that the horse was 'not worth feeding'. All these pundits were agreed that the race was lost by the horse rather than won by the pig. So the next time you hear an 'expert' call a horse 'a pig', remember that the pig ran straight as a die and as fast as he could to the trough without flinching, and then wish that all the horses you backed would run like pigs!

The Prince and the Jockey Club

Towards the end of the eighteenth century multi-runner races were being run with a number of owners putting money into the pot. This was more profitable for the winner, who took home a bigger prize, but it required a much wider course and limited the choice of venue for the race. In England, Newmarket had one of the best courses at the time—wide enough to accommodate big fields but without the prevalent sharp bends—but racing there was tightly controlled by the Jockey Club, which laid down strict rules that were stringently enforced by a panel of stewards. Any person caught breaking these rules was liable to be barred (or 'warned-off') from Newmarket Heath.

The Jockey Club's membership consisted of the most prominent horse owners of the day, including among their number the Prince of Wales, the future King George IV (1820–1830). However, it was not for jockeys in the modern sense. Founded around 1750 when the word jockey simply meant 'one who manages or has to do with horses', the Jockey Club gradually bought up Newmarket Heath, its gallops and racecourses. As its private property, the Club could bar anyone from the Heath without having to give a reason. This was the basis of its power. Should any warned-off person venture onto Newmarket Heath, the police would be called to remove the illegal trespasser. In this way the Jockey Club excluded the undesirables, the cheats and the riff-raff from their races, and their course prospered as a result.

Impressed by Newmarket's success and anxious to keep unscrupulous characters from their meetings, other racecourses decided to race under Newmarket Rules. The local stewards dealt with minor offences as before, but serious matters were passed to

Lord George Bentinck (1802–1848). The biggest gambling owner of
them all gave up the Turf for a career in politics. (*Topfoto*)

Ellis ('Honest' John Day up and John Doe at its head) arrives at Doncaster, in September 1836, as fresh as a daisy and as fit as a flea. (*Topfoto*)

Fred Archer (1857–1886). Champion English jockey from 1874 to 1886, Archer's drastic diet of a teaspoon of champagne and a glass of a purge enabled him to ride a record 2,748 winners— but sent him to an early grave.
(*Hulton Archive/Getty*)

James F. 'Tod' Sloan (1874–1933). The American jockey whose 'monkey-up-a-stick' riding style yielded 254 winners from 801 mounts in just over two flat race seasons. Feared by the local jockeys, hated by the Establishment because of his gambling friends, the stewards put the brash Sloan in his place by banning him for life in 1900.

Peter McKay (c.1885–1965), alias Ras Prince Monolulu, the tipster. He was obviously a firm believer in keeping the police on his side (Derby Day 1932). (*Hulton Archive/Getty*)

Miss Dorothy Paget (1905–1960). The biggest punter of her time and one of the biggest owners, who won the Derby with *Straight Deal* and the Grand National with *Golden Miller*. Her last Irish winner, *Fortescue*, ridden by Bunny Cox, won a Naas bumper ten days before her death. (*Topfoto*)

Miss Dorothy Paget's great horse, *Golden Miller* (1927–1957), winner of the Grand National and five Cheltenham Gold Cups. It never fell in its life, but a top jockey fell off it twice! (*Hulton Archive/Getty*)

Caughoo (Eddie Dempsey up), the 100-to-1 outsider that emerged from the fog to win the 1947 Grand National by twenty lengths. (*Hulton Archive/Getty*)

The Grand National was the biggest race of all back in 1947, and the Irish-trained winner *Caughoo* arrives back at Dublin's North Wall to a hero's welcome. Nobody cared if he had taken a short cut or had got lost in the fog! (*Topfoto*)

Captain Spencer Freeman (*right*), director of the Irish Hospital Sweepstakes Company, presents trainer Paddy Prendergast with two gold trophies for *Meadow Court*'s 1965 Irish Sweeps Derby win at a special presentation in February 1966. (*Topfoto*)

Nijinsky (Lester Piggott up), the last winner of the Triple Crown, being led in after winning the 1970 Derby for Charles Engelhard and his trainer, Vincent O'Brien. (*Hulton Archive/Getty*)

the overarching authority of the Jockey Club for assessment and punishment. As a result, if a person was warned-off by the Jockey Club, he was automatically warned-off every racecourse that raced under Newmarket Rules, so being warned-off effectively meant being unable to go racing at all—anywhere. This power enabled the Club to eliminate rough riding, blatant cheating and other offences committed by owners and riders. But could the rules deal with a person as important and powerful as the future King of England?

The Prince of Wales caught the racing bug in 1784 and subsequently assembled a large stable of horses at great cost, an expense he could not actually afford. Broke and heavily in debt, he was bailed out by Parliament, which paid his debts and increased his allowance, enabling the Prince to resume racing on an even grander scale. Splashing out the enormous sum of 2,000 guineas, the Prince secured a promising two-year-old named *Sir Thomas*, which had won its first race impressively. His decision was vindicated when the horse became the first Royal winner of the Derby in 1788. Racing basked in the patronage and success of the future monarch, whose presence at Newmarket made it fashionable to go racing there and the town was therefore able to establish itself as the headquarters of horse-racing. Flushed with success and determined to be the most important owner in the land, the Prince hired Sam Chifney, the top jockey of the day, to ride his horses and paid him a retainer of £200 a year—an unheard-of sum at the time.

The stewards of the Jockey Club were taken by surprise when the in-and-out running of *Escape*, the Prince's horse, caused an outcry on Newmarket Heath. The people—admittedly howling through their pockets—vented their anger at the stewards and demanded action on what they considered an act of robbery. The date was October 1791, the off-course betting market was in its infancy and all the serious betting took place on the racecourse. In betting parlance every bet involves a 'layer' and a 'backer': the layer is the bookmaker, backer is punter. However, as explained earlier, in those pre-bookmaker days bets were laid by the 'legs'. One such 'leg' was Vauxhall Clarke, whose ability to make a profit was partly due to his friendship with the leading jockey Sam Chifney, then at the very top of his profession. A egotistical, thirty-eight-year-old dandy, Chifney was one of the first tacticians in the saddle, perfecting the art of coming with a late run to win his races—a tactic he called the 'Chifney Rush' and which he used very effectively when winning the Epsom Derby/Oaks double in 1789.

One Thursday in October 1791 the Prince's horse, *Escape*, ridden by Sam Chifney, was an odds-on favourite to win a race at Newmarket, but instead finished a well-beaten last of four runners. Turned out again the following day, this time on a 6-to-1 chance, *Escape* well and truly turned the form upside-down by reversing the placings with two of those who had beaten him the previous day. Racegoers who had backed *Escape* on the Thursday and then opted not to back him on Friday were furious. Allegations surfaced that Chifney had pulled *Escape* on the Thursday in order to get a better price about him the next day and talk of foul play was widespread. Shocked by the hostility of the public, appalled that the Prince's horse was involved, but certain the Prince himself could have no knowledge of the incident; the stewards' first inclination was to do nothing. They were forced to act, however, when the Prince was publicly accused of being a party to the coup, and reluctantly instigated an enquiry.

The finger of blame was pointing at Vauxhall Clarke, who had apparently been laying *Escape* on the Thursday, when he was beaten, but turned to backing him the following day when he won, a fact that led to Chifney being hauled before the stewards to explain his riding of *Escape*. The jockey vehemently denied any wrongdoing, although he did admit that he had not backed *Escape* on Thursday, but did have £20 on him, struck with Vauxhall Clarke, on the Friday; at the time there was no prohibition on jockeys betting. Chifney went on to explain that *Escape* was a 'thick-winded' horse, therefore he knew he would not win the first day because he needed the run to 'clear his pipes'; having had the run on Thursday, he was cherry ripe the next day. The stewards were having none of it. They found Sam Chifney guilty of dishonest riding and refused to accept his explanation. However, the involvement of the heir to the throne, who was a substantial patron of racing, made the matter delicate. Convinced that *Escape* had been stopped unknown to the Prince, the stewards felt that action would have to be taken against Chifney, but decided to put the matter into the hands of the future King. The Senior Steward, Sir Charles Bunbury, was sent to have a quiet word with the Prince about his jockey. The quiet word turned into a blazing row when the Prince questioned the stewards' decision, pointing out that the two races were over completely different distances, two miles and four miles, respectively. Unused to having the stewards' decisions contested, Sir Charles bluntly informed the Prince that if he continued to employ Sam Chifney, no gentleman would race against him. Furious and offended, the Prince declared publicly that he had complete faith in Chifney's integrity, was satisfied that *Escape* had not been pulled and was standing by his jockey.

Believing that the Jockey Club had cast a doubt on his integrity, the Prince felt he had no option but to give up racing at Newmarket, so he closed his stable there and paid off Sam Chifney with an annuity for life. The annuity was for the life of the Prince, not of the jockey—not that it mattered because he outlived the jockey by twenty-three years and Chifney flogged the annuity for cash anyway!

The scandal had various repercussions: it showed up racing in a bad light; Newmarket town suffered from job losses and a decline in trade; but ultimately, and unexpectedly, it proved to be the making of the Jockey Club and of the town. The Jockey Club's firm stance strengthened public confidence in the Newmarket Rules. People had witnessed the stewards standing up to the Prince, despite being threatened with the loss of the Royal patronage, and in the eyes of the public justice had been served. The only loser from the affair turned out to be the Prince himself, who was forced to race his horses on minor, unfashionable racecourses for miserable prize money. Another who suffered was Sam Chifney, who was now remembered only for the *Escape* fiasco, and not his five big Classic race victories. His career never recovered because owners subsequently refused to employ him. He sold his royal annuity of £220 per annum for a lump sum, and in 1795 wrote the book *Genius Genuine* to raise funds, which gave him temporary relief. Eventually his debts caught up with him, though, and he ended up in a debtors' jail.

Sam Chifney always denied that he 'pulled' *Escape*, or did anything wrong during the race. As far as he was concerned, he did not have to stop the horse because the horse was not fit enough to win the race. This may have been the case, but the jockey did participate in a coup that effectively robbed the punters who had backed Escape, while enriching the jockey and his friends. Chifney knew full well that the public would back *Escape* on the first day, when it was beaten, and he also knew that defeat would ensure that the public did not support the horse the following day. His friend, Vauxhall Clarke, took advantage of this information by taking the public's money on *Escape* on the first day, while Sam Chifney did the same on the second afternoon. He cheated the public and brought horse-racing into disrepute: that was his crime.

A Dead Cert

Probably the first ever spur-of-the-moment betting coup involved the family of 'Old Q', James Douglas, the Duke of Queensbury (1725–1810). Better known in Ireland as the Earl of March, Old Q enjoyed a long career on the Turf, but his lurid lifestyle and willingness to cheat led to him being described as a 'monument of vice'.

The Earl of March bet Sir Ralph Gore 1,000 guineas, a tremendous sum of money at the time, that his horse *Bajazet* would beat *Black and All Black* in a match. The celebrated race was held on the Curragh on 5 September 1751. It was eagerly watched by an enormous crowd, which, it is said, wagered some 10,000 guineas in side bets. Each horse had its own set of enthusiastic supporters and the race aroused interest beyond the small racing community. The conditions of the match, which was run over four miles, set *Bajazet* to concede 7 lb to *Black and All Black*, but *Bajazet*'s groom apparently removed the extra weight before the race so that Lord March's horse had an illegal advantage. *Black and All Black* won, despite not having the agreed weight advantage. This blatant act of cheating went unnoticed until after the race, when Lord March's groom was seen giving the weight cloth back to the jockey. This was reported to Sir Ralph Gore, who immediately challenged Lord March to a duel, a challenge to his honour that his lordship was forced to accept. After a period of reflection and consideration upon the fact that Sir Ralph had never been known to miss a target with a pistol, Lord March backed down. To save his hide, and the good life to which he was accustomed, Lord March offered Sir Ralph a full apology, accepting the shame that this involved and happily and lustily lived on for another forty-nine years, enabling his family to land a lovely little coup in 1810.

Although in his mid-eighties and in declining health, the Earl of March, who had long since inherited the Dukedom of Queensbury and the nickname Old Q, continued to bet heavily on the outcome of races. In 1810 he had a number of big bets running on a big race when he died unexpectedly, which of course rendered all of his bets void. His loving family—probably just as villainous as their sire—decided to keep his death a secret for a few days, just until the race was run. They had nothing to lose because if the horse won, they would collect the money as usual, but if the horse lost, then Old Q was dead and could not pay up. Each morning they sat the lifeless body of Old Q in the window, reading his newspaper as usual, proving to passers-by that the old man was still in the land of the living. When the horse won and Old Q's last bet came up, the family collected the winnings. Soon thereafter they announced the sad news of his sudden demise!

The Trojan Horse-Box
By 1836 the off-course betting market was firmly established, with bookmakers operating out of every pub in the country. Public houses doubled up as betting shops, while vintners sponsored races and built up a huge ante-post betting business. 'Ante-Post' meant that all bets were struck on the basis of 'All in—run or not', no matter if the bet was placed ten days or ten minutes before the off. The Betting Act of 1853 would ban betting where alcohol was being served, but that was still a long way off. The pub betting business had seventeen years of boom ahead of it, but the first big off-course betting coup was about to strike.

As bookmakers found themselves taking large bets on horses about which they knew nothing, they realised that shrewd punters were cleaning them out. They needed to know where horses were likely to run and which horses were likely to run against them. In order to find out what was going on, the bookmakers employed people to ferret out and send back information from the principal training centres—a practice we looked at in the section on bookmakers. These employees monitored horses in training and reported back details of the training routine and whereabouts of horses to the bookmakers, who would use the information to anticipate where certain horses were likely to run next. These employees became known as 'touts'.

Armed with binoculars, touts would hide in bushes, in trees and in long grass, using ingenious methods of camouflage to spy on horses working on the gallops. The touts were a skilful bunch because they had to be able to identify an individual horse from a distance of at least 500 yards, assess how it was working on the gallops and monitor who was riding it in its work. Each tout carried a book with sketches of the markings of every horse that had raced, prepared by colleagues who logged the runners at the races. Every horse can be identified by its colour and the amount of white it has on its legs and face. Blazes, stars and stripes refer to white markings on a horse's face, while socks and stockings refer to white markings on the legs. Other characteristics, such as lop ears, a roman nose, a long neck or even its tail, all help with its identification. The tout's log was thus used to identify the horses on the gallops. When an unknown horse turned out on the gallops its markings were noted and it was given a 'pet name' until its real name was discovered. Touts monitored the movement of horses very carefully because this was the clue as to where they would race next.

In those days, horses were walked to each race, but the journey had to be a leisurely one otherwise the horse would be too exhausted to do itself justice on the course. This meant a horse that was in the vicinity of Newmarket, for example, was likely to be running there at the next meeting: important information for bookmakers because it enabled them to assemble a field of likely runners. Lord George Bentinck, whom we met before in the story of 'Honest' John Day, was one of the great reformers of racing, a member of the Jockey Club and a member of parliament. He was

a heavy gambler and owned a horse named *Elis*, which was showing considerable promise. Rather than run the horse in his own
name, which would have alerted the bookmakers, Lord Bentinck
ran *Elis* in the name and colours of Lord Lichfield and proceeded
to back him heavily to win the Two Thousand Guineas in the
spring of 1836, for which he considered him a certainty.
Unfortunately for Lord Bentinck and his friends, *Elis* came up
against a really good horse named *Bay Middleton* and was beaten
into second place, causing the gamble to go astray. Determined to
get back his lost money, Lord Bentinck used his friendship with
Lord Jersey, the owner of *Bay Middleton*, to do a deal: he would
not run *Elis* against *Bay Middleton* in the Derby in return for a
clear run in the St Leger. The St Leger was the last of the three big
Classic races open to colts and was due to be run at Doncaster in
mid-September, some four months later, and Lord Bentinck had
decided that this was the race to land a coup with *Elis*. He knew
that *Bay Middleton* was not going to meet his engagement in the
St Leger; the bookmakers did not. This would ensure that *Elis'*
price would be higher than it should have been. Yet even this was
not enough for Lord Bentinck, who wanted a bigger price still and
was prepared to wait for it.

Opportunist that he was, Lord Bentinck decided to make
money from his decision not to run *Elis* in the Derby—a decision
of which the bookmakers were not yet aware—by backing *Bay
Middleton* heavily. Despite Lord Bentinck's substantial bets *Bay
Middleton* was allowed to start at odds of 7-to-4, the bookmakers
having taken the view that the horse was no certainty because it
had a dodgy leg and a vicious temper and this, after all, was
the Derby. Lord Bentinck did not think *Bay Middleton* would be
beaten, and was proved right when it ran out a clear winner by two
lengths. Armed with wads of the bookmakers' cash, he attempted
to back *Elis* for the St Leger, but found that the price was much
shorter than he had expected, particularly since *Bay Middleton*
was believed to be a likely runner. The bookies were obviously not
convinced that *Bay Middleton* would run; aware that *Elis* had been
withdrawn from the Derby, they suspected Bentinck might have
had done a deal to give *Elis* a clear run in the St Leger. As a result,

Elis' odds were kept tight. Lord Bentinck's plunge on the horse in the Two Thousand Guineas had let the cat out of the bag regarding its ownership. The bookmakers now knew *Elis* was a good horse and anticipated that its owner would be eyeing the St Leger.

Not prepared to take the short price on offer, Lord Bentinck let it be known that *Elis* would not be running in the St Leger, and to emphasise the point he moved the horse from Newmarket to Goodwood, some 250 miles from Doncaster. The touts noted *Elis'* arrival, estimating that the horse was at least fifteen days away from Doncaster, and duly informed their employers. Aware that *Elis* had not been scratched from the St Leger, suspicious of Lord Bentinck and wary of getting caught, the bookmakers were reluctant to lengthen *Elis'* odds, fully expecting the horse would make the walk to Doncaster in due course.

Anxious to run his horse, but reluctant to trade at short odds, Lord Bentinck's attention was caught by a bullock-van on his estate. This small, enclosed horse-drawn cart was designed to carry a single bullock or cow short distances, and it gave him the idea of transporting *Elis* to the races by vehicle, thereby saving the horse a long, tiring walk and reducing the journey time considerably. In order to find out whether a similar type of van could be constructed to carry a horse, he approached a local coachbuilder with his idea and specifications. A design was agreed, although the purpose of the proposed vehicle was never revealed. Work began in secret, and a van was built that had its wheels running under it rather than at the sides, as was usual in those days, and designed to be pulled by six horses and to carry two. Big and cumbersome though it was, the van had padded sides and a hard-stuffed mattress on the floor, was fitted-out as a stable yet was robust enough to undertake a long journey. Lord Bentinck was delighted with his invention: everything was ready for the coup.

Meanwhile, down on the south coast of England, *Elis* was being looked after by John Doe, one of Lord Bentinck's most trusted servants. In order to convince the bookmakers that a run at Doncaster was out of the question, the horse was given a rigorous racing schedule there. Asked to run three times in two days at 'Glorious Goodwood', *Elis* won the Drawing-Room Stakes and two days later ran second in the prestigious Goodwood Cup, in which he had to take on older horses over two-and-a-half miles. Pulled out again later that afternoon, *Elis* beat his stable companion *The Drummer* to win the Racing Stakes. When *Elis* was then sent to Lewes, where he beat a high-class field, the bookmakers finally accepted that the horse was unlikely to run in the St Leger and pushed its price out. With the big race now only seven days away and the touts reporting that *Elis* was still at Goodwood, the bookmakers concluded that even if the horse met its engagement at Doncaster, having been despatched at the eleventh hour, it would arrive at the races too weary to do itself justice in what was one of the most important races in the calendar. As *Elis*' price drifted in the market, Lord Bentinck's men stepped in and took the price, but they took it for themselves and not for their boss. Livid with rage, Lord Bentinck decided to scratch *Elis* there and then and was only pacified when his commissioner agreed to lay him £1,000 at 12-to-1!

Now that he had got the better of his commissioners (that is, those who placed bets on his behalf), Lord Bentinck decided it was time to send *Elis* on its journey north, and *The Drummer* was sent with it for company. It was planned to do the journey in three parts, each leg being about eighty miles, with the horses being exercised before each leg. Sufficient hay, oats and water for the journey would be carried with the horses in the van, which would be personally driven by Lord Bentinck's trusted groom, John Doe. The journey was scheduled to begin on the Friday, four days before the race. When the appointed day of departure arrived, the journey was almost aborted before it began. When John Doe attempted to load the two racehorses into the van, an unforeseen problem presented itself: the van was too high off the ground and the ramp was too steep for horses to walk up it. Having pondered this for a while, John Doe decided to move the van to a hilly piece of ground so that it was lower than the horses, and then used an old door to extend the ramp, making it less steep. The plan worked. The docile and willing *Elis* gingerly made his way up the rickety ramp and into the van, and *The Drummer* followed in his wake.

The van was pulled by six post horses, each set of horses hired to pull the van to the next post house at a cost of one shilling per mile, per horse. The final bill amounted to £72, which made the journey an expensive one, but then the rewards would be considerable if Bentinck had, as reputed, backed *Elis* to win at least £20,000.

As the van moved north on its journey to Doncaster, it attracted considerable attention: many questions were asked, but John Doe said nothing. People stared and oncoming coaches stopped to look at this strange carriage, all of them curious to know what was inside. News of the van preceded it and crowds lined the route through the towns and villages it passed through, speculating about the cargo it contained. Some said it was fearsome wild animals on their way to a zoo, others suggested it contained criminals on their way to jail; nobody thought that it was carrying two horses to the races. On the second leg of the journey the van stopped at Lichfield racecourse, near Tamworth in Staffordshire, where *Elis* and *The Drummer* took exercise and had a proper training gallop. On Sunday, 18 September, two days before the race, *Elis* arrived at Doncaster, as fresh as a daisy and as fit as a flea. Everything was going to plan.

When the bookmakers discovered that *Elis* was in Doncaster, they were astonished and fearful—things were going very wrong. The bad news continued with the announcement that *Bay Middleton* had been scratched from the race and the reports from the touts that *Elis* looked fit and well, with no signs of exhaustion at all. The only thing between Lord Bentinck and his massive betting coup was *Scroggins*, the 6-to-4 favourite and trained by John Scott, the most successful Northern-based trainer of all time.

From the off, Lord George Bentinck and his cronies never had an anxious moment, and the bookmakers' fate was sealed when the classy *Elis* hit the front a mile from him and stayed on strongly to easily hold off *Scroggins'* late challenge by two lengths. The gamble was landed and the bookmakers paid out through clenched teeth. They had been fooled by the first racehorse van ever made, and Lord Bentinck's big gamble changed forever the way horses travelled to and from race courses. The transportation of racehorses became a thriving business and, unlike many good ideas, the originator of this one gained handsomely from his invention. It was all the more annoying for the bookmakers because they had suspected a coup from the beginning, only to get lulled into a false sense of security at the end. All's fair in love and horse-racing!

Visions of Victory

Betting by sixth sense isn't a recommended method, but every now and then a dream or intuition signals the right punt and gut instinct can lead to a good gamble. The most famous dream in racing history must be Lord Poullett's vision of the finish of the 1871 Grand National, which informed him, fully four months before the race was run, that his horse, *The Lamb*, would win with Tommy Pickernell in the saddle. He immediately wrote to Pickernell, who rode as 'Mr Thomas', telling him of his dream and offering him the ride on *The Lamb*, entreating him to keep the details of the dream a secret. As it happened, the dream came true—money always goes to money. *The Lamb* won the race and Lord Poullett landed a fortune in winning bets.

Of course, for every dream that actually comes true, thousands more fail. Every year the papers are full of 'I dreamt it won the Derby' stories, and I cannot remember one that came true! However, some years ago a man told me a story that he claimed was true and whether it was or not, it is a good story. He said he was not really a racing man, but had the odd flutter from time to time. One night he had a vivid dream: he was standing against the running rail at the start of a race, watching the horses walking around in a circle, when he clearly saw the jockey Lester Piggott crying. As Piggott and his mount came near, he shouted to the jockey, 'What's wrong? Why are you crying?' to which Piggott replied, 'I'm too light, I have not got enough weight and if I win, I shall be disqualified.' The man then suggested to the jockey that if he got up behind him on the horse, he then would be carrying sufficient weight. He immediately sprang up onto the horse behind Piggott.

The following morning he was reading his paper when he recalled his dream and decided to look up Lester Piggott's mounts. The maestro was riding at Redcar that afternoon and was booked to ride *Telephonist, Fire Worship* and—wait for it—*Passenger* in the William Hill Gold Trophy. Now there was a tip! Our friend backed it and was rewarded when *Passenger* and Piggott won the race at odds of 8-to-1. That was in 1964 and he told me the story about ten years later, but in that decade he had never had another dream, nor another bet!

For my own part, I clearly remember Wednesday, 21 June 1961. It happened to be Irish Derby day, and as a treat I was being taken to Brittas Bay in Co. Wickow with all the altar boys from St Alphonsus and Columba's Church, Ballybrack. One of the mothers came to collect me and she spoke briefly with my mother at the door before moving off. I listened as she told my mother of her dream the previous night, in which she saw three gold crowns. That was enough reason for her to have a flutter on a runner in the Irish Derby named *Your Highness*. There was no betting shop in Ballybrack at the time, so the lady stopped in Bray and put one pound each way on *Your Highness*. I have no recollection of how the result of the race became known, but I do remember trying to work out her winnings in the car on the way home: *Your Highness* won the Irish Derby at odds of 33-to-1!

Where is Trodmore?
The opening of numerous park courses in Ireland and England greatly expanded the number of fixtures because the new courses needed more fixtures in order to recoup their capital outlay. Naturally, public holidays were eagerly sought for fixtures, the August Bank Holiday Monday being a particular favourite because most people have the day off work and good weather is almost guaranteed. Nowadays the number of fixtures allowed on this day is limited by the racing authorities (at least for the time being because the competition authorities don't like this one little bit), but 100 years ago there was no such restriction. A racecourse could hold a meeting whenever it liked, and in 1898 eighteen of them decided to race on August Bank Holiday Monday. The Betting Act of 1853 had made betting shops illegal, but bookmakers operated on the streets within the law, a practice that was not banned until 1906.

Any bank holiday was a busy day for the street bookmaker, but this particular bank holiday was exceptionally busy with lots of business being done on a small jumping meeting named Trodmore Hunt. A coup was afoot on a horse named *The Reaper*, but the syndicate responsible was careful not to place too big a bet with any one bookmaker and to disguise the gamble by having a few, small, throwaway bets on other horses at the meeting. One or two bookmakers queried Trodmore—'never heard of it'—but were reassured when told, 'the card is in the papers'. Sure enough the Trodmore Hunt programme was printed in one of the trade newspapers of the day, *The Sportsman*. Although the card did not appear in the other trade paper, *The Sporting Life*, or in the dailies, that was not unusual at the time because no single paper would have the space to cover all eighteen meetings and each therefore selected only the most important half-dozen or so for inclusion.

Those were the days before overnight declarations. Three-quarters of an hour before the race the horses were declared to run and trainers tended to enter horses at several meetings, deciding at the last minute where to run after weighing up the likely opposition. Likewise, jockeys were unsure of where they were actually riding so usually accepted mounts at several meetings, even though they could attend only one of them. Owners understood this; the jockey would ride if he were in attendance at that meeting, if not, another would have to be found. If the owners and jockeys were not sure where they were going, the punters were completely in the dark, betting blindly on a horse without knowing its rider or what horses it would be lining up against. The bookmakers were in the same boat, sometimes being caught unawares when word got out that a big-name jockey was going to turn up at a small course. Their protection lay with the on-course bookmakers, whose prices are taken at the start of a race to make the SP and who were fully aware of all the facts and adjusted their prices accordingly.

The street bookmakers did receive results by telegraph from the main meetings, but for results from the likes of Trodmore Hunt they had to wait for the following morning's papers. A nasty shock awaited them when they opened their copy of *The Sportsman* on Tuesday morning: *The Reaper* had won at 5-to-1! As betting coups go the sums involved were relatively small, nevertheless the bookmakers had been heavily hit *en bloc*, particularly those based in the London area, where a very large number of small bets had been placed on *The Reaper*. It was what the bookmakers call a 'dirty result', but the occasional bad result is part and parcel of the business and has to be taken on the chin. The initial verdict was that there must have been a popular tip for *The Reaper*; there was no talk of a betting coup, nor were any rumours circulating that something might be amiss.

However, when the team of backers went to collect their winnings on *The Reaper* on the Tuesday, they were faced with an unexpected problem. Some bookmakers paid up, but many settled according to *The Sporting Life*, which had not published the results from Trodmore. These bookmakers were not interested in what was in *The Sportsman*—at the time, the newspapers occasionally differed on the starting price return and it was not unknown for them to differ on the actual winner as well. The message was clear: when *The Sporting Life* published the results from Trodmore, then and only then would bets struck at the meeting be settled. If *The Sporting Life* did not publish any results from the meeting, then all bets struck on the meeting would be void and the stake returned to the backer. This was a standard rule across the country and meant that backers were betting not on the actual result of a race, but on the result published in a particular newspaper. The backers of *The Reaper* did not appear to be aware of this rule and the subsequent row over the pay out made some bookmakers suspicious. The backers' ignorance of such a basic rule indicated that these people were not ordinary punters, which meant they must have been betting for a third party, or had access to some kind of tip. And that could only mean some sort of betting coup. Their suspicions were confirmed when the bookmakers consulted their colleagues and discovered the extent of the gamble on *The Reaper*.

Although *The Sporting Life* put the matter right by publishing the results the following day, Wednesday, a further problem arose because it returned the sp of *The Reaper* as 5-to-2, rather than the 5-to-1 quoted in *The Sportsman*. By now news of the coup was spreading, the previous form of *The Reaper* was of increasing interest, as was the unfamiliar racecourse at Trodmore—but no record of them could be found. There was no horse named *The Reaper* in training and Trodmore was not a registered racecourse. In fact, a gazetteer of the British Isles failed to even list a place called Trodmore. The truth finally dawned: the meeting had been a hoax.

The bookmakers rounded on the editor of *The Sportsman*, the paper that had printed the list of runners for the Trodmore Hunt Steeplechase meeting and published the results the following day. The editor's plea of innocence was not terribly convincing. He claimed that a gentleman representing the Trodmore Hunt Steeplechase Committee had paid a personal visit to his office, seeking coverage for its forthcoming meeting. The Committee had apparently put up generous prize money, had expected to attract a reasonable class of horse to its meeting and needed the publicity of newspaper coverage. The editor went on to explain that he was eager to help the new racecourse, particularly as it was in Cornwall, an area of England where there was not much racing, so he had agreed to cover it. Another factor was that the coverage would cost the paper nothing as the Trodmore Hunt Committee volunteered to supply the runners for the meeting and telegraph the results to the paper as they came in. How could he be expected to anticipate that someone would *pretend* to run a race meeting? The idea was preposterous. His suspicions had not been aroused at any point and furthermore the bookies hadn't questioned it either, but had willingly taken all the bets on the Trodmore meeting, even though they had never heard of it.

The editor of the other trade paper, *The Sporting Life*, knew nothing of the Trodmore meeting until his bookmaker readers complained that the results had not been published on the Tuesday. Under pressure to print the result, he postponed the investigation as to how the paper missed the meeting in the first place and copied the results from the edition of *The Sportsman*, never thinking for a moment they might have been conned. It was a simple typing error that was responsible for *The Reaper* being returned in the *Life* at 5-to-2 instead of 5-to-1, thus undermining the coup.

The facts of the matter were that there was no place called Trodmore, there was no Trodmore Hunt Steeplechase meeting and the victory of *The Reaper* was a figment of its backers' imagination. The police were called in and suspicion fell upon a group of Fleet Street journalists, who would have had inside knowledge of how the papers worked over a busy long weekend. As there was insufficient evidence to prosecute anyone, however, the case went cold and the perpetrators remained free. Despite his denials, most bookmakers believed that the editor of *The Sportsman* was in on the coup. He had printed a racecard and published results given to him by a total stranger, without making any enquiries at all and had accepted the results sent in by the stranger. Even if the meeting had been legitimate, anyone could telegram a false result, or a false starting price.

It was a successful, daring coup, but the misprint in *The Sporting Life* seriously damaged the rewards because a proportion of the winnings could never be claimed. Bets not paid out immediately were effectively losers—the winnings and the stakes being lost because they could never be collected now that the police were involved and a possible jail sentence for fraud awaited anyone that got caught. It was probably the fear of jail, rather than the maxim that one should keep quiet after a betting coup, that stopped those journalists from writing about their coup of the century!

An Opportunistic Coup

Very occasionally a successful betting coup is landed without any advance planning, when an opportunity arises out of the blue and the advantage is grabbed on the spur of the moment. A typical case occurred at Naas in the early 1970s and was so successful it changed normal bookmaker practice in relation to the paying out of winning bets.

On this particular afternoon at Naas a short-priced favourite scrambled to victory after interfering with the runner-up on the way, an incident that prompted the stewards to conduct an enquiry. The enquiry sought to establish whether the winner had caused interference to the horse that finished second and, if so, whether the interference had helped to improve its placing. The stewards had a number of options at their disposal: they could confirm the result by making no alteration to the judge's placings; they could disqualify the winner and place it behind any horse it had impeded; or they could place it last if they deemed the interference intentional. In this case, the enquiry involved only the first and second-placed horses, but the favourite, which had hampered the runner-up, was in danger of being disqualified and the bookmakers expected the result of the race to be altered. As backers of the favourite stood around anxiously awaiting their fate, an announcement was made on the loudspeaker: 'Result of the stewards' enquiry—no alteration to the judge's placings. Winner all right.' The enquiry had taken less time than anticipated and the favourite had succeeded in keeping the race.

The announcement of 'winner all right' was the signal that the result of the race was official and winning bets should be paid out by the bookmakers. On hearing it, the bookmakers duly paid out the winnings before getting on with the business of betting on the next race. Ten to fifteen minutes later, when betting on the next race was in full swing, the loudspeakers sprang to life and proceeded to give the result of the stewards' enquiry on the previous race. The bookmakers listened in disbelief as the announcer described the stewards' decision to disqualify the winner, placing it second, and to award first place to the horse that had originally finished second. In other words, the stewards had reversed the placings of the first two horses, demoting the favourite to second place. Then followed the familiar 'winner all right' announcement, followed by the Tote dividends. Bookmakers and punters were confused because this announcement contradicted the earlier announcement while making no reference at all to that earlier announcement. Pandemonium ensued as punters rushed to look for discarded winning tickets and bystanders rushed to pick up any piece of paper they could see, hoping to find a discarded ticket on the promoted winner. Seriously worried about the possibility of a double pay out, the bookmakers sent their runners to the weigh-in room to clarify the result of the race.

It was soon confirmed that the favourite had indeed been disqualified. Nobody connected to the racecourse knew anything about the first announcement that the winner had been allowed to keep the race—not even the announcer, who denied he had made any such announcement over the PA system. It was eventually discovered that the first announcement had been a hoax. It had absolutely nothing to do with the race officials, but had been broadcast from the commentator's box at the top of the stand. Apparently an enterprising punter—who had obviously backed the favourite and feared for his money—saw the empty racecourse commentator's box, climbed onto the top step at the back of the stand and wondered: what if? He did a quick investigation, realised the microphone was active, cleared his throat, put on his best speaking voice and made his own announcement—and the entire betting ring fell for it!

Red-faced with rage, the air blue with heartfelt swearing, the bookies had to pay out again, this time on the horse that had originally finished second. After this blow to their cash bags the bookmakers decided to introduce a new rule that in future winning bets would be paid a race in arrears, in other words, winnings due on the first race could be collected only after the second race had been run. This rule remained the norm for nearly thirty years, until in 1999 the Turf Club introduced measures to speed up the weighing-in process, to which the bookmakers responded by agreeing to pay out winners immediately the 'winner all right' was declared.

The Case of *Gay Future*

The famous modern betting coups, such as those that involved *Gay Future* and *Yellow Sam*, have actually been failures to the extent that everyone knows about them. The perfect betting coup is unknown to anyone except the bookmakers and the immediate connections of the horse. *Grand Visier* would be an example of a horse that landed several brilliant betting coups, yet nobody has heard of the horse its owners used to affectionately call a little post office! *Grand Visier* and horses like him are examples of how a real betting coup should be landed—in secret, silently, enabling the horse to win serious bets again and again. Everyone knows it is essential to keep quiet before a betting coup, but it is equally important to keep quiet after a betting coup as well—a point few people seem to grasp.

In the late 1960s bookmaker/owner Malachy Skelly and trainer Tom Costello landed a big gamble at Wexford, a small racecourse with a weak betting market, by including their two horses in 'doubles' placed in betting shops throughout the country (a double is a bet that requires both horses to win). Both of the horses did win, and Tom Costello put himself on the map and has never looked back since. It is likely that this little coup was the inspiration for a syndicate from Cork, fronted by local business-man Tony Murphy, which plotted a betting coup using the same formula in an attempt to win a fortune. Although the coup is often referred to as 'Murphy's stroke', insiders say the real brains behind it was Pa O'Leary, an owner, trainer and businessman who brought the Burger King franchise to Ireland. Obviously it did not suit Pa to be in the limelight when the coup hit the headlines, after all, he was a trainer licenced by the Turf Club, so he took a back seat and it proved a very wise decision.

The syndicate put a lot of effort into its elaborate plan, which entailed finding the right horse to land the coup and then keeping the whole thing secret. Eventually they settled on *Gay Future*, which had just finished third in a flat race at Naas. Formerly trained by John Oxx, *Gay Future* had finished third in a nursery (a handicap race for two-year-olds) at Dundalk before being sold to Johnny Harrington, for whom he won a bumper at Thurles, ridden by Timmy Jones, as well as finishing second in two other bumpers. The horse obviously had a bit of speed and if he could learn to jump would be a near certainty to win a lowly novice hurdle in England, which was the target. Edward O'Grady, a young Irish trainer, was instructed to purchase it.

O'Grady was told to buy *Gay Future* on behalf of Tony Collins, a stockbroker who trained in a small way at Troon, Ayrshire, in Scotland and who had been recruited to act as the official trainer of the horses involved in the coup. The syndicate had no intention of allowing the inexperienced Collins to actually do the training, however, so *Gay Future* went to the O'Grady yard at Ballynonty, near Thurles. Of course, the last thing the syndicate wanted was for it to be known that O'Grady was training the horse, which was ostensibly purchased for Collins, so it sent another horse to Scotland, a chestnut like *Gay Future*, in its place. Unlike other ringers, this horse would never impersonate *Gay Future* on the racecourse, only on the training gallops of Tony Collins while the real *Gay Future* was being intensively trained in Co. Tipperary to jump hurdles efficiently. Meanwhile the syndicate mapped out the Ulverston Novices' Hurdle, to be run at Cartmel on Bank Holiday Monday, 26 August 1974, as the race for *Gay Future* to land the coup. The real *Gay Future* was sent over to England, transferred to Tony Collins' horsebox at a secret *rendezvous* and taken to Cartmel racecourse as if it had travelled down from Scotland.

Cartmel is a hilly course in the Lake District, in the middle of nowhere, about twenty-two miles from Barrow. Locals will tell you that the course was used in medieval times for mule-racing, and in the 1970s it was only just beginning to come to terms with the twentieth century. For years Cartmel had survived on the annual two-day Whitsun fixture and had no permanent telephone—a temporary one was installed in the Secretary's office for the two days of the racing, and the number allocated changed from year to year. The old, rickety wooden stand groaned and swayed with the strain when racegoers piled in to watch a race and there was no 'blower' service in operation, which meant off-course bookmakers had difficulty sending money back to the on-course betting market. By 1974 a second two-day meeting, the August Bank Holiday fixture, had been added and the old stand had been replaced by a new, concrete, uncovered stand and the telephone situation was shortly to be addressed. There Mr A.K. Collins' *Gay Future*, trained by his owner under a permit and ridden by Mr T.A. Jones, a late jockey change, was declared to run in the 3.45pm race. The horse was bathed in soap suds to make it look as if it was 'sweating up' as it walked round the parade ring, a ploy sure to deter any big backer from having a bet on it.

The on-course betting market at Cartmel was weak, ruling out the possibility of backing the horse there, so the syndicate had to back *Gay Future* in the betting shops. To ensure that the bookmakers did not pass the money to the course bookmakers and thereby shorten up the price, the syndicate placed its bets in a series of doubles and trebles. That Bank Holiday morning, from their base at the Tara Hotel in London, a team set out to visit as many shops as they could in the area and to back three horses, all listed as trained by Tony Collins, in across-the-card doubles and trebles: *Gay Future*, *Ankerwyke* and *Opera Cloak*.

Multiple bets, as doubles and trebles are collectively known, require all horses in the bet to win, otherwise the bet is a loser. If a horse, or horses, included in the bet does not run, then bookmakers' rules provide for the bet to be reduced to a double or a single, respectively. Bookmakers always keep an eye on multiple bets, which can run into big money should all the legs win, but normal practice is to see how the first leg performs before deciding if action needs to be taken to hedge the liability. Aware of how a betting shop operates, the syndicate had planned that *Ankerwyke* and *Opera Cloak* would not be running, so the treble bets they were placing were actually single bets in disguise. It was a brilliant, perfectly planned scheme, save in one respect: a corner was cut and this one incidence of sloppiness ultimately doomed the whole coup.

By early afternoon the bookmakers were well aware of the pending coup. Some 500 or 600 betting shops in the London area had taken this treble bet, but they tarried because of the unknown permit-holder involved and their natural inclination to wait for the *Gay Future* result before reappraising the situation. There was a whiff of danger in the air, however, and the William Hill firm instructed office staff not to accept any more bets on these horses. It is said that another bookmaker made an attempt to get to Cartmel by car, but arrived too late; *Gay Future* had already won. In any event, the bookmakers were probably not really worried when the news came in that *Gay Future* had won at odds of 10-to-1. The bets were not a problem at this stage because two legs of the bet had still to run and both had to win. But the situation changed quickly when it was discovered that *Ankerwyke* had been withdrawn from its race because the horsebox carrying the horse to the races had broken down. No sooner had that news been digested than news came in that *Opera Cloak* would not run either as it too

was marooned in a broken-down horsebox. With the other two
horses in the ubiquitous trebles being declared non-runners, the
big bookmaking firms now faced a huge payout on single bets on
Gay Future at 10-to-1, the team having placed £30,000 in a series
of £5, £10 and £20 treble bets.

Rattled by a potential loss of over £250,000 and suspicious that
they had been taken for a ride, the bookmakers' security
people were sceptical about the withdrawals. The odds against two
different horseboxes breaking down on the way to the races were
high enough, but it really was a striking coincidence that the two
horseboxes carrying the two horses trained by Tony Collins could
both break down, hundreds of miles apart, at approximately the
same time. News of the coup spread like wildfire and one journal-
ist, using his initiative, telephoned the Collins' stable in Troon
seeking information. He spoke to, as Tony Collins put it, 'an
ingenuous kitchen maid who spilled the beans'. When questioned
about the whereabouts of *Ankerwyke* and *Opera Cloak*, the kitchen
maid replied that they were out in the paddock. When asked if she
was sure, she replied that she could see the two horses out of her
window, grazing. It was clear that neither *Ankerwyke* nor *Opera
Cloak* were ever going to race that day, but they had been declared
as runners, which the bookmakers claimed was a fraud. On the
basis of this information the bookmakers' trade body, BOLA
(Betting Offices Licensees' Association), issued instructions to its
members to withhold payment on the *Gay Future* bets pending an
investigation by Scotland Yard into possible fraud.

The police enquiry continued quietly until the dramatic arrest
of Edward O'Grady, John Horgan, Brian Darrer and Tony Murphy
at the 1975 Cheltenham Festival on a charge of a conspiracy to
defraud. Tony Collins was also arrested and similarly charged the
following day. An attempt was made to extradite other members
of the syndicate—Patrick O'Leary, Michael Rose and Joseph
McMahon—from Cork to face charges in England, but this failed
in the Irish courts. The charges against Edward O'Grady, John
Horgan and Brian Darrer were subsequently dropped and only
Tony Murphy and Tony Collins were brought to court. The case
took place at Preston in February 1976, lasted six days and a jury

took six hours to find the pair guilty of conspiracy to defraud. Both men were fined £1,000 and had to contribute £500 towards the costs of the hearing. When the legal case was finished the Jockey Club charged Tony Murphy and Tony Collins with a breach of its rules. Having found both men guilty, it banned them from British racecourses for ten years.

Some people argued that the syndicate did nothing wrong, but the rules of racing had been broken and the general public had been misled. Tony Collins pretended to be training *Gay Future* when the horse had never been in his stable and was actually being trained by a professional trainer. Furthermore, he had declared *Ankerwyke* and *Opera Cloak* as runners that day even though he never had any intention of running them.

The syndicate did not collect the majority of its winnings, but it did get paid out by some bookmakers in England and by all the Irish bookmakers who took its bets. Tony Murphy's careful planning was let down by overconfidence, which led to a lack of attention to detail that culminated in the decision not to send the non-runners to their respective race meetings. This lapse was in marked contrast to the efficiency and detailed planning surrounding the acquisition of *Gay Future* and the despatch of a similar-looking horse to Scotland. One simple failure to complete the minor details had brought down the coup, and the syndicate members had only themselves to blame.

The coup did nothing for the career of jockey Timmy Jones, but Edward O'Grady was destined to become one of the leading National Hunt trainers in Ireland, heading the list with eighty-two winners in 1979. While Tony Murphy was very wealthy at one stage in his life—owning an enviable yellow Rolls Royce car, one of the very few registered in Ireland—at some point his money dwindled and he was by no means a wealthy man when he died suddenly in 1982. Tony Collins survived his decade in the racing wilderness, although he said himself that he was lucky to keep his stockbroking career afloat in the wake of the bad publicity—although he was stripped of membership of the local golf course. When he eventually returned to racing he raced a horse named after himself with his good friend, the late Robert Sangster, and *Colonel Collins* ran third in the 1994 Epsom Derby. The twenty-first anniversary of the coup was commemorated at Cartmel in August 1995, when the *Gay Future* Novices' Hurdle was one of the featured races.

The Telephone Coup

A year after the *Gay Future* coup Irish bookmakers were hit for six by the *Yellow Sam* coup, landed at Bellewstown on Wednesday, 25 June 1975. Whereas the *Gay Future* coup had ended in failure because most of the betting shops refused to pay out, *Yellow Sam* managed to clobber the betting shops to the tune of £300,000 in a spectacular gamble that was executed perfectly, with every bet collected successfully. The brain behind this coup was Barney Curley, the man in the beige fedora and a punter virtually unknown to the wider public, although the bookmakers knew him well and were wary of his bets. Nowadays, Barney is recognised as one of the shrewdest planners of betting coups in the business and has pulled off many brilliantly successful gambles in the years since he first struck gold, with *Yellow Sam*.

Yellow Sam was owned by Mrs Barney Curley and trained at Newbridge, Co. Kildare, by Liam Brennan, a former jockey who started in racing with Paddy Sleator, the greatest gambling trainer of all. The race chosen for the gamble was the Mount Hanover Handicap Hurdle for amateur riders, run on the first day of the two-day Bellewstown meeting on the romantically named 'Hill of the Fairies' in Co. Meath. Nine very moderate horses went to post in what looked to be an open race, with *High and Mighty* emerging as the surprise 7-to-2 favourite, presumably because it had the services of the champion amateur rider Ted Walsh. On form, *High and Mighty* looked as if it was inferior to *Silver Road*, trained by Paddy Mullins, which had beaten it by eight lengths when the pair finished second and third at Tramore. The other two horses that featured in the market were *Alo Tynan's Satlan*, who had been placed in its last two races, and *Portballintrae*, trained by Willie Rooney and ridden by his daughter, Anne, which had been a shock winner at Navan the previous Saturday. Nobody even rated *Yellow Sam*, which had a string of 'duck eggs' in front of its name and was priced at 33-to-1.

Unknown to those attending at Bellewstown that afternoon, just after lunch a team of people began to place single bets on *Yellow Sam* to win in betting shops throughout Ireland. Unlike today's set-up, at that time many of the racecourse bookmakers had a betting shop at home and usually liked to make contact with the shop during the day, just to make sure everything was all right. But on this particular afternoon the only public telephone at Bellewstown had been commandeered by a man Barney Curley described as a 'tough sort of guy', but who anyone else would call a 'heavy'. He was on a call to a hospital, and that was that. Refusing to ring off, this chap hogged the phone for ages, effectively cutting off the racecourse from the outside world; he disappeared mysteriously during *Yellow Sam*'s race.

A minute or so before the start of the race, one of the racecourse bookmakers backed *Yellow Sam* with Terry Rogers at 14-to-1, but few of the other thirty-seven bookmakers took any money on the horse. When the field appeared over the hill it was clear that *Yellow Sam*, with Mr Michael Furlong in the saddle, was going very easily. In the end *Yellow Sam* stormed to victory by two-and-a-half lengths. The moment he passed the post the bookmakers looked it up on the card, and many of them immediately suspected there was a bookmaker somewhere who had been hit by the win. Those bookmakers with betting shops immediately became anxious and rushed to the public telephone to make contact with their offices. Their hearts must have sank when they saw the chaotic scene around the single public telephone at the back of the tiny main stand: the long, disorderly queue had disintegrated and it was every man for himself as each bookie battled for possession of the telephone.

As they listened to the recriminations about the 'heavy' hogging the telephone, it was obvious there was money for the horse SP and their shops were likely to have been hit—the only question to be answered was how much had it cost them. One of the racecourse bookmakers, who had just one betting shop in Dublin, watched *Yellow Sam* pass the post and immediately thought of a punter who had opened an account with his shop only a couple of days earlier. This punter was a greyhound man who regularly attended the Dublin dog tracks, but never went horse-racing. Gut instinct told the bookmaker that his shop had been 'done' by this account, but for how much? He later discovered that the dog punter had placed his first and only bet with the shop, by telephone: £200 each way *Yellow Sam* at SP! When the starting price was declared at 20-to-1, the punter was £5,000 richer and the bookie £5,000 poorer.

The late Terry Rogers, a leading bookmaker both on and off the course, was doubly hit that afternoon, having laid the horse at 14-to-1 in the Ring, while all of his eight shops were hit at SP and had to pay out at 20-to-1! Speaking directly through his depleted pockets, Rogers questioned the SP return of 20-to-1, which he found incredible because another bookmaker in the Ring had backed *Yellow Sam* with him just before the start at 14-to-1. Never afraid to speak his mind, Rogers suggested someone might have corrupted the person returning the SP, an allegation vehemently denied by Barney Curley. I am prepared to accept Barney's word that there was no interference with the independent people who made the returns because I was making a book at the time and remember distinctly that late movements in the betting market often did not appear to be reflected in the SP. My own observations were that the SP compilers, who also had race-reading duties, tended to leave the betting ring just before the off in order to view the race. Normally that made no difference at all because prices rarely changed in that last few seconds of betting. However, in this case the man who was returning the SP was probably seen leaving the Ring, enabling one of the racecourse bookmakers who was in on the coup to sneak a few extra quid for himself at Rogers' expense!

The full extent of the gamble did not become apparent until the following day. Some bookmakers accused Barney Curley of cheating, but, as is usually the case, the bookies who cried and shouted the loudest were those who were the least affected by the gamble. Barney was unrepentant: in his view, blocking the telephone was not wrong because the bookies would have used the telephone just to slash the price of *Yellow Sam* whereas they would not have used the phone to increase the prices of those horses unlaid in the betting shops. A deeply religious man, Barney's philosophy is that the battle between punters is nothing to do with morality but rather is a battle of wits in a 'no rules jungle', where dog eats dog and only the toughest survive. The bookmakers use every trick in their power to best the punter and the punter does exactly the same to the bookmakers; everything is fair in this war—within reason. The problem with Barney's philosophy is that it appears to allow punters to ignore the rules unilaterally while at the same time requiring the bookmakers to adhere to them.

The *Yellow Sam* betting coup is now part of Irish racing's folklore and, following an example set by Cartmel, Bellewstown officially recognised it as an event worth celebrating by running a race in its honour. On Wednesday, 29 June 2005 Bellewstown hosted the 'Seamus Murphy *Yellow Sam* 30th Anniversary Hurdle' and invited Barney Curley and Liam Brennan to a special reception, complete with VIP toilets (surely an unwonted first for Irish racing?), where they were wined and dined as that infamous day of thirty years earlier was fondly remembered. As the pals nattered nostalgically about the coup, the public and the bookies could only look on from a distance. Just as they had been excluded from the big gamble, so too were they excluded from the anniversary 'bash' in the tent. Barney reminisced to the press about the coup and remarked that 'every bookmaker paid up and I won nearly £300,000'. Proving that it is not only bookmakers who moan, he complained that all the winnings came in £1 notes and it was a terrible job counting it all! It was no surprise that the bookmakers were excluded from the party: victims are usually forgotten, but then most of them are either dead or have long since sold their shops to the chains that now dominate the off-course betting shop business.

Of the thirty-eight racecourse bookmakers who were standing in their own right in the inside enclosure at Bellewstown in 1975 only two were personally making a book there on the occasion of the thirtieth anniversary: Seamus Mulvaney and Seamus Farrell. Two others, Jim Durkin and Austin Barrett, were personally betting at the meeting in 1975, but while Jim and Austin were present on the Wednesday in 2005 they were not actually standing up, their

sons were making the book on their behalf. None of these bookmakers was in any way perturbed about missing out on the celebrations. They bet away on the 'Seamus Murphy *Yellow Sam* 30th
Anniversary Hurdle' and were rewarded when *Princess Commanche*,
the quietly supported second-string of trainer Stephen Mahon,
came from nowhere to mow down her stable companion *Oriental
Rock* and win at odds of 16-to-1. What made it sweeter was that the
Tote paid only half those odds, exposing its misleading claim that
it pays better than the bookies, which is true only when virtually
nobody backs the winner. And that, of course, is the reason why
Barney hit the bookies all those years ago and left the Tote alone!

McCreevy's Coup

The perfect betting coup involves no sharp practice of any
description, no elaborate manoeuvres in order to mislead people
and no threats or promises, just a simple punt on a horse whose
form is there for all the world to see. It is amazing how often bookmakers and punters ignore obvious form lines when a horse has
been off the course for a long time, or has run up a sequence of
seconds and near-misses. Once they become convinced that a
horse is no longer capable of producing its previous form, they
write it off as useless: the punters won't back it at any price, the
bookmakers are happy to lay it at any price. As long as the bookmakers are satisfied that a horse has been running on its merits,
they will often dismiss previous good form, quoting the old
racing adage that horses never recover from serious injury. Of
course, luck plays a major factor in the success of this type of
betting coup—the horse has to stay sound, for starters—but when
luck is on your side, you can only play it up!

Just before Christmas 1982 Aidan Walsh, a Naas businessman,
and his friend Charlie McCreevy, a local politician, landed a
gamble with *Chorelli* that was acclaimed in the Sunday newspapers
as the perfect betting coup—and it came about quite by accident. A
coup was never actually planned but presented itself fortuitously,
which was why it was so successful.

Trainer Michael J.P. O'Brien, from Newcastle, Co. Dublin, started
his racing career with Thomas J. Taaffe at Rathcoole, where his

father was head lad. Taaffe was the father of the jockeys Pat, Toss and Willie, and had trained *Mr What* to win the 1958 Grand National for David J. Coughlan, the proprietor of a firm of manufacturing chemists and the resident of *Inniskel,* a big house on the King Edward Road in Bray. When *Mr What,* with Arthur Freeman up, won at 18-to-1 there was jubilation in Bray, although this was subsequently tempered by the news that two local betting shops had been put out of business by the result! Terry Rogers stepped in and paid the punters so that ultimately the only losers were Terry and the two broke bookies!

Michael O'Brien and his brother, Leo, followed their father into T.J. Taaffe's stable, but after a few years both decided to try their luck in America. There Michael became a leading jump jockey, but at the peak of his career he suffered a terrible fall that left him paralysed and confined to a wheelchair for the rest of his life. When he had recovered sufficiently, Mick decided to pursue a training career back in Ireland and settled into the Rathbride stable on the Curragh. He quickly proved that his physical disability was no obstacle to training winners, although it did earn him the nickname 'Ironside' after the wheelchair-bound television detective. In 1980 Michael had his first really big winner with *Bright Highway* and stable jockey Gerry Newman, who together won two of England's big jumping races, the Mackeson and the Hennessy Gold Cups. At Fairyhouse on Easter Monday 1982 the M.J.P. O'Brien-trained *King Spruce* won the Irish Grand National, while its stable-companion *Sean Ogue* won the valuable Power Gold Cup the following day, pushing O'Brien towards the title of Leading Jumping Trainer in Ireland.

Charlie McCreevy was a shrewd, clever and ambitious politician who was elected to Dáil Éireann in 1977 as the Fianna Fáil candidate for the Kildare constituency. A follower of racing, Charlie was one of the first politicians to speak out against the 20 per cent rate of betting duty applied to off-course bets, which he argued was far too high. He declared that many bookmakers and punters were colluding to evade the tax and demanded that it be reduced to a proper level. His campaign led to the Coalition Government reducing it to 10 per cent in 1985. When Charlie McCreevy was subsequently installed as Minister of Finance he reduced the duty from 10 per cent to 5 per cent, in 1999, and three years later dropped it down to 2 per cent. His Budget of 2 December 1998 also abolished the on-course betting tax for punters from 26 July 1999. A chartered accountant by profession, Charlie had been associated with horse trainer Michael O'Brien since he returned to Ireland to train. There is a familial connection too: McCreevy's wife, Noeleen, is a niece of Anne O'Brien, Michael's wife.

The first horse Charlie McCreevy owned was *Go Metric*, which his old school friend Aidan Walsh bought from Rusty Carrier for £8,000 in 1979. Originally owned by George Strawbridge Jnr, one of O'Brien's staunchest supporters, *Go Metric* had been purchased by Rusty Carrier, a rich, enthusiastic, American amateur rider. After several falls, a near-miss and a disqualification, Rusty decided that *Go Metric* was not a suitable ride for him after all and wanted out. Michael O'Brien recommended the horse to Aidan Walsh and the deal was done, the friends taking a half-share each. Benefiting from the services of a professional jockey, *Go Metric* did really well for his new owners, winning four good handicap chases in 1980 before being sold on at a profit.

During this period George Strawbridge Jnr owned a nice horse with O'Brien called *Chorelli*, which he himself rode to victory in a bumper at Clonmel in December 1978. A faller in a novice chase next time out, *Chorelli* then proceeded to win four races on the trot, including a sensational six-length victory over the odds-on *Chinrullah* at Punchestown, which made him a popular fancy to win at Cheltenham. Tragically, *Chorelli* broke down on both front legs during training and never made it to Cheltenham, where its connections could only reflect on what might have been after *Chinrullah* won the Arkle Trophy by five lengths. *Chorelli* had always suffered from a bad back, but now, with a tendon on one leg bowed and the other leg wrong as well, the horse had reached the end of the road and was on his way to the factory. Aidan Walsh decided to speculate £250 to save the horse from becoming a dog's dinner. Charlie McCreevy agreed to put up £125 for a half-share and both agreed with Michael O'Brien that he could have a quarter-share if the horse ever raced again.

Aidan Walsh took the horse back to his place, where he asked the well-known horse dealer Ned Cash for advice. Following Cash's instructions, *Chorelli* was starved down to skin and bone, both forelegs were fired and the horse was put standing in a special mixture everyday. When the treatment was finished, the horse was put out into a bog, where he was to be left for three years. During the summer of 1980, Michael O'Brien went out to the bog to see *Chorelli* and found the horse in good form and apparently sound. He suggested it might be a suitable time to bring it back into training, but Aidan Walsh was most reluctant, preferring to give the horse more time to recover. However, Michael was adamant that *Chorelli* had had enough time, was sound now and could not get any sounder, and furthermore that time was a vital consideration as he was now nine years old. Charlie accepted that Aidan was far too cautious and went with Michael to the bog to collect *Chorelli* and bring it back to the Curragh. Aidan was only told of this when the horse was settled in its training routine once again, but he did not mind the subterfuge, knowing in his heart that the time had come to try the horse and he had merely been trying to put off the evil day.

As Charles J. Haughey's bitter battle to remain leader of Fianna Fáil was raging in the autumn of 1982, *Chorelli* was preparing to return to racing after a break of three-and-a-half years. Michael had assured Aidan that *Chorelli* would not be asked to race again unless it was capable of running a decent race and that if it got tailed off or pulled up, it would be retired immediately. All went well in training, the legs stood up to the exercise and the horse worked normally, albeit without showing any particular sparkle. The comeback trail began at the end of September 1982 when *Chorelli* lined up for a handicap hurdle at Gowran Park, its top weight eased somewhat by rider Kevin Doolin's 7 lb claim. Even in its prime *Chorelli* would have been hard-pressed to give weight all round in a handicap hurdle, but the horse was not fully fit and needed the race. All Aidan and Charlie wanted was for the horse to finish the course and return home safe and sound. All went well. *Chorelli* raced in mid-division, but stayed on well enough in the closing stages to finish eighth of the fifteen runners and, most importantly, his legs stood up to the ordeal and he was sound.

Stage two of the long haul back took place at Fairyhouse on 6 October, but as Charles McCreevy's motion of no confidence in his party leader was down for discussion on 5 October, he wasn't able to attend. Again the race was over hurdles, a handicap in which *Chorelli* was set to carry a massive 12 stone 7 lb, reduced by Kevin Doolin's 7lb allowance because he had not yet ridden ten winners. The horse was doing its best and the connections were anxious to see what it could do. *Chorelli* ran well, staying in a prominent position and running with the leaders until he got tired and lost his place, eventually finishing eighth of eighteen. The good news was that the horse's legs stood up to the race and he retuned to his stable sound, showing no ill effects at all.

So far, so good. The third and final stage of his comeback involved running in a steeplechase at Punchestown the following week, where *Chorelli* was set to carry a big weight over stiff fences, which would fully test the soundness of its legs. On this occasion *Chorelli*, once again an unconsidered outsider, made the running under Kevin Doolin, but his jumping was a bit rusty and the horse made a number of mistakes. In these circumstances *Chorelli* did wonderfully well to finish fifth, behind horses of the quality of *Fethard Friend*, *Poyntz Pass*, *Luska* and *King Spruce*, although it did not seem that way at the time. *King Spruce* and *Fethard Friend* had finished first and second in that year's Irish Grand National and *Luska* had won that race the previous year, yet *Chorelli* finished over twenty lengths behind and might never jump any better. The lads in the yard had already given up on *Chorelli*, whose form on the gallops was just average, and while it had run reasonably well in its races it never looked likely to win them at any stage.

Michael O'Brien's champion steeplechaser *Bright Highway*, which was expected to achieve great things over fences, had broken down after his two sensational English victories two years previously. He too was now sound again and on the comeback trail and O'Brien had pencilled in a non-handicap chase at Punchestown for the former champion's re-introduction to racing, in two months time. Noticing that the conditions did not penalise horses for big wins in previous years, Michael realised this race would suit *Chorelli* perfectly, so he entered it along with *Bright Highway*.

Over the next couple of weeks the trainer noticed a big difference in *Chorelli*, which showed some of its old sparkle on the gallops. With *Chorelli* working well, O'Brien spoke to McCreevy about the forthcoming Punchestown Chase, where *Chorelli* would only have to be half the horse it had previously been in order to beat the likely opposition at the weights. He expressed the opinion that *Chorelli* would definitely beat *Bright Highway*, which meant it had every chance of winning the race—and landing a little gamble. As the race was being run on a Saturday, the biggest racing day of the week in those pre-Sunday racing days, a strong betting market was ensured and it was likely that *Chorelli* would be overshadowed by *Bright Highway* and be generously priced.

Grasping the situation immediately, McCreevy told O'Brien not to tell Aidan: 'a nice guy who will tell everyone'. Charlie took charge of doing the commission himself. He would get the stable's money on and would also back the horse for Aidan, although he would not know it, and nothing would be said to anyone. Everything seemed to be coming right at the right time for *Chorelli*, a nice payday before Christmas is always sweet and Saturday, 11 December 1982 was the date, the race was the Punchestown Chase, a two-and-a-half mile race over fifteen fences. All the pre-race publicity concerned the comeback of the top-class steeplechaser *Bright Highway*. He was the champion everyone wanted to see and the press wanted to write about. *Chorelli* was completely overshadowed by his stable companion's return to racing, which suited Messrs O'Brien and McCreevy just fine as the trainer was not asked one question about *Chorelli*. One thing was done deliberately to keep the bookmakers off the scent: the stable jockey Gerry Newman was put up on *Bright Highway*, leaving the young stable apprentice, Peter Walsh, to ride *Chorelli*. Everyone assumed that the stable jockey had had the choice of rides and would have chosen the more fancied horse of the two.

The bookmakers installed Michael Cuddy's *Drumlargan*, trained by Edward O'Grady and ridden by Tommy Ryan, as the 6-to-4 favourite, while *Tacroy*, ridden by the leading jump jockey

Frank Berry was second favourite at 2-to-1. Michael O'Brien's supposedly first-string *Bright Highway* was a 3-to-1 shot; *Royal Dipper*, trained and ridden by John Fowler, was priced at 4-to-1; *Chorelli*, ridden for the first time by Peter Walsh, was an 8-to-1 shot; and the two rags, *Owen's Image* and *Like-A-Lord* were offered at 20-to-1.

Suddenly, unexpectedly and dramatically a flood of money came for *Chorelli* as Charlie McCreevy and his mates waded in, its price dropped like a stone … 7-to-1, 6-to-1, 5-to-1, 4-to-1, 3-to-1 … and the market was turned on its head. No strokes were pulled and no lies were told, this was a straightforward gamble and the bookmakers only had themselves to blame because they had offered too big a price about a horse that, although inferior to *Bright Highway*, was not far short of top class in his prime. They had written off *Chorelli* and were now going to have to pay the price. One of the features of that afternoon was how the bookmakers priced *Bright Highway* at odds as low as 3-to-1. Certainly *Bright Highway* was a top-class horse at its best and was being ridden by the stable jockey, but it had been off the course for two years because of injury and its wellbeing had to be taken entirely on trust. At the off there were three joint favourites—*Chorelli*, *Drumlargan* and *Tacroy*—all at 5-to-2; *Royal Dipper* had gone out to 7-to-1; and *Bright Highway* to 10-to-1.

Bright Highway and *Royal Dipper* made the running from *Drumlargan*, with *Chorelli* in touch just behind. Four fences from home *Chorelli* loomed up to dispute the lead, only for his progress to be checked by a jumping error at the third last. Allowing his mount time to settle, Peter Walsh did not panic but waited until he was in the straight before kicking *Chorelli* clear of *Drumlargan* and *Big Dipper*. Danger loomed when the stylish Frank Berry produced *Tacroy* with a typical late run to challenge after the last fence, breaking his whip in the process, but *Chorelli* was too good and pulled away again to win by a couple of lengths. Victory was sweet for the owners of *Chorelli*, and O'Brien had another good reason to be pleased: he had trained *Tacroy* earlier in its career and was very disappointed when the owner, Ned Tunney, took the horse away from him.

When *Chorelli* passed the post in front, Aidan Walsh's delight was purely the satisfaction of seeing his decision to save the horse from the knacker's yard vindicated. He was only told of the successful betting coup, and his share of the spoils, while standing in the winner's enclosure after the race, when he was invited to join the big party being given at the Manor Inn in Naas that night to toast the gamble. The Manor Inn, at the time owned by Denis Curry, was the establishment favoured by racing people and was a perfect place for the party The bill, when it was eventually tallied, came to over £2,000 and was put down on Aidan's account. When Aidan Walsh recounts the story of the *Chorelli* betting coup, he humorously tells how his friends stole the horse from his bog, then did not tell him of the upcoming gamble and finally hit him with the bill for the celebrations. He has a good sense of humour!

The gamble successfully landed, *Chorelli* returned to the Curragh sound and it looked as if it might yet have an opportunity to fulfil some of its former promise. O'Brien aimed *Chorelli* at the valuable Findus Handicap Chase at Leopardstown's Christmas Festival, where it would be taking on the talented up-and-coming chaser *Ivan King*, as well as *Tacroy*, again. *Ivan King*, under a particularly strong ride from Paddy Kiely, got up to beat *Chorelli* by three parts of a length, but the old horse lost nothing in defeat and might have won but for a couple of jumping errors. With its form good enough to be entered for races at the Cheltenham Festival, *Chorelli* ran a preparatory race in the P.Z. Mower Chase at Thurles on Thursday, 24 February 1983. The conditions of the race ensured that *Chorelli* was meeting its Leopardstown conqueror *Ivan King* on 22 lb better terms, encouraging punters to make the horse a hot odds-on favourite to reverse the placings. Gerry Newman rode *Chorelli*, the 2-to-1 ON favourite, while Peter Walsh, who had ridden *Chorelli* in its two previous races, now took the mount on *Great Hays*, which was in the field to act as a pacemaker for the favourite.

The two stable companions raced off in front, together from the start, streaking past the stands into the first bend. At that point on the course there were a number of dolls marking out the route, but in the heat of the moment Peter Walsh got confused, swerved to keep inside the dolls, as he thought, but in fact ran his mount off the course, taking *Chorelli* out with him, too. Realising Peter's error, Gerry Newman thought quickly, pulled up his mount and retraced his steps to the point at which he had run off the course and re-entered the race, well behind the field. In a dramatic exhibition of *Chorelli*'s talent, Gerry sent his mount in pursuit, gradually reducing the leeway, until finally joining *Ivan King* at the head of the field five fences from home. *Chorelli* and *Ivan King* then fought out an exciting duel over the next four obstacles, coming to the last neck and neck and a dozen lengths clear of the remainder. *Chorelli* had every chance at that point, and probably would have won the race but for the disaster that struck. Out of the blue his leg broke a couple of strides from the fence and Gerry was unable to pull him up, so *Chorelli* had to jump it with a broken leg. The horse got over the fence, landed on three legs and stood stock still at other side as Newman was vaulted off its back. Although the formbook states that *Chorelli* fell, that was not actually the case, in fact the jockey dismounted after jumping the fence. The injury to *Chorelli* left *Ivan King* in a clear lead and it sauntered home to victory, though it finished lame and was found to have broken down during the race.

Poor *Chorelli* had to be destroyed where it stood. Gerry Newman and Peter Walsh were hauled before the stewards, who fined each of them a hefty £250—five-and-a-half times the riding fee—for going the wrong side of the doll. It was a bad day all round. As Michael O'Brien sat in his familiar 'ironside' van distraught and being comforted by Aidan Walsh and Charlie McCreevy, Eamonn King, the owner/breeder of *Ivan King*, came over to commiserate with Michael on the death of *Chorelli*. It was a sporting gesture from a man whose own horse had been seriously injured and illustrates the competitive sportsmanship that exists in Irish national hunt racing.

Trainer Michael O'Brien rates *Chorelli* as one of the best horses that he ever trained, bearing in mind its history of back trouble, its comeback from serious leg injury and its impressive demolition of the talented *Chinrullah*. An examination of its carcass after death revealed that the horse's hind leg had given way in a place where an old injury had only partially healed. Unnoticed by anyone, this injury was another hurt the poor horse had to suffer leaving one to wonder what it might have achieved had it remained free of injury!

A Thorough Job

The best and biggest betting coup of recent years was landed with *Boccaccio* at Leopardstown in the summer of 2004. The general public never heard about this coup, which was described by David Power, the leading on-course bookmaker, as 'the best job I have ever seen'. The Ring soon found out who was behind the coup, which hit the off-course betting shops heavily although some of the money inevitably got back to the course.

During this summer period midweek fixtures at Leopardstown were poorly attended, mainly because construction work on the M50 motorway made the place inaccessible in the rush-hour traffic. The market thus weakened, the money would have to be placed off the course in the betting shops. The ingenuity of this coup was the way it got around the usual problem of the money being sent back to the course and reducing the odds on offer. Barney Curley had got around this problem by blocking a telephone, while the *Gay Future* syndicate disguised a single bet as a treble, but the organisers of this coup did everything by the book and still beat the system.

Over 100 people were involved in a military-style operation to back *Boccaccio* in as many betting shops as they could. Stationed in big towns in England and Ireland, these people were ready to put money on *Boccaccio* when the 'first show' came in from Leopardstown. The 'first show' is the list of prices taken from the on-course bookmakers when they first put up their prices and which is relayed live to the betting shops. The shops regularly take bets at fixed odds according to the 'show', a practice that is normal and therefore will not arouse the suspicion of the betting shop staff. The invisible army of punters who were working the coup were not told the name of the horse until a half-hour or so before the race. The syndicate had decided that its golden rule was to be that on no account would a penny be put on the horse at morning prices—no matter what price was offered against *Boccaccio*. The reasoning behind this was that in the morning the market is notoriously weak, the prices are very sensitive and very small bets can send the price of the horse tumbling. The syndicate did not want to mark the bookies' cards prematurely just to get a small sum of money on at an exceptional price. The bets were therefore to be placed later—no exceptions. On finally receiving the name of the horse, the punters moved into place and the gamble was on.

When the first show came in from Leopardstown, *Boccaccio* was priced at 6-to-1 and each member of the team moved in to take that price in his chosen betting shop. Having done their homework and knowing the strength of the shop, each team member took the price to a stake ranging from £200 to £1,000, depending on how much that particular shop would be prepared to take without a referral to the shop manager or to head office. When the second show came in *Boccaccio*'s price was reduced to 5-to-1 and the team repeated the action, backing the horse at the fixed price according to the revised show. This was repeated with each new show that came through. With the show price being taken in the shop, the SP of *Boccaccio* was irrelevant to the success of the coup, so it did not matter if the money got back to the course, which of course it eventually did. The off-course betting shops were cleaned out, as were the racecourse bookies, but no bookmaker could cry foul because those who had executed the coup had acted completely within the rules and had done nothing wrong. The syndicate was estimated to have taken over £1 million from the bookmakers in total—a good day's work by any measure!

Furious at the loss, but with no cause for public complaint, the bookmakers complained among themselves and simply could not take it on the chin. Suspecting that the person who organised the coup might own all or part of *Boccaccio* but was not the registered owner, the bookmakers decided to stir the pot by lodging a complaint with the stewards regarding the ownership of the horse. This created some hassle for the horse's trainer, Michael Grassick, who had to explain in detail to the stewards the precise ownership of *Boccaccio*. It was a red herring, of course, because Michael Grassick does not bet and had nothing at all to do with the betting coup. He merely trained a horse that a form expert happened to believe was a 'racing certainty' and put its money down accordingly. They did nothing other than bet.

Using the Tote to Catch the Bookies

The Totalisator, popularly known as the Tote, is a mechanical betting system based on the *Pari-Mutuel*, which was pioneered in France. The system works by putting the punters' stakes into a pool, from which a deduction is made to cover costs, then the number of winning units is divided into the sum of money in the pool to get a dividend. The disadvantage for punters is that the odds are not fixed, so when placing his bet the backer has no idea how much the return will be in the event of his selection coming up trumps. On the other hand, the Tote can be very competitive when conditions are in its favour: usually in open races with large fields, on big days, when it has a large number of people betting with it in relatively small and consistent stakes.

By 1891 the *Pari-Mutuel* had developed sufficiently to allow the French government to give it a monopoly; bookmakers were banned and all bets had to go through the machine. Unfortunately for punters, the government helped itself by taking a hefty tax out of each pool for the Exchequer, then there was an additional deduction for the benefit of French racing and finally there was the deduction to cover the *Pari-Mutuel's* expenses. While the excessive deductions from the pools were bad news for punters, it was of no concern to French owners, trainers or breeders, who were pacified by the grant of a significant sum that would go to fund racing and prize money. With no bookmakers to compete with, the *Pari-Mutuel* could actually take what it liked from the pools, so down the years the government gradually increased its tax. Expenses rose too, the unions got a grip on the company and it was all too easy to recover increased costs by taking a bigger cut from the pool.

The first instance of a mechanical betting system being used in the British Isles occurred at York racecourse in 1871, when eight betting machines were put on display. The machines only accepted half-crown (2/6, or 12^1/$_2$p) bets, with the number of bets taken on each horse being displayed on a big dial. Each machine made a separate return so punters were encouraged to seek out the machine that had taken the least bets on the horse they wanted to back; but the odds were not fixed, as they would be with the book-makers. The experiment was not a success, mainly because the high minimum stake put a lot of punters off and the erratic dividends, which fluctuated wildly from machine to machine, left many dissatisfied with their winnings.

The introduction of the *Pari-Mutuel* in France had led to a big increase in the prize money available there and the banning of bookmakers had been done without much trouble. Casting envious eyes across the Channel, British owners and breeders (it should be remembered that Ireland was part of the United Kingdom until 1922) clamoured for a Tote monopoly. The *Pari-Mutuel* in France had proved it would work and would bring riches to horse-racing, ensuring much bigger prize money for them, paid for by the punters. Shamelessly this wealthy class lobbied the govern-ment for a Tote monopoly to be introduced in Britain and Ireland, unabashed that they were demanding a tax on the poor to pay for the pastime of the wealthy. Their case was that without a monopoly British racing would collapse, all the owners and breeders would transfer to France, with the resultant loss of employment and exports. They stressed that a Tote monopoly would ensure proper salaries for stable lads, a greater reward for jockeys and the system was working well in almost every other racing nation. The interests of punters were dismissed completely, with the wealthy openly accusing those who demanded rights for punters as being selfish by trying to retain a method of betting to which they were more accustomed to or simply preferred.

Naturally, the bookmakers, not wishing to be put out of busi-ness, opposed the concept of a Tote monopoly and their inspired tactics were so successful that they managed to delay the intro-duction of the Tote for nearly forty years. Their lobbying policy was to point out the potential of the Tote to raise substantial revenue, to warn the government not to give away what were in effect tax-raising powers to an unelected, wealthy minority. Playing off one side against the other, it worked like a dream. The horse-racing industry had formed a group of owners, trainers and breeders to deal with the government, and its brief was to be allowed run the Tote for the benefit of racing. The government demanded to run the Tote itself and to retain some of the revenue as tax, but the Racing Group strongly resisted that concept. The debate smouldered without anything being done, and nothing could be done until the government passed legislation. The result was an *impasse* that lasted until 1928.

During this *impasse* the Irish Free State was founded, the Dáil replaced Westminster as the sovereign Irish parliament and the new government had more important issues to consider than establishing a Tote, not to mention the complex matter of a Tote monopoly. Ireland was a poor country at the time, money was badly needed to build up the institutions of the new State and as a means of raising revenue the government decided to legalise betting shops, run by bookmakers in 1926. This bill ran into considerable opposition from anti-gambling groups and Tote monopoly advocates. In response the government conceded that the Act would be temporary, and would be renewed after two years to enable a full assessment of the social impact of betting shops. The government also agreed to establish the 'Interdepartmental Committee on Irish Racing'. The Committee reported its findings in 1927, one of which was that a Tote should be operated under a licence granted to the Turf Club and the Irish National Hunt Steeplechase Committee.

Meanwhile in Britain a private member's Bill to establish a Tote was introduced in the House of Commons and eventually passed, control being vested in a body known as Racecourse Betting Control Board, a statutory body responsible to the Home Office, and the Tote first operated there at Newmarket on 2 July 1929. Ireland was not far behind. The government introduced the Totalisator Act in 1929, granting a fifteen-year licence to a body consisting of Turf Club and Irish National Hunt Steeplechase Committee members, representatives of racecourses, breeders, owners and trainers to run the Tote for the benefit of horse-racing and to make a 10 per cent deduction from the pool. The Tote opened for business in Ireland for the first time on Easter Monday, 21 April 1930 at Fairyhouse.

The Tote introduced a new bet that was to prove very popular with punters. It was the forecast bet, in which the backer had to nominate the horses that would finish first and second in any given race. It did not take the betting shops long to realise the bet's potential and they began taking forecasts from punters—paying them Tote odds. For years all went well, the Tote was happy for the bookmakers to take these bets once they paid it a licence fee and betting shops had another product for customers until one day the sky fell in! During days when there was no horse-racing or when there was a lengthy interval between races, to keep the punters in the shops the bookmakers began to sponsor greyhound meetings to be run at these particular times. Known as BAGS meetings— Bookmakers' Afternoon Greyhound Service—they were run at minor greyhound tracks purely for betting shops to bet on them and the bookies paid the costs. These meetings were sparsely attended, on-track betting with the bookies and the Tote was tiny, the dogs running were moderate and only die-hard punters had an interest but they proved to be a valuable earner for the betting shop during slack times. These meetings had a 'blower' service, a telephone linking bookmakers to the track, which meant that any large bets received in a shop could be passed on to the on-course bookies and so reduce the returned price and of course the punters potential winnings.

One afternoon in early 1964 Les Carey, at the time the biggest bookmaker in the East End of London, who operated about twenty shops in the area trading under the name of George Brent, began getting reports of unusual bets being taken on a dog running at Dagenham. This was the local greyhound track, which was staging a BAGS meeting that day. His shop managers were reporting to the firm's head office at London Road, Romford, that they were getting a number of £1 place only bets on a certain dog at Tote odds. This meant that the bet was a winner if the dog finished either first or second. Normally a stake of only £1 was not worth a second glance, but it was very unusual for punters to back an odds-on favourite for a place at Tote odds for such a tiny amount and the number of these small bets indicated some sort of coup. With the dividend likely to be in the region of 1-to-10, a

price not at all attractive to those planning a coup, Les Carey
became suspicious. Knowing that the market down at Dagenham
was weak, he decided to pop down to the track and cover the liability himself. Gathering together three of his staff, which included
Barry Dennis, now a well-known bookmaker in his own right, Les
Carey took them straight to the Dagenham Greyhound Stadium,
where the four of them went to the Tote windows and put £200
for a place on the dog, which had been laid in the offices. The
intention was to reduce the Tote place dividend if the dog won or
was second, lessening the pay out in his shops, which would have
been substantial had there been what is called in the trade 'a freak
dividend'; i.e. one that is much larger than anyone would have
expected. Les and the boys were very pleased with themselves
when the dog won and the Tote place dividend paid poorly. But
they had ruined somebody's coup.

Meanwhile, John Turner, Terry Orwell and Harry Cohen, the
local characters behind the coup, were devastated: weeks of work
and organisation gone, almost for nothing, because the small
dividend ensured a tiny return for their efforts. Shocked and frustrated that their payday had been spoiled, they began blaming
each other until they spotted Les Carey at the track. Their initial
surprise at seeing the bookie there, instead of in his office, turned
to rage when the penny dropped that it was he who had foiled
their coup. Rounding on the bookmaker, their angry jeers of abuse
quickly led to fisticuffs, a *mêlèe* ensued and the police were called.
Having broken up the fight the police arrested all of them, including Les Carey and Barry Dennis, took them down to the local nick,
where the arguments continued but tempers cooled. Harry
Cohen, who ran an illegal gambling joint in the area, complained
bitterly to Les that his actions had cost them a fortune because
they had placed bets in nearly every betting shop in London.
Carey replied that they should have left out the local bookmaker
or, better still, let him in on it, then everything would have gone to
plan. As Carey explained how the coup should have been done,
that the bets should have been placed on the forecast, rather than
the weird place bet on a favourite, the recriminations stopped and
everybody listened. There and then a new plan was hatched, all

had suddenly become pals, nobody wanted to press charges and all left the police station dreaming of a big coup.

The new plan involved the forecast bet, which was to place the first and second dog in the correct order. This bet was very popular in betting shops and unlikely to arouse the suspicion of the manager. However, they would have to wait for the right race, one in which two out of the six dogs had no earthly chance of winning or being second. Making the Willow Rooms their headquarters, the team drew a map of all the Dagenham Tote windows on a blackboard, identifying each with a number. Men would be assigned to each window and, to ensure that no mistake could be made on the day, a young man was sent to the dog track to surreptitiously chalk the numbers on each window. The original team concentrated on getting the bets on in the betting shops, while Les Carey put up the cash to put into the Tote pool in order to ensure that there would be an unusually high, or freak dividend, on the winning forecast bet. The plan was rehearsed over and over while they waited for the right race to come up.

It duly did on a Tuesday in June 1964 when the 4.22pm race from Dagenham contained two 33-to-1 chances in the six-dog race, the pair looking to have no earthly chance of reaching a place. The coup was on! The plan counted on two of the four remaining dogs finishing either first or second, so a four-dog combination bet was placed in betting shops throughout the country, which guaranteed a winning return once neither of the two outsiders finished in the first two. A four-dog combination bet was common in betting shops, it consisted of twelve bets, the usual stake being two shillings, the sum to which the Tote dividend was declared. This bet was known as a twenty-four shilling (£1.20) combination, but the team went for a really big killing and a team of men were sent to place £6 and £12 combinations in as many betting shops as they could. The stake per bet was 50p, which meant that if the bet came up the backer would be entitled to receive two-and-a-half times or five times the declared Tote dividend.

The second part of the plan involved a smaller team going down to Dagenham dogs, each carrying a money belt like those worn by traders in the London markets, which contained £100 in silver coins. Three men were allotted to each window. The first was to keep placing forecast bets on the two no-hopers until the race started, the two men behind were there as cover should members of the public, waiting in the queue to bet, start giving trouble. If the first man was forced to move away from the window, then the next member of the team would take over and do exactly the same thing. One designated man would place one bet only on the other twelve combinations, in order to ensure a dividend, because if there is no bet on the winner the Tote returned the stakes to the punter. When he had done this, he returned to backing the designated forecast (i.e. the two no-hopers) for as long as he could, until the race started. The team were actually rigging the dividend, not hitting the Tote at all, but to get an inflated dividend they had to stop ordinary punters from having bets on the Tote.

The plan worked perfectly: the first man in line successfully placed the bets without being suspected and the second and third managed to prevent the public from betting on the Tote without too much trouble. The moment the traps opened the bet was looking good, the two outsiders were struggling and clearly were not going to feature. Now it did not matter which dogs finished first or second—the bets were up and the coup had been landed. At the finish a dog named *Buckwheat*, a 5-to-2 shot, beat *Dancing Nell*, the 7-to-4 favourite and the two outsiders finished fifth and sixth—the bookmakers were about the receive the shock of their lives!

The Tote had taken £1,100 in bets on the two outsiders and only twenty-four shillings (£1.20) in total on the other four dogs, all placed by Les Carey's team. Having deducted their percentage, the Tote declared a dividend of £942.13.6, which meant that each combination bet placed in a betting shop now was worth either £2,500 or £5,000, depending on the stake—at a time when the average man earned £870 per annum! Barry Dennis was only a junior member of the gang yet his share was a whopping £20,000! As Barry prepared for his wedding, which was to take place the following Sunday, no doubt he thanked his lucky stars for such a wonderful wedding present and a financially secure start to married life.

Amazed by the size of the dividend from Dagenham, Extel, who relayed the results and the prices to the betting shops via an audio system, decided to delay the announcement of the dividend while it attempted to seek clarification. Aware of the winning bets, the delay in the declaration of the dividend perturbed the proprietors of betting shops and caused rising concern in the head offices of the big bookmaking firms. Alarm turned to panic when the dreaded announcement to the shops came half-an-hour late: 'This is the Tote dividend for the 4.22 race at Dagenham and it is correct … £942.13.6!' With each shop facing a payout of at least £2,500, well beyond its capacity to pay on the day, many firms were facing ruin. Les Carey had done the job too well—the dividend was too big, the money won from individual shops was much too large; the bookmakers could not pay and did not pay. Instead they demanded an enquiry. Some of those entrusted to collect the winnings were offered £50 in settlement, which a few of them agreed to accept. However, Les Carey instructed his people not to accept such a derisory amount as they would collect in full in due course. Barry Dennis married Marian the following Sunday, going on honeymoon still confident of banking his fortune on their return. It was not to be—Barry never received a penny!

The sheer size of the winnings destroyed the coup. The bookmakers produced a man who claimed to have been assaulted while trying to place a bet on the race at the Dagenham track. This was bad news for the coup because it indicated that the public was physically and fraudulently prevented from going to the Tote windows to place a bet on that race. Although those who monopolised the Tote windows that afternoon vehemently denied that anybody was assaulted or interfered with, and claimed that they never even saw that man at the track, the coup was in trouble. Here was a witness saying he was fraudulently prevented from having a bet on the Tote, giving the bookmakers the right to declare the bets void and return the stakes. Holding out to the bitter end, Les Carey steadfastly refused to collect the stake money because it would mean accepting the decision and he never did.

The Dagenham betting coup was the beginning of the end of bookmakers taking forecast bets at Tote odds, an interim limit of

two time the Tote dividend was introduced while the bookmakers
compiled a chart forecast, based on the prices of the dogs
involved. Terry Rogers was one of the first bookmakers to compile
such a chart and it became the basis of the official one issued
shortly afterwards. A list of odds ran across the top, as well as
down the side of the chart and the price of the first horse or dog
was taken from the side and aligned with the odds of the second
horse or dog taken from the top, the dividend being printed in the
box. By the time the chart was replaced by the Computer Straight
Forecast, Les Carey had sold the George Brent Betting Shops to
Mart Lane, now part of Corals, which he did in 1968, and the
Dagenham Greyhound Stadium had long since been closed down.

Irish punters enjoyed the stories of the Dagenham coup, which
fired the imagination of backers as they thought of ways to beat
the bookie, hoping for the big payday that never seemed to come,
but it was soon forgotten. Irish bookies were unaffected by that
particular coup, it did not cost them money and only the
bigger chains realised the dangers of accepting bets at Tote odds.
One day in 1978 an owner of a fancied greyhound put £100 on it
in his local betting shop, while his wife had a £5 on it in a shop in
Limerick city centre. The dog won at 4-to-7 ON, the owner
collected £57 winnings and was well pleased—until he heard that
his wife had picked up a profit of £18 on her fiver. It transpired
that she had placed the bet in the bookies at Tote odds, which paid
just over 7-to-2, and the owner immediately saw an opportunity
for a betting coup. Not knowing much about bookmakers, betting
or the Tote, he decided to visit his friend Eric Browne to find out
more. Eric was a butcher and a bookmaker in Listowel town and
was well-known for his gambling brain, as well as for his connections. He arrived in the shop when Eric was out the back in the
middle of killing sheep, but on utterance of the word 'coup', the
killing was abandoned for the day and the pair got talking about a
'real killing', with the bookies as the victims, and the whole coup
was planned at the back of the shop.

At that time many of the betting shops in Ireland were run by one-
to two-shop operators: none of the big British bookmaking chains
had shops here and although there were two Irish chains, Kilmartin's

and Richard Power, these were tiny compared to Ladbrokes or William Hill. In the informal atmosphere of a small industry, the local bookie shops accepted any bet, provided it involved small stakes, and laying a bet at Tote odds was not a problem. Eric knew the coup would have to be kept small, but the driving force behind the planning was the thrill of landing the coup more than the money it would yield. Everything was planned and ready to go. Now they waited for a suitable greyhound to land the spoils.

Eric's friend, the late Con Murphy from Abbeyfeale, provided the opportunity with his dog *Ballydonnell Sam*, who was a virtual certainty in a race at Mullingar, being quoted as a 3-to-1 ON chance. On the day of the race they backed *Ballydonnell Sam* at Tote odds in small stakes in as many betting shops as they could between Listowel and Mullingar, eventually placing a total of £600 on the dog. When they had finished this task, the team headed for the greyhound track, where they would ensure that the Tote there paid a good dividend. The Mullingar Tote in those days was very small indeed with only a handful of windows in operation, all of which were covered by Eric's team. Each team member had a fist-ful of £20 notes which was offered for a bet of 20p on *Ballydonnell Sam*. When the change from the £20 was received—a tenner, a fiver, four £1 notes and 80p in coin—the tenner was then offered for another 20p on the dog. This was done until all the notes were gone. Then the team member would produce another £20 note and the merry-go-round began all over again. There were chaotic scenes at the Tote, which ran out of change, delaying the process deliciously, but the team were very worried about an extra window, which they feared would open at any moment. They had miscalculated the number of windows available to the Tote and did not have enough personnel to cover it properly. One man was half-watching it and he was not really sure what he would do if it suddenly opened but, fortunately, the Tote was so preoccupied in getting more change that it never did. The team placed 1,200 bets of 20p with the Tote that evening, only one of which was put on *Ballydonnell Sam*, which resulted in an outlay of £240. *Ballydonnell Sam* won the race, the coup was landed and the cost of the little operation with the Tote was only £40.40 because the winning dividend was £199.60 for their 20p bet—the Tote paying odds of 997-to-1! On paper the team had won an incredible £598,200 from the bookies. Just like Dagenham, turning the paper profits into ready cash was likely to be a problem, and so it proved.

Getting the money on and landing the coup had gone exactly to plan, but the extraction of the winnings from the bookmakers proved virtually impossible. Many shops simply could not pay up and those that could went looking for the rulebook to limit the damage. A few paid up having imposed a limit of 100-to-1 on the bet, but most of the shops either voided the bet or settled it at the SP odds of 3-to-1 ON, on the grounds that the rules stated they did not accept bets at Tote odds at greyhound meetings, even though they frequently did so. As the day wore on the team found that betting shop proprietors were pointing out a notice clearly displayed on the wall, outlining details of the limits and restrictions on greyhound bets, which they asserted was there when the bet was placed. More than one betting shop owner was caught red-handed putting up the limit retrospectively; but all claimed that this was in their rules anyway. The punters were not getting paid and that was that.

Faced with a blank refusal to pay, those who had pulled off the coup had only two options open to them: accept the situation, or object to the licence of the defaulting bookmakers. The latter course of action is not as simple as it sounds. Even if they had convinced the Garda Superintendent that the bookmaker had defaulted, rather than voided the bet according to his rules, the bookmaker had the right of appeal to the Circuit Court. This involved costs and a court appearance in the witness box, as the bookmaker's counsel probed the goings-on at Mullingar, which was likely to prove embarrassing because everyone knew that the public were prevented from having a bet. With that option a non-runner, the beneficiaries of the coup had no choice but to accept what they were given—and they were given very little!

Mathematicians Master the Tote
Like Dagenham, the Mullingar coup had not affected the Tote itself, its dividends had merely been manipulated in order to hit

the bookmakers who accepted bets at Tote odds. Gradually, and inevitably, human ingenuity began to look at the Tote itself. For years and years nobody ever thought the Tote could be a victim of a betting coup as it was not a bookmaker, it did not offer fixed odds and, even if pools were manipulated, it would only affect the dividend. They were wrong. It is true that the early betting coups involving the Tote actually hit bookmakers who were taking bets at Tote odds and not the Tote itself—but that was about to change. The first point of attack was when big punters began taking advantage of the Tote's commitment to pay all dividends in silver. The basic unit was two shillings, so the Tote guaranteed that its lowest dividend would be 2-to-6—in other words 4-to-1 ON. When a horse was priced at shorter odds than this in the betting ring, punters and bookmakers realised they could obtain the fixed price of 4-to-1 ON because of this guarantee. As more people availed of this generosity, the more expensive it became for the Tote, which had to subsidise the pool to sustain the payout. This forced a rule change. The new rules meant the new minimum dividend was now £1.10, a fixed price of 10-to-1 ON.

In the 1990s a syndicate in Ireland began to operate against the Irish Tote, using a scheme it had employed successfully in Britain. The syndicate chose its races very carefully. The ideal race was one over hurdles, with a favourite that looked a 'certainty', and had eight runners. Using the Tote's systems to its advantage, the syndicate would invest about £10,000 on the race, putting about £9,000 on the favourite for a place, that is for the horse to finish either first, second or third. This favourite would be about a 3-to-1 ON shot to win the race with the bookmakers, but the syndicate was happy to get 10-to-1 ON for the place which, barring a freak accident, was simply picking up money. The syndicate then placed £100 on each of the seven other runners, again for a place, and awaited the result. It did not matter which horse won the race: the coup came up once the favourite finished in the first three.

The syndicate usually chose a hurdle race for the coup and the one instance when it deviated from that successful formula the coup came unstuck for the first and only time. Choosing a flat race with an odds-on 'certainty' trained by Aidan O'Brien, the coup failed because this 'good thing' finished outside the first three. It usually selected its races carefully, was very patient, being prepared to wait for weeks on end for the right race, which made sense because one failure could wipe out seven or eight winning coups.

The system worked by investing a large sum of money on one horse, which the syndicate believed was certain to finish in the first three, and using the Tote's formula of dealing with the place pool to legally manipulate the dividends. To get the place dividend, the Tote divides the total place pool three ways, for the first-placed horse, the second-placed horse and the third-placed horse, having first deducted its expenses from the pool. It then divides the total number of units on each horse into the pool on that particular horse, arriving at the dividend for the three placed horses. The syndicate was going to win some money if the favourite finished in the first three, but the real point of the coup was to back other horses for a place and get the benefit of an artificially high dividend, which meant that it got its stake money back twice.

For example, when the syndicate put its money down on the favourite for a place and it finished in the first three, the Tote would deduct its expenses from that bet and then divide it three ways. Let us assume, for simplicity sake, that the syndicate's bet was £12,000 after the Tote had deducted its expenses, then £4,000 would go into the pool on each of the first three horses home. There would be other bets in the pool as well, those of the general public, but let us ignore these because they do not change the position materially; nor does it matter if the favourite wins the race or just finishes second or third. After the race the three place pools have £4,000 in them, but there will be 11,300 units on the pool of the favourite (the syndicate's £12,000 less the seven bets of £100 it had on each of the other runners). When the Tote divides the number of winning units into the pool it produces a dividend of 35p for each £1 invested, but it has a minimum dividend of £1.10, which means that the Tote must put £8,475 of its own money into the place pool on the favourite in order to honour its minimum dividend policy. Then there are the other two places to be paid out. Again, leaving out the public's bets, the two remaining

Tote place pools contain £4,000, there are 100 winning units on each, producing a freak, inflated dividend of £40 on each of the placed horses. The syndicate would get odds of 40-to-1 a place about a horse that may only have been a 5-to-1 shot to win the race! The syndicate had won on the race, but the Tote, despite deducting its expenses, had produced a massive loss because of its dividend policy. In order to stop the syndicate, the Tote had to get the government to change the law regarding Tote betting.

The Last Charge of the Mugs
The dictionary definition of the word 'mug' is given as a noun with three different meanings: first, it is a large drinking vessel with a handle for use without a saucer—its real meaning; second, it is a slang word for a person's face; and third, it is slang for a person who is outwitted easily. It is the latter meaning of the word that is used in betting parlance to mean a person who is a regular loser. A 'typical mug' in the gambling world is a person who has a bet everyday, and usually puts a large number of horses together in a multiple bet in an attempt to win a large sum of money for a small stake should the impossible happen. Mugs are destined to lose, but once in a blue moon it comes up for them and when it does the bookmakers take a real hiding. Fortunately for the layers, the mugs immediately resume their habits of a lifetime and the windfall trickles back to the bookmakers over the next few years. Nonetheless, the unexpected betting coup gives hope to all those millions of small betting shop punters who bet to pass the time.

The last big coup by the unknown punter occurred in 1996, on Saturday, 28 September to be exact, when the leading jockey Frankie Dettori rode all seven winners at Ascot. Every mug punter in the land had, as per usual, doubled, trebled and accumulated all Dettori's mounts in multiple bets. The bets were the usual fare on a Saturday afternoon: the stakes were small, although there were many of them, and if a quarter of the money had been placed by unknown faces, every bookmaker in the land would be rushing to head off a forthcoming betting coup. As usual though, the bookmakers ignored this liability; after all, the last disaster, from their point of view, had occurred in June 1992 when Pat Eddery rode seven winners from eleven mounts at two meetings and the beneficiaries were regular customers. Frankie would probably ride one or two winners on a good day, a treble was possible, but a four-timer would be exceptional and there was a real chance the rider might draw a blank. It was, as I've described, a typical Saturday in a betting shop.

For the unknown punter to land his coup, Frankie Dettori had to do what no jockey had ever done before: ride the winners of all seven races on the card. Gordon Richards and Alec Russell were the only jockeys ever to have ridden all six winners on the same card. Richards, or Sir Gordon Richards as he was to become, did so at Chepstow in 1933, which was part of a sequence of an incredible twelve consecutive wins, while Russell achieved his milestone at the now defunct Bogside meeting in Scotland in 1957. Several jockeys had ridden six winners at an individual meeting without riding all the winners that day, notably George Fordham and Fred Archer (twice each), Mr Ted Wilson, Mr Charlie Cunningham and the more familiar Willie Carson. In Ireland, two jockeys have gone through the card, but on both occasions only five races were run. On 8 September 1900 at Cavan the Liverpool-born jockey Frederick 'Tich' Mason rode all five winners, a feat equalled by Frank Morgan fourteen years later at Downpatrick, on 12 March. At Navan in 1949 the brilliant Martin Molony rode the winners of all five races open to professionals, the sixth being a bumper that was restricted to amateurs.

A firm favourite with the public, Lanfranco Dettori is the son of the Italian jockey Gianfranco Dettori, remembered here for his flying visits to England in the mid-1970s to ride horses belonging to owner Carlo D'Alessio, notably *Bolkonski* and *Wollow*. When Frankie showed interest in following his father into racing, he was sent to Luca Cumani, an Italian who was training at Newmarket and for whom his father had ridden previously. Young Dettori quickly displayed ability and flair, becoming the Champion Apprentice in 1989, and successfully bridged the gulf between an apprentice and a fully-fledged jockey. Twenty-three-year-old Dettori really hit the headlines in 1994, winning his first Classic when *Balanchine* won the Oaks. Three weeks later the pair struck again when the filly won the Irish Derby at the Curragh. Owned by Sheikh Maktoum Al Maktoum and Godolphin Racing and trained in Dubai by Hilal Ibrahim, *Balanchine* was the first ever British or Irish Classic winner to be trained in the Middle East. The following September a treble at York brought his seasonal total past the 200 mark, making Frankie Dettori only the sixth jockey to ride 200 winners in a flat season in Britain, joining an exclusive club whose members included Fred Archer, Tommy Loates, Sir Gordon Richards, Pat Eddery and Michael Roberts. Young Frankie was not finished yet though, ending the season in a fanfare of glory as he rode *Barathea*, trained by Luca Cumani, to victory in the Breeders' Cup Mile, thrilling the crowd with his flamboyant leap from the saddle when he won, in the style of Angel Cordero, the recently retired Puerto Rican jockey who had ridden 7,056 winners in the USA.

Returning to that fateful Saturday at Ascot in September 1996, as the results came one by one the bookmakers could not believe their eyes:

First Race: 2pm, Cumberland Lodge Stakes (Group 3) (3yo+) £31,400. 12 furlongs (7 Ran).
1: Godolphin's *Wall Street* USA (L. Dettori) 2/1fav. Trained: Saeed Bin Suroor. Won by ½ length.

Second Race: 2.35pm, Racal Diadem Stakes (Group 2) (3yo+) £58,350. 6 furlongs (12 Ran).
1: Godolphin's *Diffident* FR (L. Dettori) 12/1. Trained: Saeed Bin Suroor. Won by a short head.

Third Race: 3.20pm, Queen Elizabeth II Stakes (Group 1) (3yo+) £199,020. 8 furlongs (7 Ran).
1: Godolphin's *Mark of Esteem* IRE (L. Dettori) 100/30. Trained: Saeed Bin Suroor. Won by 1½ lengths.

Fourth Race: 3.55pm, Tote Festival Handicap (3yo+) £50,102. 7 furlongs (26 Ran).
1: Herbert Allen's *Decorated Hero* GB (L. Dettori) 7/1 (from 12s). Trained: J.H.M. Gosden. Won by 3½ lengths.

Fifth Race: 4.30pm, Rosemary Handicap (Listed) (3yo+)
£19,129. 8 furlongs (18 Ran).
1: Godolphin's **Fatefully** USA (L. Dettori) 7/4fav. Trained: Saeed
Bin Suroor. Won by a neck.

Sixth Race: 5pm, Blue Seal Conditions Stakes (2yo)
£12,335. 6 furlongs (5 Ran).
1: J.C. Smith's **Lochangel** GB (L. Dettori) 5/4jt-fav. Trained: I.A.
Balding. Won by 1/2 length.

Seventh Race: 5.35pm, Gordon Carter Handicap (3yo+)
£14,655. 16 furlongs (18 Ran).
1: Seisuke Hata's **Fujiyama Crest** IRE (L. Dettori) 2/1fav. Trained:
M.R. Stoute. Won by a neck.

The last of the seven winners, *Fujiyama Crest*, was a 12-to-1 chance
in the morning, but the racecourse bookmakers had opened it up
at only 3-to-1, anticipating heavy off-course support for the horse.
It duly came, forcing the price down to 2-to-1, which many racecourse bookmakers considered a false price, encouraging them to
hold liabilities they would normally hedge. It scrambled home
from a horse ridden by Pat Eddery, hoovering an estimated £18
million out of the nation's betting shops in the process and bringing about a massive, but temporary, transfer of wealth from the
rich to the poor. Frankie described the day as 'a dream come true',
while his father, who was enjoying the sun in Gran Canaria and
casually following the racing results on the teletext, was incredulous and assumed there had been some mistake. It had been a
black day for bookmakers, but things quickly went back to normal
the following afternoon when Frankie Dettori managed only one
win from seven rides. The 'mugs' had had their day in the sun!
Punters come and go, gambles win and come unstuck, but the
bookies go on and on!

PART 4
THE CROOKS,
THE CHANCERS AND
THE WIDE SHAMS

'A racehorse is an animal that can take several thousand people for a ride at the same time.'

ANON

Although this book describes many coups, strokes and fraudulent practices, it would be wrong if readers got the impression that horse-racing was as bent as a corkscrew. It is not. Less than 1 per cent of the 2,000 or so horse-races run in Ireland every year are open to suspicion, which is not at all bad for a business in which money plays such a huge role. Nonetheless, it is the case that where money is involved people will be tempted to cheat, which is why we have rules and stewards to enforce them. God might love a trier, but the stewards and the industry most certainly do not and when people attempt to cheat, they need to make sure their plan is watertight—but few seem to manage this, thankfully! Our 'rogues gallery' has the odd outright crook, but mostly these are cases of opportunism, of being human and failing to resist temptation and of that most common affliction in horse-racing: a rush of blood to the head!

The Ringer

A 'ringer' is the racing term for the illegal substitution of one horse in place of another. One of the earliest cases in which the deliberate use of a ringer was discovered occurred in Ireland over 150 years ago. In this case an owner, who was a pillar of the Establishment, deliberately substituted an older and consequently much stronger horse for a younger one in order to win a valuable race and land a gamble in the process. Edward Ruthven, a member of the Turf Club, Irish racing's governing body, and MP for Kildare (a constituency that includes the Curragh), was a keen racing man. In October 1835 he swept the boards at the Curragh when *Caroline* and *Leinster* won all three of the valuable two-year-old races there. Well-developed and well-backed, both horses won so easily that onlookers believed Mr Ruthven had not one but two champion racehorses in his possession—a very rare occurrence. Had Mr Ruthven left it there, all would have been well, but he could not resist going back to the well again.

Lord Milltown, one of the leading owners of the time and breeder of Russborough, beaten in a run-off for the St Leger, saw an opportunity to make money by challenging Mr Ruthven to a match on handicap terms between *Caroline* and his colt *Fusilier* for a stake of £100. He hoped that an elated Mr Ruthven would accept that *Fusilier* would carry 7 stone 7 lb and *Caroline* 8 stone 7 lb—terms that were very much against *Caroline*—and was confident that there was no two-year-old filly in the land that could concede a stone to *Fusilier*. Foolishly, Ruthven could not resist, despite the harsh terms put on *Caroline*, and accepted the challenge. The following week *Caroline* and *Fusilier* lined up for the match and, to the consternation of Lord Milltown, the filly beat the colt easily, despite her burden. The manner of her victory astonished experienced race-watchers. It was the performance of an outstanding two-year-old, or perhaps a good three-year-old! The easy victory raised some suspicions, but most people refused to even consider the notion that a person of Mr Ruthven's standing could be involved in cheating of any kind. Lord Milltown, on the other hand, was convinced Mr Ruthven had done just that. Amazed by the result, Lord Milltown refused to believe there was a two-year-old in the land that could demolish *Fusilier* at those weights, sensationally going as far as making a public allegation that *Caroline* was an 'early foal'—a euphemism for a horse that is older than its declared age. Demanding that his vet be allowed to examine *Caroline*, Lord Milltown was taken aback when this was met with agreement and disappointed when his vet, being inexperienced in these matters, could not say for certain that *Caroline* was a three-year-old. Nevertheless, Lord Milltown went ahead and lodged an objection with the stewards to the effect that *Caroline* was not a two-year-old, as described.

Edward Ruthven retorted that Lord Milltown was simply trying to score a political point, being a supporter of his political opponents, and that it was merely part of a dirty tricks campaign. This defence worked well because the public debate split along party political lines and the issue became a game of political football, which clouded the facts and distorted impartiality. The result of this was that, amid the political argument, nobody really cared what age the horse was. With public sympathy on his side, it looked as if the venerable MP would escape unscathed, but then matters deteriorated for Edward Ruthven. Out of the blue, two other owners objected independently to *Leinster* on the grounds that it was a three-year-old and not a two-year-old, as described. *Leinster* was Ruthven's other champion two-year-old and this second objection, which could not be dismissed as a political dirty trick, brought the real issue into sharp focus once again. Did the MP cheat, or did he not? What age were *Leinster* and *Caroline*?

The only evidence against Mr Ruthven was the word of a prominent Curragh vet, an employee of Lord Milltown, who stated that he was of the opinion that *Caroline* was a three-year-old, but he could not be absolutely certain. Lord Millton wanted *Caroline* and *Leinster* examined by a leading vet from England, which he claimed would settle the issue once and for all. Ruthven countered by lodging all the relevant documents pertaining to *Caroline* and *Leinster*, from conception to the training stable, to prove the whereabouts of each horse throughout its life, and naming witnesses who would testify in support of these facts. Essentially the case boiled down to Lord Milltown's request that both horses be produced for examination by a panel of experts and Edward Ruthven's refusal to accept this was necessary, arguing that *Caroline* had been examined by Lord Milltown's own vet. When the stewards sided with Lord Milltown, Ruthven objected to the Turf Club hearing the case and refused to allow any English witnesses examine the horses, and then declined to take any part in the inquiry. The case proceeded in his absence, witnesses were produced who identified *Caroline* as a three-year-old English mare named *Becassine*, and *Leinster* as the three-year-old *Old Bill*. The stewards accepted this evidence as proof that both horses were three-year-olds and upheld Lord Milltown's objection. Exposed as a cheat, Edward Ruthven, MP for Kildare, was disgraced. He was forced to resign as a member of the Turf Club and disappeared from the racing scene. Two years later he lost his parliamentary seat.

A Dead Ringer
Memories of the Irish case had faded when the most infamous ringer of them all, running as *Running Rein*, won the Derby nine years later, landing a fortune in bets and lining up another fortune in the years to come from stud fees. The Derby is restricted to three-year-old horses. Obviously, if an older horse could run in

the Derby at level weights with the three-year-olds, it would have a considerable advantage—that was the thinking behind the attempt to win the Derby by substituting an older 'ringer' in place of *Running Rein*.

The real *Running Rein* was a bay colt by *The Saddler* out of *Mab*, foaled in 1841 and bred by C.R. Cobb, who sold him to a Mr Goodman—actually a reckless gambler named Goodman Levy, who was using a false name. *Running Rein* made its racecourse debut in a two-year-old event at Newmarket in October 1843, running in the name of Mr A. Wood, a corn merchant. It was backed down from long odds to 3-to-1 and duly won. The big gamble aroused interest in *Running Rein*, his well-developed physique was commented on and rumours of a 'stroke' began to surface. The Duke of Rutland, owner of the second-placed horse, lodged an objection to *Running Rein* on the grounds that the horse was not as described on the race card. The stewards conducted an enquiry.

At the enquiry the chief witness was a groom who was in the employ of Mr Cobb when *Running Rein* was foaled and he was called to confirm the identity of the horse. When the groom confirmed that the horse running under the name *Running Rein* was indeed the horse that had been foaled out of the brood mare *Mab*, the case against the horse collapsed. The stewards overruled the objection and *Running Rein* was confirmed the winner.

The rumours continued to persist throughout the winter, however, encouraging the stewards to hold a private investigation into the movements of *Running Rein* from the time he had been sold to Mr Goodman until he was passed on to Mr Wood. The stewards also monitored other horses that had been in Mr Goodman's possession at the same time, but one could not be traced—a bay colt named *Maccabeus*. Bred by Sir C. Ibbetson in 1840, *Maccabeus* was by *Gladiator* out of the *Capsicum* mare and had been sold to Mr Goodman in 1841. Evidence began to surface that Mr Goodman might have switched the two-year-old *Maccabeus* with the yearling *Running Rein* in 1842, passing the horse on to Mr Wood to cover his tracks. The stewards decided to wait until *Running Rein* ran again before taking further action, but the matter was suddenly and unexpectedly taken out of their hands.

A few days before the Epsom Derby, where *Running Rein* was expected to make his seasonal debut, a number of owners and trainers with runners in the race petitioned the stewards that *Running Rein* might not be that horse at all. They requested that its mouth be examined by a vet to determine the horse's age before it was allowed to run in the Derby. Horse dealers had developed a system of measuring a horse's size with their hands (one 'hand' being equal to 4 in.) and a horse's age by its teeth. Obviously a three-year-old horse is infinitely more valuable than one aged sixteen, yet long ago a buyer had only the vendor's word regarding its age, which was not satisfactory. By the nineteenth century there was a bit more information to go on, and horse dealers would look at the teeth of a horse before buying it, first to make sure they were healthy, but also because they knew that if a horse was 'long in the tooth', it was old. In time the system of judging the age of a horse by its teeth became refined. A horse has six incisor teeth on the top and six on the bottom of its mouth. The middle pair is called the 'centrals', the next on either side the 'laterals' and the two outer teeth the 'corners'. The 'centrals' cut through the gum at two-and-a-half years of age and are fully up and level at three years; 'laterals' cut at three-and-a-half years and the 'corners' at four-and-a-half years. A horse has a full set of teeth when it is six years old. While horse dealers were experts on the teeth of horses, vets did not have any real experience of aging horses and often invited an experienced dealer to confirm their findings.

For some reason, which is hard to fathom today, the Epsom stewards decided to allow *Running Rein* to run in the Derby without any examination, declaring they would call an enquiry and withhold the stakes if the horse won. The stewards obviously had no idea just how determined Mr Goodman and his fellow conspirators were to land £50,000 in winning bets! Further drama followed when an objection was lodged against another runner, *Leander*, owner by a German named Lichtwald, on the grounds that it was a four-year-old. Again, the stewards postponed the enquiry until after the race.

The betting at Epsom was 5-to-2 favourite *The Ugly Buck*, 3-to-1 *Ratan* and 10-to-1 third-favourite *Running Rein*. The conspirators made sure that the favourite and the second favourite were not going to win. Jockey Sam Rogers agreed to stop his mount, *Ratan* but John Day junior, rider of *The Ugly Buck*, refused to co-operate—surprisingly, in view of his family's pedigree—forcing the conspirators to resort to other tactics. The race was a fiasco. Not content to have a year in hand with their horse, the conspirators had strategically placed 'no-hopers'—horses patently not good enough to win such an important race—to foul and impede other fancied runners, particularly *The Ugly Buck*. The corrupted jockeys soon put paid to the chances of *The Ugly Buck*, balking and impeding it by foul riding. The rider of *Running Rein* joined in, deliberately crashing into the only possible danger, *Leander*, which was brought down and broke its leg. With all the fancied runners duly disposed of, *Running Rein* now had only *Orlando* to beat, ridden by the trustworthy, competent champion jockey Nat Flatman. Flatman had evaded all the fouls to throw down a challenge to *Running Rein*, but the four-year-old beat him by three parts of a length.

After the race there was pandemonium because Mr Goodman and his pals attempted to collect their winnings, but the book-makers did not want to pay given that there was to be an enquiry. Bets are not usually subject to technical objections—which can take weeks or even months to resolve—and many people, completely innocent of the coup, had backed *Running Rein* and were reluctant to leave the Epsom Downs without payment on their winner. Matters were made worse when the stewards announced that the enquiry would be deferred until pending legal proceedings were completed. This allowed the conspirators to collect most of their ill-gotten gains, leaving the innocent and naïve Mr Wood to defend himself against Colonel Jonathan Peel in the courts. Colonel Peel, a brother of the incumbent British Prime Minister Sir Robert Peel, was the owner of *Orlando* and was claiming the prize on the grounds that *Running Rein* was actually a four-year-old named *Maccabeus*. Mr Wood vigorously denied the allegation, declaring that he had acquired the three-year-old *Running Rein* fair and square, had never owned *Maccabeus* and had most certainly not switched the horses.

Meanwhile, the stewards had decided to enquire into the identity of *Leander*, which had been the subject of a protest prior to the race. Having broken its leg in running, *Leander* had raced all the way to the line on three legs and a stump before being shot on humane grounds. The stewards now insisted the head be removed and sent for dental examination. Several eminent vets declared that *Leander*'s teeth were those of a four-year-old horse, an allegation the owner denied vehemently, but enquiries failed to identify which horse it actually was. Nevertheless, with the evidence before them, the stewards declared *Leander* a ringer and 'warned off' the owner for life. On being informed that he could never go racing again virtually, Lichtwald was furious and declared that the vets did not know their business. Slamming British justice, he stated that the case against him was flawed, that *Leander* was definitely not a four-year-old, which allegation the vets and the stewards had presented as a fact, and he knew this because Leander was actually six years old!

The *Running Rein* case proceeded slowly through the courts. Several actions were pending, but in due course a judge demanded that Mr Wood produce *Running Rein* for examination and the whole case collapsed. The cessation of legal proceedings enabled the stewards to re-open the enquiry into the race and into the true identity of *Running Rein*. Once satisfied that *Running Rein* was actually *Maccabeus*, the stewards disqualified the horse and awarded the Derby to *Orlando*.

If rogues wish to take a lesson from these cases, it is this: one has a reasonable chance of getting away with running a 'ringer' provided it is done only once and the 'ringer' is fed to hounds as soon as possible after the race. This kind of scam is best suited for landing a betting coup rather than winning a major race because betting winnings will normally be paid out within minutes of the winner passing the post. Subsequent objections do not affect bets, but prize money is subject to the winner fulfilling the conditions of the race and passing the routine dope test. Although veterinary medicine is light years behind human medicine, vets can now accurately tell a horse's age from its teeth and there are now comprehensive records of a horse's markings for identification purposes. So the best ringer really is a dead ringer!

Jockeying for Position

From the earliest days of horse-racing there have been examples of people determined to win—at all costs. Nobbling, foul riding and false descriptions of horses were commonplace until the rules of racing were established. While the rules restrained the cheats and imposed penalties on them when they got caught, they did not eliminate the root problem—people were still looking for a loophole. One way for a jockey to get an advantage in a race is to carry less weight than that allotted to him, which is the reason behind the strict weighing-in and weighing-out arrangements at race meetings. The first attempt to actually rig the scales took place at Newmarket in 1863. A horse named *Catch 'em Alive*, trained by William Day, won the prestigious Cambridgeshire Handicap at the skinny odds of 4-to-1. William Day had won a fortune just three years earlier when he had taken both the Cambridgeshire and Cesarewitch Handicaps. Believing him to be very hot in handicaps, the public tended to follow his horses and backed them at any price. So of course, *Catch 'em Alive* was a popular winner— and an expensive one for bookies.

After the race, when the winning jockey Sam Adams returned to the scales, he was unable to draw the correct weight. Holding the whip said to be the one he had carried in the race, Adams barely made the correct weight, but the owner of the runner-up, *Merry Hart*, objected immediately to his weighing-in with anything at all in his hands after he got on the scales. As a heated argument raged between the Clerk of the Scales, the connections of the winner and the owner of the second horse, Adams had to remain where he was while the stewards were summoned. Charges that the whip was the biggest and heaviest ever seen at Newmarket were countered by reminders that the public had backed the winner heavily and there would be a riot if the race was lost for the sake of 2 lb. Nonetheless, the stewards ruled that Adams could not weigh-in with a whip, which meant that *Catch 'em Alive* would lose the race. The second horse, *Merry Hart*, whose rider had already weighed-in all right, was about to be awarded the race, but the stewards were interrupted when James Grimshaw, rider of the third horse, *Summerside*, also weighed-in 2 lb light. Grimshaw protested that something was wrong because he had weighed-out correctly, saddled the horse himself and no one could have tampered with his lead weights. This statement, together with the almost unprecedented case that two of the first three horses had weighed in exactly 2 lb light, led the stewards to order an examination of the scales. It was discovered the scales had been tampered with.

The stewards decreed immediately that *Catch 'em Alive* be declared the winner because they were satisfied that had the scales not been defective when Sam Adams weighed-in, he would have drawn the correct weight. The stewards ordered a full enquiry into the incident and offered a £50 reward for information leading to the discovery of the culprit—a bookmaker or his agent being the prime suspects. However, it transpired that the bookmakers had no hand, act or part in the deception, which actually had not been carried out to influence the outcome of the race. Although the person who tampered with the scales was never caught, it was well-known that it was the jockey who had ridden *Merry Hart*. Contrary to expectation, his only motive in tampering with the scales was to keep the mount on *Merry Hart*, which he was in danger of losing because he would have to put up 2 lb overweight.

The jockey had wasted hard all week to get his body weight low enough to ride at the weight *Merry Hart* had been allotted. But when he weighed himself on the morning of the race, he found that he had not lost enough weight and that even if he used the lightest and most uncomfortable saddle possible, he would still not be able to meet the correct poundage. Fearing that the owner would replace him with a jockey who could do the weight—2 lb can make all the difference in a close finish—and not wishing to lose the ride, the jockey decided to conceal the fact from the owner and to fix the scales so nobody would notice. Sneaking up to the scales at a quiet moment, he placed 2 lb of lead on it so that it would register 2 lb lighter than the actual weight being measured. The effect of this was that every horse in the race would appear to be carrying the allotted weight, but in fact every runner was carrying 2 lb more than its allotted weight. None of the horses would be penalised, however, because every runner would meet on the same terms allotted by the handicapper, except carrying an unseen 2 lb extra.

It was all pretty harmless, or so he thought, but the jockey had forgotten that there were two scales in operation at Newmarket—although only one, located in the top stand, was used to weigh in the winner and the placed horses. He had doctored the scales in the top stand, but a number of jockeys had used the scales in the lower stand to weigh-out before the race, among them Sam Adams and James Grimshaw. They had weighed-out at the correct weight from the accurate scales, but on weighing-in, this time on the tampered scales, they were 2 lb lighter. The culprit had weighed in and out on the same scales, therefore drew the correct weight when he returned to scales. The rule at the time was that only the first three home were required to weigh-in, which meant the culprit was unlucky that the riders of the first and the third had weighed-out from the 'wrong' scales. On the other hand, he was very fortunate that Admiral Rous, a man who seemed to be able to sniff out villainy, apparently failed to realise that the rider of *Merry Hart* had weighed-in correctly on the incorrect scales. Had he insisted that all three weigh-in again, once the scales had been put right, he would have found that *Merry Hart*'s jockey went to scale 2 lb heavier than the others, and his true crime would have been exposed.

All the jockeys realised what had gone on, but none reported the culprit, despite the substantial £50 reward—an indication of the comradeship that existed among them. All realised that no harm had been done, that the result of the race was not affected, but that this petty offence, if detected, would have resulted in a savage penalty for the unfortunate jockey. Perhaps Admiral Rous also felt some sympathy for the starving jockey and turned a blind eye as it was an untypical lapse by this normally astute senior steward not to require the three jockeys to weigh-in again once the scales had been corrected.

The Scales of Justice

For many years the rules of Irish racing allowed a rider to weigh-in 1 lb light in flat races and 2 lb light in jumping races and still be allowed to keep the race. This was to take into account possible loss of body fluid through sweating during the race. The rule had to be changed about eight years ago when it became obvious that some trainers and/or jockeys were abusing this leeway to 'get an edge'. The issue came to light when one winner failed to draw the correct weight and had to be disqualified. A piece of foam that did not weigh as much as 2 lb and that was part of the saddle came loose during the race and fell out. It was assumed that the jockey must have lost some weight during the race as well, and the combination of the two resulted in the horse being disqualified. It was very unfortunate and exceptional and was unlikely to happen again. But it did happen again, and again, all within a period of a few months.

At first the stewards examined the possibility that riders were losing more weight during races than previously, but their investigations soon revealed a more sinister reason. Apparently some jockeys (probably egged on by trainers) were deliberately shedding 2 lb after they had weighed-out, knowing they would not be disqualified for weighing-in 2 lb lighter than they weighed-out. In a jumping race 2 lb in weight is equivalent to a couple of lengths: enough to swing the balance in a closely fought finish! However, by leaving no room at all for minor weight loss, such as that incurred through sweating or the accidental loss of a piece of foam, the once very rare occurrence of a horse being disqualified because the jockey failed to draw the correct weight became a more frequent event—much to the consternation of racegoers. The Turf Club acted quickly, reducing the margin allowed in jumping races to 1 lb, thus bringing it into line with flat-racing rules. That had the desired effect. The practice was eliminated and the disqualification of a winner because the jockey could not draw the correct weight is once again a very rare occurrence in Irish racing, which is as it should be!

Down the years there has always been some jockey or another seeking to gain an advantage by evading the rules. It began with jockeys seeking to anticipate the start. When this was banned they began to fight like cats for the best positions in the line-up, with senior jockeys blatantly intimidating the younger ones and crossing and rough riding commonplace. The stewards responded by making it an offence for a jockey to disobey the Starter's instructions and by introducing a draw for positions at the start of flat races. The introduction of the camera patrol, which recorded the whole race for subsequent viewing by the stewards, clamped down on the deliberate foul riding that had become known as 'jockeyship' and made racing safer and fairer. Jockeys got into the habit of carrying the whip in their outside hand, the trick being to swing the whip extravagantly when hitting, or feigning to hit, their own mount, making sure that if any horse behind came too close, it got a good smack on the nose. The swinging whip and the bang on the nose would invariably make the strong-finisher flinch and lose valuable ground. Other tricks of the trade, such as leaning in ever so slightly on another horse, pushing it off course, or squeezing off another runner, usually executed by two or more jockeys in cahoots, have to be done with much artful subtlety nowadays, but it still goes on. Pinning a horse against the rails is certainly an art that lives on in modern racing and most jockeys object strongly, and rightly so in my opinion, when another jockey attempts to come through on the inside of a mount. The latter manoeuvre can often lead to the racing equivalent of road rage. One common trick of the trade that jockeys can still employ without fear of a penalty is shouting. A well-timed yell at an inexperienced young horse can startle it, causing it to throw up its head and lose ground, or can distract a rival jockey, or get him to move over.

It is not often that the seedier side of racing is brought into the public arena, but when it does make an appearance the allegations can be sensational. But then, of course, it is all too easy to make allegations. A court case in July 1895 considered the case of jockey William Taylor, who claimed wrongful dismissal against James Daly and William Hilliard, the proprietors of a stable at Castleknock, Co. Dublin. Taylor stated that he had been hired as a stable jockey in January 1894 for a period of three years, at £50 per annum plus £1 per week for expenses. Taylor was a twenty-five-year-old Englishman who had served his time with a leading Newmarket trainer and had come to Ireland in 1890 to ride the horses of Warren Jackson. When Jackson died just before

Christmas 1893, Harry Peard, the vet and manager of Cork Park racecourse, introduced Taylor to James Daly and he it was who had written out the terms offered to the jockey.

James Daly of Liffeybank, Islandbridge, Co. Dublin, a leading horse dealer, gave evidence that he had installed his son-in-law, William Hilliard, as his trainer and had won the Grand Steeplechase de Paris with a horse named *Royal Meath*. Daly alleged that Taylor had been working secretly for the bookmaker John Reece, who was getting him to stop horses for his benefit and using his private trainer, Robert Orton, as a go-between. He further alleged that the horse *Shylock*—trained by William Hilliard for Bertha Dewhurst, wife of Captain Robert Henry 'Bob' Dewhurst of the Fourth Hussars, himself a well-known amateur rider—had been stopped deliberately by Taylor when favourite to win the Navan Plate at Boyerstown on 30 April 1895. John Reece turned up in court to deny vehemently that he had ever asked Taylor to stop horses, through Robert Orton or anyone else. He defended his reputation, saying he had been in the bookmaking business for many years and had never been involved in any malpractice nor had his name been linked to any scandal.

The case was put to a jury, which found for William Taylor and awarded him £100. Taylor may have won the case, but it was a Pyrrhic victory because it ended his career as a jockey. Tainted by the allegations, no Irish owner or trainer was willing to risk putting him up and he was forced to return to England, where he was taken on by trainer Jack Fallon. Taken to Druid's Lodge in the wilderness of Salisbury Plain, William Taylor was a virtual prisoner, like the rest of the staff, but in his case it did serve to keep him well out of the way of temptation.

Mistaken Identity

While it is true that most ringers are used deliberately in order to mislead the bookmakers and the public, it sometimes happens that horses get mixed up accidentally. Whether the horse owner is innocent or not, in all cases a horse that runs in a race improperly described is automatically disqualified, irrespective of how the mix-up occurred.

The most famous accidental 'ringer' was the winner of the 1880 Derby, *Bend Or*, ridden brilliantly by the legendary jockey Fred Archer, who performed this feat with a broken arm in a sling and one leg reputed to have been over the running rail as the pair rounded the sharp Tattenham Corner bend. Chasing from behind, his whip flashing, Archer forced *Bend Or* to catch the flattering *Robert the Devil* right on the line, winning the race by a head for the Duke of Westminster and his trainer, Robert Peck. Charles Brewer, the bookmaker who owned *Robert the Devil*, was distraught, having thought his horse was winning easily. He had turned to his friends in delight only to discover, when his eyes reverted to the race, that the picture had changed radically. Bitterly disappointed, Brewer blamed his jockey, E. Rossiter, for throwing away the race and was utterly convinced that *Robert the Devil* was a better horse than *Bend Or*. Most observers agreed with him that Rossiter had been completely outridden by Archer and had lost his head in the closing stages of the race when the latter rallied his mount.

According to the convention of the time, it was not the 'done thing' to lodge an objection against the winner of the Derby. The race had been decided on the course, the best horse on the day had won and it was generally believed that a horse ought not win the greatest horse race in the world on a technicality. However, the following week Charles Brewer received information that, if true, would ensure *Bend Or* would be disqualified; he therefore had no compunction about lodging a formal objection. Ignoring the social opprobrium and defending his action on the grounds that *Robert the Devil* was the better horse and deserved to be declared the Derby winner, he objected to *Bend Or* on the grounds that it had been improperly described as being by the stallion *Doncaster* out of the brood mare *Rouge Rose*. One of the Duke of Westminster's former stud grooms had informed Brewer that *Bend Or* was not *Bend Or* at all but was in fact *Tadcaster*, a horse of the same sex and age and by the same sire, but out of the brood mare *Clemence*. The groom alleged the two horses had become confused after they left the Duke's Eaton stud as yearlings to go into training.

The stewards held an enquiry into the parentage of *Bend Or*, which revealed a disturbing laxity at the Duke's Eaton stud, where records of identification were not kept properly, the process largely being dependent on the grooms to keep tabs on the identity of the young horses. This reliance on the grooms to know which horse was which constituted bad practice, but at least *someone* did know one from the other. But when a horse left the stud for the training stable it was a different matter. If two of them got mixed up on the way, there were no procedures in place to discover the error. The absence of proper records, while an indictment of the Duke's code of practice, also meant, of course, that the only evidence against *Bend Or* was the statement by this groom, who had been sacked recently. The stewards could find no corroborating evidence at all. Alongside this problem, they were also mindful that the objection had been lodged by a bookmaker from a humble background against the powerful Duke of Westminster, the richest man in England and a very generous patron of horse-racing. The circumstances being what they were, the stewards set aside the groom's evidence on the grounds that he was a disgruntled employee and dismissed Brewer's objection, stating that they were satisfied the horse that finished first was described correctly as *Bend Or*.

With the benefit of hindsight it is now clear that the stewards made the wrong decision: the horse that won the Derby was almost certainly *Tadcaster* and not *Bend Or*. The groom never recanted his evidence—actually swearing on his deathbed that he had been telling the truth—and the later offspring of the respective dams proved that matter conclusively. The subsequent offspring of *Rouge Rose*, the dam of *Bend Or*, proved to be utterly useless on the racecourse while *Clemence*, the dam of *Tadcaster*, did breed foals that went on to win races. Many among the breeding and racing community were far from convinced that the stewards had made the right decision, with the result that the future offspring of *Clemence* were watched carefully on the off-chance that she might have been the dam of the Derby winner rather than of the useless *Tadcaster*, as the records indicated. Within a couple of years it became obvious that *Clemence* was the classy brood mare and not *Rouge Rose*. Her filly foal of 1881, also by *Doncaster*, so resembled *Bend Or*, right down to similar peculiar dark marks on the body, that it was undeniable she must be that horse's own sister. In a desperate attempt to quash the rumours, the Duke of Westminster decided to mate *Clemence* with *Bend Or*. This was a strong statement that he, for one, had no doubts about the latter's parentage because if the allegation were true, this mating would be a case of incestuous inbreeding of mother with son. The resulting filly vindicated the doubters by being worse than useless! By the time *Clemence* foaled another chestnut filly by *Doncaster* in 1885, the foal was openly described as being 'an own-sister to *Bend Or*'.

There can be little doubt that the stud groom, disgruntled or not, was telling the truth. He was the one person who could identify the two colts, which had probably got mixed up, just as he alleged, with *Tadcaster* being the good horse and *Bend Or* the useless one. The confusion was completely accidental—the Duke owned both horses and both dams and all the subsequent offspring of both mares remained in his ownership and went into training, so he had nothing to gain from the mix-up. However, the rules of racing unequivocally require a horse to be identified properly. In this case, *Bend Or* wasn't and therefore should have lost the Derby.

Stooping to a New Low

Beating the system is a trainer's job, but cheating is another matter entirely and is strictly against the rules of racing, and against the principles of sportsmanship. Such considerations have not stopped owners and trainers breaking the rules in order to get an advantage over the opposition. There is a basic rule of thumb at work here: the more desperate the financial position of the owner or trainer, the more audacious and flagrant is the rule-breaking.

One of the best horses ever to have raced in Ireland was *Barcaldine*, but it had the misfortune to be owned by George Low, who was a crook. Fred Archer rode five Derby winners in his short but brilliant career and he rated *Barcaldine* as superior to all of them. Undefeated in Ireland, *Barcaldine*'s career suffered because its owner was perpetually broke, the prize money was never sufficient for his profligate needs and consequently he was always looking out to make some extra money from the horse in any way he could. George Low, whose brother was the successful livestock auctioneer Gavin Low, bred *Barcaldine* in 1878 from his mare, *Ballyroe*. By choosing the stallion *Solon* as a mate for *Ballyroe*, George Low inbred at a time when this was not fashionable. Furthermore, he inbred very closely because *Solon* was out of a mare known as *Darling's Dam*, which was by the great Irish sire *Birdcatcher*, and *Darling's Dam* was also the grand-dam of *Ballyroe*. The experiment, or perhaps accident—who knows?— worked because the offspring of this mating was the inimitable *Barcaldine*.

Barcaldine exploded on to the Irish racing scene at the Curragh in the autumn of 1880 when it hacked up in the Railway Stakes, the most valuable flat race of that year, and beat the Anglesey Stakes winner and subsequent Irish Derby winner *Master Ned* out of sight. The following month *Barcaldine* contested three top-class two-year-old races in as many days, winning all three—the National Produce Stakes, the Beresford Stakes and the Paget Stakes—again defeating *Master Ned* each time. Trained by Tom Connolly and ridden by John Conolly (who was not related to the trainer), *Barcaldine* was the top Irish two-year-old of the year, having won four races to the tune of £1,334. The jockey family of Conollys, one of whom was assistant trainer to Tom Connolly, who died in 1883, revealed in later years that the horse never got a proper preparation for its races because when George Low got short of cash he would instruct the trainer to run the horse at the very next Curragh meeting. The trainer was ordered to run the horse in as many races as possible, whether or not it was fit or was suited to the distance and conditions of the race.

In those days most of the valuable races had early closing dates—the horses were entered for big races as yearlings, before they had gone into training, let alone before they had raced. This was done purely to boost the prize fund because every owner who had a yearling and aspirations of winning a decent race had to enter the horse and pay the entry fee, even though he had no clue as to its ability. Naturally, most of those entry fees were lost without getting a run, but the horses that were scratched left money in the pot for the others to win. George Low evidently had sufficient ready cash to enter up *Barcaldine* in all the valuable two-year-old races of 1880, but he failed to enter the horse in the 1881 Irish Derby, or in any of the English Classic races. It cost £15 to enter a horse in the Irish Derby back in 1879, which was a big sum, and Low was probably broke at the time, so *Barcaldine* could not contest Ireland's most prestigious race for three-year-olds.

Instead, *Barcaldine* began its three-year-old career in the Baldoyle Derby. Seven horses opposed the champion, including a revenge-seeking *Master Ned*, but only Garrett Moore's well-bred filly *Theodora* made a race of it, the others being beaten by a distance. Conceding 36 lb, *Barcaldine* beat *Theodora* by a length, a performance of the highest class as it was the only occasion on which the filly was beaten and she simply hacked up in her two subsequent races. If any further endorsement of *Barcaldine*'s ability were needed, *Master Ned* provided it by winning the Irish Derby; *Barcaldine* had beaten *Master Ned* easily in five previous races!

At that Irish Derby meeting, which took place on the last Tuesday, Wednesday and Thursday in June 1881, *Barcaldine* ran on each of the three days, winning three Queen's Plates to bring his seasonal prize money total to £761. *Barcaldine*'s appearance at the Curragh meeting surprised everybody because the horse had been entered to run in the Northumberland Plate, which was run at the same time. While the Curragh races had a pot of just over £100, the Northumberland Plate was worth £905 to the winner and was a big betting race, therefore would have provided George Low with an opportunity to land some worthwhile bets, and *Barcaldine* certainly looked to have the form to steal victory. So why had Low chosen to stay at the Curragh? The story came out later.

In June 1881 Low was broke, had no access to credit and was therefore unable to bet on his horse, so he engaged in what we would nowadays call 'lateral thinking'. He approached a leading bookmaker and offered to scratch *Barcaldine* from the race in return for a payment of £1,000. Low knew that *Barcaldine* had been heavily backed ante-post by the general public and that the stakes would be lost if the horse did not run, so he reckoned the bookmaker would gladly part with the 'grand' to get the horse out of the way and save himself a heap of cash. Unfortunately for Low, the man he chose was an honest bookie who not only refused to pay up but passed on the details of the illicit approach to the Jockey Club. The upshot was that George Low was 'warned-off', barring him from attending racemeetings or racing horses. The Turf Club confirmed the ban, which came into force on 11 July 1881 and forced Low to transfer ownership of *Barcaldine* to his brother, Gavin. Not satisfied that George Low had disposed of his entire interest in the horse, the Turf Club refused to accept any entries for *Barcaldine* until it was incontrovertibly proved that George Low was no longer the owner, or part-owner, of the horse. Low responded by trying a number of ruses to keep the horse while giving the impression that he no longer was the owner—but without success.

For over a year the *impasse* continued, during which time the unbeaten winner of eight races could not be raced, although in its prime. *Barcaldine* was forced to stay off the racecourse from 30 June 1881, when it was a three-year-old, until 4 May 1883, when it was five—the period of its prime, thus depriving it of showing the greatness that its ability surely merited. Eventually the stewards' tenacity forced George Low to accept defeat and *Barcaldine* came up for sale at public auction, the property of a gentleman [*sic*] at Newmarket, England, on Thursday, 12 October 1882. Knocked down for 1,300 guineas to the bid of Robert Peck, one of the most successful gambling trainers of his time who had retired at the end of 1881, *Barcaldine* was sent to the nearby Beverley House stable of James Hopper.

When *Barcaldine* eventually reappeared on a racecourse, in May 1883, it won three races in succession, including the Orange Cup at Royal Ascot, before landing a big coup for Peck. The horse was entered for the Northumberland Plate, but Peck somehow managed to convince the touts that *Barcaldine* was in his box at Newmarket; the horse was on its way to Newcastle for the race. The deception enabled Peck to back the horse to win the race at odds as high as 50-to-1: an incredible price about a horse that had been unbeaten in its eleven races, notwithstanding its burden of

9 stone 10 lb. When it transpired that *Barcaldine* was in fact at Newcastle and the champion jockey Fred Archer would ride it, the bookmakers were shocked and the odds tumbled down instantly to 11-to-2. *Barcaldine* maintained its unbeaten record, completing a sequence of twelve victories on the bounce and earning a fortune in bets for Peck. It's a good thing horses don't bear grudges!

Tod Sloan: Father of the Modern Jockey

Horses will not race naturally nor will they chase little animals like dogs do: means must be employed to make them race, those means being jockeys. The term 'jockey' comes from a little Jack (boy), a term first used to describe those who were associated with horses. The job of a jockey is to make a horse race, to keep it on the course without hampering the other runners and to pace it over the distance. Two hundred years ago it was thought that a jockey's sole function was to get a horse going, to steer it while urging it to run at its fastest and to pull it up when the race was over—all relatively simple tasks that any horse-rider could manage. In those days a horse was usually ridden in its races by its groom, but any competent rider would do once he was fit. In other words, the art of jockeyship had not yet been recognised. Over time, it gradually dawned on owners that some men were infinitely better than others when it came to race riding and the services of those jockeys were in constant demand. This in turn led to the successful riders taking up the job on a full-time basis, establishing the professional jockey.

Once it became apparent that weight was a major factor in the outcome of races, it became essential for a jockey to be small and light in order for him to secure enough rides to earn a living. Racing stables began recruiting boys as young as ten to sign up as apprenctice jockeys, mainly to provide cheap labour in the yard. Only a small proportion of these apprentices ever made the grade as a jockey but when the stable did get a good young jockey, whose services were in demand from other trainers, the apprentice's master retained half the boy's riding fee for himself. A good apprenctice was worth real money, which was the incentive for trainers to teach young lads the art of race riding. Obviously, it was important that trainers did not waste time training young boys to be jockeys if they were going to be 6 ft high and weigh 11 stone at age sixteen. Height had the major bearing on a person's weight and racing stables quickly learned that the average boy grew taller than his mother. Therefore, all prospective apprentice jockeys were interviewed in the presence of their mothers—and ones with tall mothers were rejected out of hand.

The handicap system had to respect the frail legs of the thoroughbred horse so the range of weights introduced for racing ranged from welterweight (10 stone or 140 lb) to featherweight (5 stone 7 lb or 77 lb), which included the saddle and the jockey's riding boots. All jockeys used to ride with a 'straight back', using a long stirrup, which everyone agreed was very stylish and nobody dared to question whether it was the most effective. Any jockey who deviated from this accepted style was condemned as having an 'ugly seat'. Tommy Lye (1837–1866) was the first jockey to ride with a shorter than usual stirrup, but the consequent loss of leg power, which meant he couldn't kick his mount to make it run faster, forced him to become over-dependent on the whip. George Fordham (1837–1887) refined Lye's style, making it more effective and less reliant on the whip and in doing so became one of the great jockeys of his day until challenged by his great rival, Fred Archer (1857–1886). These two brilliant jockeys were honest and rode in a distinct crouching style, leaning forward rather than backwards in a finish. They were keen rivals and fierce competitors, but it was Archer who caught the imagination of the public and reigned supreme as champion jockey from 1874 until 1886, the year of his death. Tall for a jockey, Archer had to waste hard to keep his weight down and after a severe bout of wasting fell ill in November 1886. During this illness he shot himself with a pistol, which he always kept by his bed as a protection against burglars. He was only twenty-nine years old. In his seventeen years as a jockey, Archer rode 2,748 winners and was champion jockey thirteen times. Shortly before his death, Archer made a celebrated visit to the Curragh, taking three mounts at the meeting of 21 October 1886. Having won on the first two, *Cambusmore* and *Isidore*, Archer was beaten into third place on *Black Rose*, behind the amateurs Tommy Beasley (*Spahi*) and Willie Cullen (*Lord Chatham*). Archer's record number of wins in an English season, 246 in 1885, stood until beaten by Gordon Richards in 1933, a year in which Richards rode eleven consecutive winners.

The success of jockeys with an 'ugly seat' did not alter the opinion of owners and trainers that the normal English riding-seat was the best, the most beautiful and the one all aspiring jockeys should imitate. Indeed, owners and trainers tended to shun riders who did not ride in the conventional style. Things were very different in America, however. Over there, stirrups were decidedly shorter and all jockeys crouched towards the horse's neck. The first jockey to ride in England in the American style was Willie Simms, who arrived on the English racing scene in 1895. A figure of amusement, Simms was dubbed 'the monkey up a stick' and was not supported by owners, getting only nineteen rides, which yielded him four wins and five places. Unfairly written off as a failure, Simms returned home, but another veteran of the American scene arrived to take his place. Tod Sloan (1874–1933) arrived in England in 1897 and was a much better jockey than Simms. He was fast away at the start and his judgment of pace was so impressive it was as if he had a precision clock in his head. Sloan was about to revolutionise the way racehorses were ridden all over the world.

Sloan had watched how the black jockeys rode at country meetings in America, and it impressed him. He copied their style: crouching up the horse's neck during a race rather than sitting back in the saddle as all the other jockeys did. He was immediately successful, but the New York racetracks were not the best environment for an ambitious jockey. Racing there had come under the influence of a criminal element, which the politicians were anxious to disperse. Doping, dishonesty and crooked bookies were rampant, to say nothing of the social problems that excessive gambling was bringing to ordinary families. In response, a law was introduced to ban racing in New York State. This turn of events inclined Sloan to look to Europe for his future. Towards the end of the 1897 flat season twenty-three-year-old Sloan began his racing career in England and had instant success. His style was new and

Owner Jane Samuel leads in a victorious *Captain Christy* and its thirty-seven-year-old jockey, reformed alcoholic Bobby Beasley, after winning the 1972 Sweeps Hurdle at Leopardstown. The veteran jockey described *Captain Christy* as the most brilliant jumper in training, but a little bit crazy! (*Topfoto*)

Mick O'Toole, trainer of *Dickens Hill* (Irish 2000 Guineas), *Davy Lad* (Cheltenham Gold Cup) and *Chinrullah* (Sweeps Hurdle) and of most winners in Ireland in 1971, serves the dearest breakfast on the Curragh—as Mike Dillon of Ladbrokes discovered to his cost! (*Sportsfile*)

Jockey Pat Eddery and trainer Vincent O'Brien had the worst day in their racing lives when *El Gran Señor* was beaten by *Secreto* in the 1984 Epsom Derby. The public blamed Eddery, and O'Brien was red-faced because he had declared the horse to be the best he had ever trained. The defeat meant a staggering $80 million bid went down the Swanee! (*Topfoto*)

Charlie McCreevy— racegoer, punter, racehorse owner, Kildare TD, government minister and now European Commissioner. (*Topfoto*)

'A dream come true' for Frankie Dettori after *Fujiyama Crest* won the last at Ascot on 28 September 1996, giving the jockey a clean sweep of all seven races on the card. It was a 'nightmare come true' for the bookies, who were hit for six no less than seven times—but they got over it. (*Empics*)

Winning trainer Michael Hourigan polishes the Hennessy Cognac Gold Cup, which was won by *Beef or Salmon* at Leopardstown in February 2006—yet another 'mouthwash' helping to clear the bad taste left by *Cushie King VI* many years before. (*Empics*)

Barney Curley, the 'wide sham' in the beige fedora, moaned that his £300,000 winnings on *Yellow Sam* all came in £1 notes. (*Getty*)

Dermot Weld, *Ansar* and jockey Paul Carberry after winning the 2001 Galway Hurdle. *Ansar* has won seven races at the Galway Festival meeting, including successive Galway Plates in 2004 and 2005. (*Inpho*)

John P. McManus from Co. Limerick, ubiquitous owner, fearless punter, tormentor of bookies—one who knows the odds. (*Inpho*)

Joe Walsh, the Turf Club's Chief Security Officer, escorts *Carrig Willy* and jockey T.A. Quinn back to the scales after winning the 1980 Sweeps Hurdle. Trainer Mick O'Toole was over the moon, but the result left Mike Dillon of Ladbrokes as sick as a parrot. (*Lensmen*)

Gentlemen on horseback clamour to bet among themselves in this picture dating from 1800. In those days ordinary people had to find a 'leg' to have a bet as the modern bookmaker did not yet exist. (*Hulton Archive/Getty*)

The Epsom betting ring on Derby Day 1874, swarming with loose bookies rambling all over the place, seeking bets. (*Hulton Archive/Getty*)

English street bookie Bill Beasley makes up his bets and counts his cash at home in 1949, while the law turned a 'blind eye' to what was an illegal practice. Off-course cash betting was legalised in Ireland in 1926, but British punters had to wait until 1961. (*Hulton Archive/Getty*)

A tic-tac man shows the Tattersalls Ring prices to the bookmakers betting on the Downs at Epsom in 1970. Faster than a walkie-talkie, tic-tac allowed the bookmakers chat silently to each other throughout the day without being overheard! (*Empics*)

unmistakable: riding short, with his knees up near his chin, sitting up at the horse's neck in the style of a modern jockey. The English racing fraternity laughed when they first saw Sloan perched up on the horse's neck, but the smiles were quickly wiped from their faces. Sloan swept all before him in the closing few weeks of the flat-racing season, riding twenty winners and fifteen places from just fifty-three mounts, and instilling a wholesome fear among the English jockeys. So successful was the American over the next couple of years that the off-course bookmakers introduced a special deduction of 5 per cent from the winnings on any horse ridden by him.

In 1898 Sloan secured a retainer from Lord William Beresford, who had realised that his instant success was no fluke. The retainer allowed him to settle in England permanently, which he now did, resuming where he had left off on the course. Sloan rode winner after winner, but his popularity with the public was not matched within the small racing fraternity. Feared by the English jockeys, disliked for his brash arrogance and his nationality, Sloan was insensitive to the resentment he was causing and did his case no favours by surrounding himself with a gallery of rogues and unde-sirables, who were betting heavily on his mounts. To make matters worse for Sloan, there followed hot on his heels into England a stream of refugees from the banned New York racetracks, present-ing stiff competition for the locals. These immigrants consisted of trainers, jockeys and a retinue of touts and hangers-on—some were good, most were bad and a few were downright nasty. All of them loved to bet and before long the immigrants were cleaning out British bookmakers as the rules of racing struggled to come to terms with a new threat. Doping to win replaced 'nobbling' as the biggest threat to the integrity of racing, and the foreigners were experts at it. Human nature being what it is, the natives threw up their hands in despair and shouted foul at every opportunity, overlooking the good innovations the Americans brought with them (before finally copying them): the Americans used light, aluminium racing places instead of the heavy English horseshoe, they stabled their horses in airy stables rather than the traditional English hot-houses and the jockeys had the proverbial 'clock in the head', enabling them to judge the pace of a race perfectly.

English owners, trainers, jockeys and bookmakers were screaming at the Jockey Club to take action against the Americans, accusing them of doping and fixing races. Although some undoubtedly were engaged in malpractice, the Americans were really a convenient scapegoat for the failures of English jockeys and horses. British horses, trainers and jockeys were the best in the world, according to themselves, but how could they compete against a pack of foreign dopers and cheats? The Jockey Club stewards were especially irritated by the gamblers and low-lifes that surrounded the American jockeys, by the encouragement given to the hangers-on through the dissemination of confidential information and by the rumours that the jockeys were betting and receiving financial presents from gamblers. The British were particularly riled at the idea of jockeys parting with stable secrets.

Sloan had the largest retinue, villains to a man, and they were all betting heavily and winning. Naturally, the stewards began to watch him like hawks. Aware of the substantial sums being bet on his mounts and fearful that it might compromise the integrity of racing, the stewards were alert for any sign of cheating or rule-breaking. Reports came to their attention which seemed to indicate that not only was Sloan betting but he was also receiving cash presents from people for tipping them winners. Jockeys were forbidden to bet and were not allowed to receive a present from any person, other than the owner of a horse they had ridden. The stewards bided their time, waiting for firm evidence and the right opportunity to pounce on Sloan. They did not have to wait very long.

Sloan and his entourage decided to go for a big coup on *Codoman* in the 1900 Cambridgeshire Handicap, which was run at Newmarket, the headquarters of the British Turf. The horse had been heavily supported in the ante-post market and it was evident that Sloan and his pals were going for a big touch at 14-to-1, but rumours began to circulate that other jockeys riding in the race were being intimidated. One man who took the rumours seriously was Irishman J.C. Sullivan, who had backed his own horse, *Berrill*, to win a tidy sum. Aware of Sloan's attempt to 'ready up' the race, Sullivan instructed his trainer, Philip Behan, to engage the best apprentice in Ireland to ride *Berrill* and to keep the rider's identity secret as long as possible. Behan choose nineteen-year-old John Thompson—famous afterwards as the first Irish jockey to ride in a style similar to Sloan—and kept both horse and rider well away from Newmarket until the last minute.

The afternoon of the race came and Sullivan and Behan would not let Thompson out of their sight, fearing Sloan would get to him with his threats. In the parade ring before the race, the Irish group stayed well away from the connections of *Codoman*, which was where Sloan would be, and made sure that young Thompson was the very last jockey to mount. They sent him to the start late and with a stern warning to keep well clear of Sloan, at all costs. Thompson arrived at the start as the runners circled round the Starter, who was taking the customary roll call. As the Starter called the roll, Sloan and Thompson played hide-and-seek as the latter weaved in and out between the other twenty-two horses, successfully evading the American. Thompson did as he was instructed and jumped off in front, where he was safe from inter-ference by Sloan or other jockeys in on his coup. The tactics worked. *Berrill* was never headed and beat *Codoman*, and a furious Tod Sloan, into second place. Throughout the closing stages of the race, the Irish apprentice could clearly hear Sloan's abuse and threats from behind, ordering him to pull his mount so that *Codoman* would win.

As Thompson silently made his way to the weigh-room, a livid Sloan was right behind him and could not contain his fury. In the passion of his rage, which was building to a crescendo, the American jockey forgot himself completely and was still reeling off a tirade of abuse and threats as Thompson sat on the scales to weigh-in, now within earshot of the stewards. This was the perfect opportunity to bring the cocky American jockey to heel, but the stewards decided to wait twenty-four hours before calling Sloan before them. The following day Tod Sloan stood before the Newmarket stewards, brash, cocky and full of confidence, not realising that he was in serious trouble. The stewards informed Sloan that they had information confirming that he had placed a number of big bets on *Codoman*, as well as being promised a cash present by a certain gentleman if the horse won. They reminded him that jockeys were forbidden to bet and to accept presents from persons other than the owner of the horse. Sloan admitted the offences, but pleaded ignorance of the rules because he was used to the American system, where jockeys were allowed to bet on their own mounts. He also admitted that Frank Gardner had promised him a cash gift running into four figures if *Codoman* won the race, but again stated that he was unaware of breaking any rule. Having heard Sloan's explanation the stewards repri-manded him severely and the jockey left the room without a care in the world. He rode three more winners at that Newmarket meeting, and then rode a two-year-old named *Encombe* to victory by a head to record his 254th winner in England from 812 mounts. Little did poor Tod realise, or anybody else for that matter, that it was his last winner!

Although the flat-racing season dragged on into November, Sloan had always intended to return home after that Newmarket October meeting for a well-earned rest. Before he left England he accepted a retainer to ride the horses of the Prince of Wales in 1901, a prestigious post that sent Sloan to the very top of his profession. He made arrangements to return in the spring as the Royal jockey, and then boarded a ship for his homeland.

During his holiday, Sloan was casually reading an American newspaper when a paragraph caught his eye: '... the English Jockey Club had announced that J.F. Sloan had been advised not to apply for a licence to ride for the coming season.' Besides preventing him from riding in England, the ban was certain to be applied by the governing bodies of all the racing nations, putting him out of work. Sloan was shocked and bewildered: this was the first he had heard of any ban. He had admitted to the stewards that he placed bets on his own mounts, but had strongly denied ever stopping a horse, arguing that he wanted to win too much. Sloan had also denied abusing John Thompson after *Codoman*'s defeat at Newmarket, but with their own eyes and ears the stewards had witnessed him doing just that. As he wrote fifteen years later:

My one and only Turf misdemeanour was betting—nothing else during my whole career. I admitted this to the stewards in 1900. I have not retracted in these pages, but I have repented that I was ever such a fool. It cut me off at the age of twenty-five. Having 'done' fifteen years I can only pray that some day, in a spirit of clemency, that mercy will be shown to a transgressor—who would never transgress again, even to the extent of a fiver.

(*Tod Sloan by Himself*: London, Grant Richards, 1915)

Tod Sloan may have been glossing over the full extent of his 'betting misdemeanours', which were more serious than mere betting, but he cannot have imagined that he was finished for life. But he was. He was never again granted a licence to ride, despite repeated requests to the Jockey Club for a pardon. Certainly, Sloan did threaten and abuse Thompson and did attempt to induce jockeys and owners to stop their horses to allow *Codoman* to win the race. It was also common knowledge that he was a heavy gambler who would bet on anything and that he surrounded himself with gamblers, many of whom had no visible means of support. However, even accepting that Tod Sloan was no angel and corruption engendered by the American invasion had to be stamped out, the life sentence he received from the Jockey Club was savage. It is hard to escape the conclusion that the stewards were unduly hard on Sloan because of his arrogance and nationality and their own self-righteousness and prejudice, which shut out all feelings of mercy. It is interesting to note that Fred Rickaby, a leading English rider of that period, had his licence withdrawn in a similar manner in 1902 for 'having associated with persons of bad character', but in his case the ban was lifted after three years. There was no mercy for Sloan. The jockey was never given another chance, and a great talent was lost forever. In spite of his repentance, the loss of his licence did not stop Sloan's gambling habit, unfortunately. He carried on until he was caught running an illegal gaming house in London in 1915 and was deported by the authorities as an undesirable alien.

The *Mitigate* Mystery

Back in 1954 racecourse gossip was full of accusations that *Mitigate*, the runaway six-length winner of the Irish Lincolnshire Handicap at the Curragh, was not that horse at all. In other words, a 'ringer' was said to have turned out in its place. A winner of three races at two years old, including the Birdcatcher Nursery at Naas over five and six furlongs, *Mitigate* flopped on its three-year-old debut over seven furlongs at Baldoyle on St Patrick's Day, but improved considerably on this run while landing some nice bets as it won the Irish Lincolnshire over a mile. The Curragh stewards hauled trainer Brud Fetherstonhaugh and jockey Bert Holmes before them, seeking an explanation for *Mitigate*'s dramatic return in form. The trainer blamed himself, stating that with the ground so wet he had not given the horse enough work, which error he had only discovered when it ran badly at Baldoyle. During the twenty-day interval between the races he had rectified this, hence the improvement in the horse's form.

The stewards accepted the explanation, but people in the betting business remained suspicious. *Mitigate*'s subsequent form only served to add grist to the rumour mill concerning the possible use of a ringer. Pulled out twice over a mile at Royal Ascot, *Mitigate* got well and truly turned over on both occasions, appearing not to get the trip and failing to even reach a place in three subsequent races in Ireland. The following year it was the same old story: not mapped in a repeat attempt in the Irish Lincolnshire before a flop in a Leopardstown Handicap brought down the curtain on its career. With the exception of that scintillating performance at the Curragh, *Mitigate* did not train on after a good two-year-old season, indicating that the rumours about a switch of horses in the Irish Lincolnshire might have had substance to them. We shall never know, but some of us will continue to wonder ...!

The Fabulous Four and the Dead One

About twenty-five years ago a gentleman with bookmaking connections got news of a non-trier at Galway: the horse would not win, and if the horse managed, by some fluke, to get into a position from which it might possibly win, the jockey would jump off. The horse was not going to win the race—that much was sure. Armed with this information, our gentleman set about profiting from it. If he had stopped to think about it, he might have wondered how much a jockey's life was worth. What did he consider to be the going rate for a jockey to risk his life and limb by jumping off a horse travelling at nearly forty miles per hour and falling on ground as hard as concrete, amid a *mêlée* of flying hooves? But he didn't think about it, he didn't consider that at all—he had a 'dead one' and was determined to exploit it.

Our friend recruited four bookmakers to collect the money but, for obvious reasons, they must remain anonymous, so I will call them by the fictitious names of Robert, Mark, Bob and Billy. The four were betting in pitches that were placed strategically on different lines in the betting ring, their job being to get as much money as they could out of this 'dead' favourite, no matter what price had to be offered in order to attract bets. Recruiting bookmakers was not as simple as it sounds; many bookmakers refused to have anything to do with the plot, particularly as they could not be told any details about the coup. Nonetheless, four bookmakers did give in to temptation and agreed to participate.

The 'dead one' in question turned out to be a horse named *Bay God*, which was running in a flat handicap on the day *O'Leary* won the Galway Plate for the legendary trainer Paddy Sleator and his stable jockey, Bobby Coonan. *Bay God* opened a warm favourite at 6-to-4, but the 'fabulous four' promptly offered 2-to-1, taking money on the horse as fast as their clerks could book the bets. Never doubting for a moment that *Bay God* would be beaten, the four filled their satchels, oblivious to the fact that there was a fortune for the horse. As far as they were concerned, there was no issue: *Bay God* had no earthly chance of winning because its trainer, Paul Doyle, could not 'train ivy up a wall' while the jockey, J.V. Smith, 'couldn't ride a bike'. In their smug delight at their coup, they managed to overlook some important facts: on paper, *Bay God* had a right chance, having been placed in each of its three races since winning at Limerick, all of which were a higher class of race than the one in which it was now running. They allowed their judgment to be clouded by the promise of cash, a fatal error for any bookmaker.

The sheer volume of money for *Bay God* forced its price to contract to 7-to-4, only to be pushed out to 2-to-1 again as the 'fabulous four' took on all-comers. At the off the four were still offering the best price in the Ring with 9-to-4 against *Bay God*, but the SP reporters had to return the horse at 7-to-4 because that was the general price on offer; four individual bookmakers cannot determine the SP return. Poor Robert, Mark, Bob and Billy: what mugs they were! *Bay God* was nearer to being a certainty than a 'dead one'. Despite being badly hampered when the early leader dropped back rapidly, *Bay God* recovered the lost ground to hit the front inside the final furlong ... and won! Not only did the horse win, it won by one-and-a-half lengths. The four bookmakers were shell-shocked, and now faced a bumper pay out with insufficient cash and punters baying for their winnings. Other bookmakers loaned them money so they could pay the punters, and the Racing Board also helped by cashing cheques, while some winners agreed to wait for their money. It was somewhat ironic that the kindness and honesty of colleagues and punters helped them out of a mess created by their cynicism and dishonesty.

It was a terrible shambles altogether and the 'fabulous four' paid a very high price for their involvement. Robert dropped dead some months later, killed by a combination of the shock of the result and the subsequent financial problems it brought on him. Bob never made a book again, vanishing out of the business and leaving behind a trail of bounced cheques, outstanding loans and unpaid bets. Billy also packed in the bookmaking business but, unlike Bob, honoured every cheque, every loan and every bet. Mark, the smallest bookmaker of the four, sold some of his pitch positions in order to stay in business, which he did in a very small way for some years afterwards. Before his death, which occurred a few years ago, he told me that *Bay God* had broken his heart, destroyed his business and cleaned him out so badly that he never again returned to Galway.

The Ultimate Dead One

The best 'dead one' I ever witnessed ran some years ago in the last race at the pleasant Kilbeggan course in Co. Westmeath. One bookmaker appeared to know that the short-priced favourite would not win. Although not one of the big layers, this bookie was offering higher odds against the favourite than anyone else, which in itself was not particularly revealing at first because the horse was very easy in the market. What did arouse suspicion was that he priced only one horse in the race, went the biggest price in the Ring and whenever another bookie matched his price, immediately put up a bigger one. He would only have got about a few hundred pounds out of the horse—Kilbeggan punters are generally modest 'bettors'—but it was a nice little touch just the same.

Once the race got underway, so confident were the bookie and his clerk that the horse would not win that they began to dismantle the joint. By the time the field passed the stand with a circuit to race, the pair were ready to leave. In order to exit Kilbeggan racecourse, one must cross the course, which is of course barred by stewards while racing is in progress, so the pair walked down to the barrier and waited for the horses to pass. From that vantage point, about 100 yards from the winning post, they watched the favourite get well and truly stuffed. As the winner was pulling up, I could see the bookmaker heading into the car park for a quick exit before the traffic.

'Nice one!' you might say, but believe it or not it did that book-maker no good at all. In my experience those bookmakers and punters who depend on strokes never seem to prosper in the end. That bookmaker has long since gone out of business, having given back the ill-gotten gains many times over.

The same can be said of the three bookmakers who had the dead one in Naas, which resulted in a full-scale enquiry by the Turf Club. The first inkling I had that something was up was when the bookmaker beside me was going to war trying to lay a certain horse. When his clerk silently gestured to me with a finger stroked across his throat, it was clear that the horse was 'dead'. It certainly was and it duly got beaten. However, members of the Racing Board staff got wind that something odd was going on and before the race began reported to the stewards that the betting trends indicated the horse was not going to win. The three bookmakers got away with the spoils, but the owner, trainer and rider of the horse had many anxious weeks as the enquiry continued before eventually being let off due to lack of evidence.

The Importance of Keeping One's Wits

People are always on the lookout for easy money if they can get it, and one particular trainer found a very satisfactory way to make training pay. This trainer, who flourished in the 1970s, syndicated horses when the practise was in its infancy. However, he did it with a twist, secretly selling a number of half-shares in the same horse to different people, while retaining a half-share himself. All these horses ran in the name and colours of the trainer and all was well so long as these horses were no good. Unfortunately, one of them won unexpectedly at long odds one evening at Limerick Junction, exposing the scam. With a dozen people all claiming to be the owner jostling for position around the winner in the enclosure, it was clear something was wrong. The trainer had disappeared, but the scam was exposed. To this day that ex-trainer is probably still scratching his head wondering, how on earth did that horse win?

It does serve to show just how naïve owners can be. I have always said that rich men lose their marbles when they come into racing, which is amazing because they are obviously smart enough to succeed in their own way of business. For some reason, when they get involved in racing they all too frequently become lambs, ready to be fleeced, and mostly through their own stupidity. I recall one particular owner who had spent an awful lot of money on a filly, albeit a well-bred one, from which he intended to breed in due course. It was important that the filly win a race, as that would make her infinitely more valuable as a broodmare, but she was finding this very difficult to do, despite running well. There was always an excuse: the ground was too firm; the ground was too soft; the filly needed more time; the distance was wrong; and so on. The owner had no idea whether he should persevere with racing her, or to retire her to stud. His friends advised him to engage the jockey Nicky Brennan to ride the mare and give his opinion. Brennan had a reputation of being a good judge of a horse he had ridden and of giving an honest opinion to an owner. The owner agreed to try this avenue and Brennan was given the ride. When he dismounted, the filly having finished a moderate fifth, he did not reel out another excuse. He told the owner the truth: 'She is no use, Sir, don't persevere with her.' The doting owner was dismayed and annoyed by the jockey's candid comments, disregarded the advice and afterwards bad-mouthed Brennan at every opportunity. No wonder jockeys only tell owners what they want to hear!

Hitting the Mark

Here is some anecdotal evidence to illustrate the lengths people will go to in the name of winning—and how hit and miss their tactics can prove to be! One such incident took place at a 'flap', that is a pony race meeting not run under the rules of racing. A punter put £100 on a pony with a bookie I knew well. I would not have expected him to accept such a large wager at a flapping meeting, nor would he have done so save that he knew he could get the pony stopped for £25. The money was despatched to the owner, who instructed his young jockey to pull his mount and stop it from winning. Twenty-five quid in the hand was worth a lot more than the £5 prize, and it was accepted eagerly. The race was run, the pony was beaten and the punter had no idea what had happened. He ought to have been wary, though: in attempting to make a big hit, he left himself wide open to an underhanded retort—his bet was simply too big for the game.

One desperate, stony broke punter decided to give the horse he fancied in a race some assistance. After backing the horse in the betting ring, the punter took up a position by the rail in the Silver Ring enclosure, about two furlongs from the finish. He reached into his bag and pulled out a pellet gun he had stashed there and prepared to give his horse a little gee-up on its way past. He took a pot shot at the horse's rear as it raced past ... and missed. Obviously the poor chap could not hit winners, not even with a pellet gun: the missile missed the intended horse and struck one of the rank outsiders instead. The idea was a good one though, as evidenced by the fact that the struck horse took off like a rocket, galloped past the leaders and won the race! The jockey knew something had happened, that the horse had reacted to some outside force, and an examination after the race discovered the pellet wound in its rear. It's a small story, but it has a number of morals!

Ring-fencing the Ringer

A recent exposé of the use of a ringer concerned a race run at Leicester on 29 March 1982, when a two-year-old named *Flockton Grey*, trained by Stephen Wiles and ridden by Kevin Darley, won a race over five furlongs by an incredible twenty lengths at odds of 10-to-1. Its owner, a millionaire businessman named Ken Richardson, was believed to have collected only £36,000 out of the £250,000 in winnings due to him, the remainder being withheld by the bookmakers pending an investigation. It was the manner of *Flockton Grey*'s victory, rather than the gamble, that made the bookmakers suspicious because the horse had won like a champion two-year-old. On investigation it was discovered that a substantial gamble on the horse had taken place in the North of England. Following complaints by the bookmakers, the Jockey Club asked their security man, George Edmondson, to make enquiries and he later passed the case over to the Humberside fraud squad.

By that time Edmondson had uncovered enough evidence to expose the use of a ringer: *Flockton Grey* was not the horse that ran that day; an older horse, a three-year-old named *Good Hand*, had run in its place. A barrister in the subsequent law case described this 'as a sixth-former running against a class of eleven-year-old schoolboys'. Four months after the race the stewards disqualified *Flockton Grey* on the grounds that it had not been under the care of its trainer, Stephen Wiles, who trained at Flockton, near Wakefield, for the stipulated period of fourteen days immediately preceding the race. The trainer had given evidence that *Flockton Grey* had never been in his stable, the horse having been driven to Leicester racecourse by Peter Boddy, who also took it away immediately after the race. It was left to the police to prove the case of fraud.

It transpired that a man named Colin Mathison, a close friend of Ken Richardson, had claimed a grey horse named *Good Hand* after it had finished fourth in a two-year-old selling race at Ripon on 15 August 1981. *Good Hand* was a grey horse, similar to *Flockton Grey* but a year older, and it was alleged that this was the horse that ran at Leicester. Charges were brought against Ken Richardson and in June 1984 a jury convicted him of conspiring to defraud bookmakers. Richardson was fined £20,000, received a suspended nine-month jail sentence and ordered to pay £100,000 towards the cost of the prosecution. His accomplices, Colin Mathison and Peter Boddy, also appeared in court. The former was fined £3,000, while Boddy received a conditional discharge but was ordered to pay £2,000 towards the costs of the case.

Once the court proceedings were complete, Ken Richardson was brought before the Jockey Club and warned-off the Turf for twenty-five years; Colin Mathison was banned for fifteen years; Peter Boddy was disqualified for three years.

However, Richardson discovered that the police had not produced some photographs at the trial and briefed his lawyers to appeal the case to the Home Office on the grounds that this fact made the conviction unsafe, unsatisfactory and wrong. The photographs were of *Good Hand* and showed clearly that the horse had a large white star on its forehead, whereas the photographs taken of *Flockton Grey* at Leicester showed no sign of this distinctive white marking. Home Secretary Michael Howard rejected the appeal in 1993, but three years later Richardson obtained permission to seek a judicial review of Howard's decision. This time Michael Howard agreed the case should be referred back to the Court of Appeal.

After a three-day hearing the case finally ended on 5 December 1996, fourteen years and 251 days after the race had been run, with the Court of Appeal rejecting the appeals lodged by Ken Richardson, Colin Mathison and Peter Boddy. Richardson's defence had been that the horse that won at Leicester was not *Good Hand* but a similar-looking grey horse that was totally unconnected with him or his associates. The three appeal judges held that the evidence supporting the contention that *Good Hand* was the winner was very strong. Justice Poole stated: 'Any other conclusion would mean that somewhere, untraced, is yet another unknown grey with an identical leg scar. Such a conclusion beggars belief.' Lord Justice Rose stated that the non-disclosure of the photographs had not affected the safety of the convictions. He went on to say that only two other greys with a scar on the right off-foreleg were registered with Weatherbys, the keepers of the *General Stud Book*, and neither could have been racing at Leicester on the day in question.

In keeping with good practice in such cases, *Good Hand* disappeared after the race but was discovered by police eight months later in a Yorkshire field, alive but in a poor state. *Flockton Grey* was useless as a racehorse and never ran again, although he was schooled as a steeplechaser. Now virtually white in colour, the contested horse lives in retirement with Sharon Dick in the village of Wales, near Sheffield.

God saves the Bookies from the Half-Bred King

Even in this modern age, when every horse has a passport with details of its markings and confirming its identity by blood test, horses can occasionally get mixed up. This confusion can happen by accident or by design, or sometimes by a bit of both!

In 1990 *Passer By*, a thoroughbred bay gelding by *Lomond* owned by Sir Anthony O'Reilly and trained by Vincent O'Brien, was good enough to win three flat races as a three-year-old. At the end of that season Sir Anthony O'Reilly transferred the horse to the stable of Michael 'Mouse' Morris for a jumping career, which started well enough with a win at a maiden hurdle in Killarney in 1991. Next time out it put up a tame performance when a well-backed odds-on favourite at Bellewstown, so was then tried in blinkers, but again flopped in a valuable hurdle at Killarney. Sir Anthony O'Reilly was not interested in keeping lowly handicap hurdlers in training, particularly those with leg problems, so *Passer By* was sold off and quickly forgotten by the racing community.

During the summer of 1994 Co. Limerick trainer Michael Hourigan was asked to train a gelding of uncertain pedigree, which in racing parlance is called a half-bred horse. The trainer was told that this young horse was showing some ability and the owners wanted to use it to land a big gamble. Although Hourigan did not know the owners, he agreed to train it; after all, it was summer time, a quiet time in a jumping stable. The trainer had no reason to be suspicious as the horse, officially named *Cushie*

King VI, had a valid passport and all the documentation appeared to be in order. *Cushie King VI*'s pedigree could not be traced back according to the rules of the *General Stud Book,* so it could not be registered in that publication. Neither had it been registered in the *Register of Half-Bred Horses*, so the owner had to apply to the Turf Club to have it named for racing. Horses named in such a manner are allowed to race in Ireland only, they cannot run abroad, and are distinguished by the suffix 'VI'. Usually horses in this category turn out to be rather slow hunters, although the vast majority of them are actually thoroughbreds or had a lot of pure blood, being usually bred out of unregistered stock or from horses of uncertain parentage. *Cushie King VI* was registered as a bay gelding, foaled in 1988 by *Euphemism* out of a mare by *On Your Mark*, whose pedigree was untraced but which had the look of a racehorse and its work indicated that it had a bit of ability.

Hourigan, who had started out with Charlie Weld, was one of the lesser-known jockeys on the Irish circuit before taking out a licence to train in 1973. In the early years Michael found it difficult to get horses to train because he had not ridden winners for the wealthy owners who dominate racing, and was therefore forced to combine his training operation with running a pub in Rathkeele. It was not until St Patrick's Day 1979 that he trained his first winner, *Ramrayja*, but it was the break he needed and within three years his name was fourth position in the list of leading Irish National Hunt trainers. Hourigan's success with *Deep Bramble*, winner of the Kerry National and the Ericsson Chase during the autumn and winter of 1993, confirmed that he had the ability to train top jumping horses. This talent was incontrovertibly proven a couple of years later when he trained the popular top-class chasers *Doran's Pride* and *Beef or Salmon.*

When he agreed to train *Cushie King VI*, Michael Hourigan made one mistake: he was inveigled to run the horse in his own name even though he did not own the horse or have a share in it. This was a deliberate ploy by those who knew the real identity of the horse, but was also a technical breach of the rules and it was to cost Michael a lot of money afterwards. The owner of *Cushie King VI* wanted the horse to win at one of the Northern racecourses,

Down Royal or Downpatrick, and was very confident of taking every penny out of the bookmakers' satchels when it did win so. The horse was working well as far as Michael was concerned and was ready to win first time out, but the owner wanted *Cushie King VI* to have a quiet run before the planned coup. A maiden hurdle at Dundalk was selected for this purpose. Perhaps Michael should have been a bit suspicious about the reclusive owner and his speedy, precocious half-bred, but he wasn't. Unfortunately, he never got round to considering how he came to get such a good horse without any effort on his part; his mother was dying at the time so he had more serious matters on his mind.

Making its racecourse debut at Dundalk on Thursday, 15 September 1994, unconsidered and unfancied, *Cushie King VI* was up against a good horse named *Divinity Run*, who was the medium of a big gamble. Hourigan did not attend the meeting, remaining by his mother's bedside instead, but he instructed jockey Kevin O'Brien not to hit the horse or to knock him about, but to win if he were able. As it turned out, *Cushie King VI* caused a big upset by beating *Divinity Run* by a neck, much to the annoyance of its owner, who was surprised and disappointed. Kevin O'Brien was impressed with the horse, reporting back to the trainer that *Cushie King VI* had 'blown up' but, in the manner of an experienced or a talented racehorse, managed to get a second wind to run on again and win.

A fortnight later *Cushie King VI* was back in action and fancied to win a handicap hurdle at Downpatrick—the race that had been earmarked for the big coup. Its Dundalk victory scuppered all hopes of a big price and *Cushie King VI* started the 5-to-4 favourite, but was disappointingly beaten into second place, O'Brien explaining that the horse refused to go on when asked. This behaviour indicated that the horse was a 'jade', meaning a worn-out horse rather than one at the start of its career, and in hindsight this was a clue to the fact that all was not as it appeared.

Mrs Hourigan died on 5 October 1994, and shortly afterwards Michael received a phone call from a man he knew who informed him that the horse he was training under the name *Cushie King VI* was actually *Passer By* and had previously raced under that name.

Alarmed by the implications, Michael Hourigan immediately tele-phoned Michael Keogh of the Turf Club and requested an urgent meeting, which was arranged for the following day. When he met Keogh, the trainer reported to him: 'I have won a race with a ringer!' Michael Hourigan told the story of how he had got the horse, invited the Turf Club to blood-test *Cushie King VI*, which was in his yard, and offered his full co-operation. The stewards held an enquiry into the identity of the horse, found it to be *Passer By*, which had been re-registered improperly under a different name, disqualified the horse from its races at Dundalk and Downpatrick and warned off its owner, P.J. Tynan. Michael Hourigan was exonerated from any wrongdoing and the case was officially closed.

But the nightmare was only beginning for Michael Hourigan. Stripped of all its winnings, *Cushie King VI* was eating its head off in the yard while no training fees were being paid. The person who had given Michael the horse to train claimed to have no money to pay the bills, but said Michael could keep the horse in lieu. This offer was accepted, but another problem arose when three people turned up at the yard claiming to be the owners of *Passer By*, but refused to accept any responsibility for the bills. A wrangle over the ownership of the horse and liability for the training fees devel-oped, agreement could not be reached and the three went to court to recover the horse.

When the case was called up, the Turf Club and Michael Hourigan had to appear in Birr Court, in Co. Offaly. *Passer By* was still in Hourigan's yard, nobody was paying the bills, a substantial account had run up and it was rising by the day. The judge declared *Passer By* to be the property of the three who had claimed it and dismissed the case against the Turf Club. However, he refused to accept that Michael Hourigan was a completely inno-cent party because *Cushie King VI* had run in his name. As a result, he refused to give an order for the cost of the accrued training and keep bills and ordered Michael Hourigan to pay the costs of the court case if the man who had claimed to own *Cushie King VI* failed to do so. Needless to say the purported owner did not come up with the money, leaving Michael to deal with a legal bill for

£15,000, as well as being left to whistle for his training fees! It left a sour taste in his mouth, but fortunately *Doran's Pride* emerged as a refreshing mouthwash and lifted the trainer into an infinitely brighter and more pleasant limelight.

Passer By, reunited with its real name and its rightful owners, emerged in the 1996 point-to-point season, winning a race at North Tipperary when owned by Bernie Owens of Mullingar, trained in Kildare by Peter McCreery and ridden by Mr Richard Keogh.

PART 5
THE CONTROVERSIES

'Live in the best society yourself, but always run your horses in the worst, unless they are very good ones.'

CAPTAIN J.O. MACHELL

Steeplechasing: the early days

Of all the racehorse owners I have come across during my study of the history of racing the one I most admire is Lord Glasgow, a man who famously found it both difficult and tiresome to think up names for his many racing horses. As a result, some of his runners sported ridiculous names, such as *I Have A Name Now, Give Him A Name*, or *He Is Not Worth A Name*. But at least they were original in an age when the naming of horses led to confusion and deliberate abuse of the system. Worse still, horses were permitted to race unnamed!

The spectacular growth and popularity of steeplechasing during the first half of the nineteenth century was surprising because that particular code of horse-racing was completely un-supervised. The Jockey Club issued licences for flat and hurdle racing, but had no rules to cover steeplechasing. It was carried on with only basic rules regarding foul riding and carrying correct weights. Local people were appointed to act as stewards for the day, but their only disciplinary power was the ability to disqualify a horse; they could not suspend or fine a rider. Lacking a body to supervise the identification and naming of horses, the conduct of jockeys or the registration of ownership, confusion reigned and this situation was exploited by unscrupulous persons as a mask to conceal deliberate malpractice, giving wrongdoers the freedom to do virtually as they pleased. Scandals, coups and suspicious incidents abounded, the public were being ripped off and steeple-chasing was dubbed the 'illegitimate sport' by the press.

'Something should be done about it' was the catchphrase of the time, but nobody did anything until a newspaper, *Bell's Life*, took the initiative in November 1862 and published a list of forty-one rules under the heading of 'Steeplechase Reform'. The publication of these rules encouraged the Jockey Club stalwart Admiral Rous to get involved, that great reformer of flat-racing and the greatest authority of the day on the rules of racing. Worried that the free-for-all in jumping might have implications for the integrity of flat and hurdle racing, the Admiral gave the paper's campaign a big lift by intervening with suggestions to improve those basic rules. The Admiral's updates and additions were published as an appendix to

Weatherby's Racing Calendar, and his influence led to the establishment in 1866 of a committee to enforce the new rules. The National Hunt Steeplechase Committee worked in co-operation with the Jockey Club, which gave it full control of hurdle-racing as well. These developments in England led to a list of steeplechase rules being included in the 1866 *Irish Racing Calendar* and a similar body, the Irish National Hunt Steeplechase Committee, was established in 1870 to enforce them.

The scandals that caused public outcry usually cropped up in the big betting events, such as the Aintree Grand National. The race was founded in 1837, although the racecourse, for some stupid reason, refuses to recognise the first two winners, *The Duke* and *Sir William*. The latter was bred in Ireland by William Battersby and won the big race in the 'yellow, ruby buttons & cap' of Allen McDonogh, who owned, trained and rode the eight-year-old to a thrilling victory. *Sir William* was probably fortunate that *Lottery*, the greatest chaser in England, missed the 1838 Grand National, preferring to run in the St Alban's Steeplechase, in which he was sensationally beaten. Allen McDonogh had a high opinion of *Lottery*, describing it as 'the best horse in the world, for he could trot faster than any of the rest of us could gallop'. Others thought the same because the horse was excluded from a meeting at Horncastle, where the conditions were advertised as 'open to all horses except *Lottery*.' *Lottery* came to Liverpool in 1839 and won the Grand National with James 'Jem' Mason in the saddle. During the race *Lottery* and Mason sailed over Captain Martin Becher's head, who was sitting in the water as they cleared the brook on their way to a long since forgotten victory. Mason is unknown nowadays, unlike the Captain, who never actually rode a winner of the Grand National but whose ducking in the brook christened it 'Becher's'. *Lottery* returned to defend his crown in 1840, but was used in an unsavoury incident of public deception.

John Elmore, the owner of *Lottery*, also owned another useful steeplechaser named *Jerry*, on whom Jem Mason had won the Leamington Steeplechase. Both horses were set to run in the Grand National and Mason took the mount on *Lottery*, which was a significant pointer to the respective chances of the two horses.

The punters followed the clue, backing *Lottery* heavily. When the jockeys emerged from the weigh-room and walked to the paddock, there was considerable surprise when Mr B. Bretherton, the man who replaced Mason on *Jerry*, was clad in the colours of a Norfolk squire named Mr Villibois, rather than in those of Mr Elmore. Rumours started to fly and the talk was that *Jerry* was in fact owned by Lord Sheffield. The confusion over the ownership of *Jerry*, coupled with the suspicion that Mr Elmore still owned the horse and had decided to win with it, caused *Lottery*'s price to drift alarmingly and suddenly there was a new favourite, *The Nun*, on whom, the previous year, Allen McDonogh had remounted to finish fifth.

Six of the thirteen runners were Irish, one of those being *Valentine*, ridden by his owner, John Power of Gurteen, Clonmel. Apparently, Power had struck a large bet that he would lead the field over the stone wall and he blazed off in front at such a fast gallop that only *Lottery* had the pace to go with him. By the time they reached the canal turn on the first circuit, *Valentine* had got away, establishing a clear lead as his rider raced to the wall. *Valentine* made a dreadful blunder at the brook, however, but Johnny Power made such a spectacular recovery that this part of the brook has been known as 'Valentine's' ever since. The jumping error allowed *Lottery* to get on terms with *Valentine* and a battle royal followed to the wall, which Mr Power was determined to reach first. For some unknown reason, Mason was equally determined to thwart him and the pair rode like demons as they faced up to the obstacle neck and neck. It looked as if a judge would be needed to determine the fate of the wager, but whereas the pair took off to jump the wall together, *Valentine* cleared the wall with a brilliant leap while *Lottery* hit the top of it and fell, bringing down *The Nun* and two others with him and leaving only five horses standing with another circuit to race.

Valentine battled on bravely, but *Jerry* was lying in wait and used its reserves of stamina to win the race easily. The general public felt cheated: *Lottery* seemed to have been ridden into the ground, and the integrity of steeplechasing received another blow. While some of the public mistrust that surrounded the sport was due to the confusion caused by a lack of regulation, this incident ensured the persistence of the public impression of steeplechasing as a sport in the grip of rogues intent on robbing the punters.

A Coterie of *Peter Simples*

The naming of horses running in steeplechases was haphazard to say the least. For example, during the early 1850s there were no less than three horses named *Peter Simple* running together in the big races. All three were half-breds—in other words not eligible for inclusion in the *General Stud Book*, the official register of thoroughbred horses—but, in addition, five thoroughbred *Peter Simples* were foaled between 1831 and 1859. Of the three steeplechase horses named *Peter Simple*, one was a grey horse by *Arbutus*, foaled in 1834; the second was a bay gelding by *Patron*, foaled in 1838; and the third was another bay gelding by *Patron*, whose year of birth is uncertain. The grey *Peter Simple* ran in the Grand National without winning it, easily identified by its colour, but Turf historians have concluded that only one of the two bay-coloured *Peter Simples* ever ran in the race. The bay *Peter Simple* is recorded as the second horse to win the Grand National twice, but some informed sources refused to accept that the *Peter Simple* that won the race in 1849 was the same *Peter Simple* that was successful in 1853. Few historians have bothered to wade through the inaccurate statistics and flimsy evidence that still exists from those far-off days, usually being satisfied with a press report that states that the 1853 winner had won the race previously.

The grey *Peter Simple*, easily the best horse of the three, first ran in the Grand National in 1841, carried top weight twice, started favourite once and was placed three times. A popular chaser in the English Midlands, the grey *Peter Simple* tended to run rather free and made his last appearance in the race when a twelve-year-old, in 1846. Meanwhile the bay *Peter Simple*, owned by Finch Mason and ridden by Tom Cunningham, won the Grand National three years later, on his first attempt. Cunningham, who also trained the horse at his stable in Beverley, Yorkshire, had a son who told the prolific racing writer John Fairfax-Blakeborough that this *Peter Simple* was not the same horse that won the race in 1853. This information tends to be dismissed nowadays, but in my opinion a close inspection of the records seems to support his contention.

In six outings in the Grand National between 1848 and 1854, the bay *Peter Simple* (assuming it is the same horse) ran in the name of five different owners and was ridden by five different jockeys. We do know that *Peter Simple* was an eleven-year-old when it won the race in 1849; we also know that it started favourite the following year, was a neglected 33-to-1 shot in 1851 and in 1852 was unconsidered in the betting, priced at odds in excess of 100-to-1. Yet the 1853 winner named *Peter Simple* started well fancied at 9-to-1! How could a real no-hoper, who had failed to finish in each of the previous three years, suddenly become a live fancy when past its best at the age of fifteen? This anomaly has been accepted on the basis that the going was heavy in 1853, conditions which suited the *Peter Simple* that won in 1849, but then how can it be explained that its SP the following year, when it was a geriatric sixteen-year-old, was just 12-to-1 on going that was good? Is it not more likely that a different *Peter Simple* ran in 1853 and again in 1854? Finch Mason sold his *Peter Simple* two days before the 1850 Grand National was run, but two of his horses, *Miss Mowbray* and *Oscar*, finished second and third to *Peter Simple* in 1853. Surely if *Miss Mowbray*, winner of the race in 1852, and *Oscar* had been beaten by one of his cast-offs, Mason would have mentioned it in his book, *Heroes and Heroines of the Grand National*?

The Question of the Whip
Tod Sloan's success with the 'forward seat', his innovative riding position, ensured it would be adopted by jockeys everywhere because it helped horses to run faster, although nobody at the time understood why. Modern science has subsequently proven that when a horse carries a weight, the place where that weight will affect the horse least is over its centre of gravity, in other words, on its withers, which is just at the base of its neck. That is exactly where Sloan crouched during a race, up the horse's neck, plumb over its centre of gravity, which not only distributed his weight correctly but also allowed better streamlining and less wind resistance.

Once the merits of the 'forward seat' became clear, all flat jockeys altered their style of riding virtually overnight and stirrups became shorter and shorter down the years. Naturally, jockeys who rode over jumps were keen to try to adapt the forward seat to their code and their stirrups too got shorter, but the general adoption of the new seat in jump-racing was a much slower process. The jump jockey was forced to compromise on the matter of streamlining because there was no point being perfectly streamlined if you are going to be sent whistling over your mount's head at the slightest jumping blunder. But even given that, in the jumping game jockeys now ride very short, and while it does produce more winners, it also increases the risk of being unseated and sustaining collarbone injuries.

The main drawback of the modern seat is that a jockey does not have the full use of his legs to squeeze, kick and encourage the horse to run faster, and the easy option is to rely on the whip instead. As stirrups got shorter, the whips got longer and more and more jockeys used it more and more. A 'win at all costs' mentality was creeping into racing, with owners demanding that jockeys give their horse plenty of stick to guarantee victory. The 'stick jockey' became king; the 'quiet jockey' was dismissed as useless in a finish. The upshot of all this was that horses were being whipped willy-nilly.

Appalled that jockeys were beating horses already galloping at full speed, animal rights campaigners began to highlight the practice, particularly the casual whipping of horses during the closing stages of races when their finishing position was already determined. The animal rights lobby put pressure on the racing authorities to stop what was termed 'a barbaric cruelty', while television pundits reviewing the closing stages of races would count the number of strokes dished out by the various jockeys. Outside racing circles, particularly among television viewers, the issue was causing more and more concern—even if those participating in the sport did not realise it—and huge demands were being placed on the stewards to do something about it.

Out of the blue, the stewards declared war on the misuse of the whip—although what actually constituted misuse had not been properly defined. The 'making an example of' victims were the Irish jockeys Tommy Ryan and Joe Byrne, who got a three-month ban from race riding after winning races at the 1980 Cheltenham Festival.

Tommy Ryan won the first race, the Sun Alliance Novice Hurdle, on *Drumlargan*, trained by Edward O'Grady. His mount had hung badly on the run-in, but rallied under the strong use of the stick to head the rank outsider, *Farmer*, close home. Ryan had apparently hit his mount seventeen times after jumping the last hurdle and hit his mount again after passing the winning post, despite having won the race by two lengths. Joe Byrne got into trouble the following day when beaten by a short head on *Batista* in the *Daily Express* Triumph Hurdle. In Byrne's case the stewards were reacting to 'feedback' they received after he had ridden *The Vintner* a close-up third in the valuable Greenall Whitley Breweries Chase at Haydock Park, where his use of the whip appalled a number of television viewers.

Even in Ireland, where we are more relaxed on this issue, the use of the whip was raised in the Dáil in 1980 when Dr Noel Browne asked Minister of Agriculture Ray McSharry, whose brief included horse-racing, to introduce a bill to ban the use of the whip by jockeys.

It was true that some National Hunt jockeys, riding much shorter than they used to, relied too heavily on the whip to urge on their mounts, but the sudden outbreak of war against this method of riding, before proper guidelines had been agreed, resulted in jockeys being tried by television. For a time a dual system applied, at least it did in Ireland, with the stewards being much harsher on whip offences when a meeting was televised and therefore viewed by a non-race-going public.

Eventually, guidelines were put in place to regulate the matter and the whip controversy died down. Everyone now accepts and understands the rules in this regard. The politically correct thing to say is that the whip does not make a horse go faster and tends to sour a horse. Many jockeys will tell you that a horse will produce a greater effort if shown the whip rather than dealt a belt of it! I am not so sure. I am rather persuaded by my memory of the finish of the 1972 Epsom Derby, a race that was decided by the whip: Lester Piggott gave his mount, *Roberto*, an almighty crack close home and the horse surged forward to pip *Rheingold* by a short head. It was the whip that did it, there's no mistake.

The Ismay Curse

One of the most sensational renewals of the Derby Stakes took place at Epsom in 1913, when the favourite, *Craganour*, the top two-year-old of the previous year, was sensationally and controversially disqualified. *Craganour*'s owner was Charles Bower Ismay, a younger son of Thomas Ismay, founder of the White Star Shipping Line, which owned the doomed liner *Titanic*. His brother, Joseph Bruce Ismay, was on board that terrible April night in 1912. Bruce Ismay managed to survive by climbing into a lifeboat with the women and children, and rumours were rife that he had achieved this by dressing up as a woman.

On his return, Ismay was shunned by polite society, which felt he had let the side down by not dying like the gentleman he was supposed to be, so he decided to lie low for a while and bought a retreat in Co. Galway. His absence from English society meant that some of this odium began to rub off on other members of the family, particularly as the '*Titanic* enquiries' produced numerous allegations of reckless behaviour by Captain Smith and Bruce Ismay, who was chairman of the White Star Line. It was alleged that Ismay had urged the Captain to try to beat an Atlantic speed record, that he instructed the radio operators not to pass on ice warnings from other ships in case they made Captain Smith slow down, and that he had caused an inadequate number of lifeboats to be provided because he had declared the ship unsinkable. Ismay did not help his case with his attitude in the witness box, which was furtive, evasive and unco-operative. The prolonged enquiries publicised the bravery of some of the passengers and revealed a shocking tale of cowardice, prejudice and indifference among some of the crew, to which the Ismay family became inextricably linked in the eyes of the general public.

Bruce's brother, Charles Bower Ismay, courted controversy of his own on the racecourse. His 1913 racing year started badly when the stewards investigated two of his jumpers, which had won in the same week, because both had shown abnormal improvement from previous form. The stewards hauled Ismay's trainer, Tom Coulthwaite, before them and found him guilty of not running the horses on their merits in the previous races. Making an example of Coulthwaite, a leading trainer who had trained two winners of the Grand National, the stewards withdrew his licence to train indefinitely and eight long years would pass before he got it back.

At the start of the flat season Ismay again found himself embroiled in unwelcome publicity when *Craganour* was controversially beaten in the Two Thousand Guineas, the first big race of the year. Ridden by Bill Saxby, *Craganour* had shot clear of the field, looking all over a winner, but the jockey took things a bit easy in the closing stages and was nearly caught by a late challenge from *Louvois*. Although the two horses were on opposite sides of the track, virtually everyone present believed that *Craganour* had beaten *Louvois* by at least half-a-length. Alas for Bower Ismay, the one person on Newmarket Heath that afternoon who did not see it that way was Charles E. Robinson—and he was the judge! During an acrimonious post-race argument, the judge found himself besieged on all sides by people questioning the decision and in his defence asserted that 'What they should be saying is that Saxby ought to have won'.

The upshot of this was that Saxby was sacked and replaced on *Craganour* by Danny Maher. Maher was in the saddle when *Craganour* won his next race, the Newmarket Stakes, reversing the placings with *Louvois*, who was beaten into third place. Maher, who was Lord Rosebery's jockey, was expected to ride *Craganour* in the Derby until it was discovered that Lord Rosebery also had a runner in the race. Although Lord Rosebery was happy to release Maher so that he could ride *Craganour*, in an admirable display of loyalty the jockey refused to ride against his employer's horse. This resulted in a bizarre display of 'musical chairs' as the French-based American jockey Johnny Reiff, who had ridden *Louvois* at Newmarket, now took the mount on *Craganour*, and Bill Saxby now switched to *Louvois*.

As the Derby runners rounded Tattenham Corner and into the straight on that June afternoon, with the rank outsider *Aboyeur* leading the field, unseen from the stands, a tall woman ducked under the rail into the path of the oncoming horses. Raising her arms as she faced the horses that were bearing down upon her, she was immediately bowled over, the horse who had knocked her falling and landing on top of her. The horse was *Amner*, owned by HM The King, and the woman was Emily Davidson, a militant campaigner of the suffragette movement. The horse struggled to its feet and ran off after the others, leaving the jockey Herbert Jones lying unconscious and Miss Davidson dying on the ground.

Meanwhile, the race continued with *Craganour* producing a challenge, joining *Aboyeur* to dispute the lead, while *Shogun* and *Day Comet* were closing up behind. Under pressure, *Aboyeur* began to hang away from the running rail, colliding with *Craganour*, and an angry Johnny Reiff responded by trying to push *Aboyeur* back. As *Aboyeur* drifted off and then back onto the rail, *Shogun* tried to get through the gap on the inside, but was abruptly cut off when *Aboyeur* was pushed back. Again *Aboyeur* drifted left and again was pushed back and a persistent barging match resulted, which was eventually won by *Aboyeur*. Coming right off the rail inside the last fifty yards, *Aboyeur* forced *Craganour* wide with him, the pair in turn hampering *Great Sport* and the fast-finishing *Nimbus*. By the time the permanent gap had come on the rails, *Shogun* had no more to give, but *Day Comet* and *Louvois* had every chance of coming through, if good enough. Six horses flashed past the judge, Charles Robinson, in a close bunch, and this time he definitely made a mess of it. Robinson called *Craganour* the winner by a head from *Aboyeur*, with *Louvois* a neck away in third, *Great Sport* fourth and *Nimbus* fifth, but he completely failed to notice *Day Comet* on the rails. Photographic evidence subsequently proved that *Day Comet* definitely finished third and Robinson had blundered badly by not placing him in the first five, prompting more complaints about his competence.

As Bower Ismay proudly led *Craganour* in to the raucous roars of those who had backed the favourite, shouts of 'objection' emanated from the bookmakers, who were hoping to promote the case of *Aboyeur*—a real long shot. Although it had been a rough race, there was a convention that owners did not lodge objections in the Derby, plus Edwin Piper, the rider of *Aboyeur*, declared he had no cause for grievance. In those days all racecourse announcements were by signal: a blue flag indicated that the winner was all right, a red flag confirmed that an objection had been lodged. The flagman was sighted lining up the blue flag, but was stopped by an official. The connections and those who had backed the favourite watched in dismay as the blue flag disappeared and the red flag began to ascend, signalling an unprecedented objection to *Craganour*, lodged by the Epsom stewards themselves on the grounds of jostling *Aboyeur*. Backers of the favourite were stunned, the connections irritated and Edwin Piper went ashen with worry, fearing the wrath of the stewards for not keeping a straight course.

Lord Rosebery, Lord Wolverton and Major Eustace Loder were the stewards on duty that day, but Lord Rosebery took no part in the deliberations. Although he remained in the stewards' room, he did not participate in the decision because he had a runner in the race. In due course the stewards delivered their shock verdict:

> The stewards objected to the winner on the grounds that he jostled the second horse. After hearing the evidence of the Judge and several of the jockeys riding in the race they found that *Craganour*, the winner, did not keep a straight course and interfered with *Shogun*, *Day Comet* and *Aboyeur*. Having bumped and bored the second horse, they disqualified *Craganour* (placed last) and awarded the race to *Aboyeur*.

Craganour enjoyed the ignoble distinction of being the first horse to be disqualified in an English Classic race since *Zanga*, which lost the 1789 St Leger for jostling.

When the revised result was announced there was pandemonium as the bookmakers loudly cheered the 'skinner'—*Aboyeur* was a 100-to-1 shot—and backers of *Craganour* loudly disputed the decision. *Craganour*'s connections were understandably bitter, but many impartial observers felt an injustice had been done, basing their opinion on a number of grounds: *Aboyeur* had not kept a straight course either, having clearly come off the rails in the closing stages; it had been a rough race, but Johnny Reiff was not the only offender; neither Edwin Piper nor any other jockey had lodged an objection to the winner; the whole business had been prosecuted and judged by two men. It was also considered strange that the stewards, having objected on the grounds of jostling, had added the extra charges of not keeping a straight course and interfering with other runners. Furthermore, there were doubts over the evidence of the judge, who had completely missed *Day Comet*, while the jockeys were regarded with suspicion because there was a foreign jockey involved, the France-based Johnny Reiff, and Bill Saxby's evidence was considered particularly unreliable.

Several members of the Jockey Club subsequently expressed doubts about the decision, prompting Lord Rosebery to issue a statement defending it. He could hardly have said otherwise, but certainly Major Loder had doubts and expressed them during an illness that was to kill him the following year. The great jockey Steve Donoghue had no doubts either, writing in his autobiography, *Just My Story*:

> The whole thing was a terrible tragedy, and the verdict was a most unpopular one, as nine out of ten of the onlookers considered the second to be quite as much to blame as *Craganour*.

Donoghue had ridden in the race, on *Bachelor's Wedding*, on which he subsequently won the Irish Derby, and had a clear view of what was going on ahead of him. He went on to say:

> It was very unfortunate that just at that time there was a tremendous amount of bad feeling between the French and the English jockeys, as so many owners were bringing over French jockeys to ride their horses in all the important races and the English jockeys left standing on the ground keenly resented this.

Donoghue goes on to recount Saxby's jocking off *Craganour*: 'His evidence was taken by the Stewards and jockeys are like other people, only human, and here was surely a golden opportunity for anyone to get his own back. Anyhow, Saxby's evidence certainly turned the scale against *Craganour*.'

Bower Ismay gave notice of an appeal, but it was dismissed on the grounds that it had not been lodged in time. He then applied to the courts for an injunction, which he was granted and which prevented the stakes being paid out. His feelings of injustice increasing with each passing day, Ismay became determined that *Craganour* would never run in England again and promptly accepted an offer of £30,000 for the horse from an Argentine breeder. On foot of this he decided to drop the court proceedings.

Golden Miller

Twenty-six-year-old Miss Dorothy Paget caused a stir at the 1931 Bloodstock Sales by buying young horses extensively and expensively. Residing at Leeds Castle, Maidstone, Miss Paget was reputed to be one of the wealthiest heiresses in the country and was a cousin of the Whitneys, the wealthy American horse-racing family. Having bought horses, she took the Beechwood Stables, Exning, where she installed Basil Briscoe, a former amateur rider and a keen huntsman, as her trainer and tasted immediate success with *Golden Miller* and *Insurance*, the Champion Hurdler of 1932 and 1933. Her first jockey was Ted Leader, who rode *Golden Miller* to the first of his five successive Gold Cup victories in 1932, the same year he won the Champion Hurdle on *Insurance*, but following a row with the owner later that year was sacked and replaced by Billy Stott. Stott rode *Golden Miller* and *Insurance* to their second doubles at Cheltenham in 1933.

Having ridden *Golden Miller* to victory in his last six races, Stott was jocked-off the horse in the Grand National. Ted Leader was brought back to take the ride and the excuse offered to the public was that Leader was more experienced around Aintree, having won the race on *Sprig* in 1927. Leader afterwards claimed that Stott himself requested the change, believing that he was too short-in-the-leg to assist *Golden Miller* over the big fences and also because he had an attractive alternative ride on *Pelorus Jack*. In any event the racing public felt that Billy Stott had been treated badly and

Miss Paget and Basil Briscoe received much criticism for the switch. In the race *Golden Miller* tended to jump to the right, then began to make mistakes before he finally came down at the Canal Turn on the second circuit. Meanwhile, Billy Stott was leading the field on *Pelorus Jack* and was still there jumping the last fence, although being challenged by *Kellsboro' Jack*. Unfortunately, *Pelorus Jack* fell at the last, leaving *Kellsboro' Jack* to win the race. Leader reported back to Briscoe that *Golden Miller* was unsuited to the big fences and would never win at Aintree. Typically, Miss Paget and Briscoe ignored this advice.

Shortly after that Grand National, Billy Stott was injured in a car crash, depriving him of a sixth successive National Hunt jockey championship. Although he did ride in races again, he was only a shadow of his former self, his condition was obviously deteriorating and the thirty-four-year-old jockey passed away shortly after. With Stott dead and Leader deciding to turn to training, Miss Paget decided on Gerry Wilson as her new jockey, despite Wilson's uneasy relationship with Briscoe. Wilson was the son of a horse dealer, whose business depended on his ability to straighten out faults in horses before selling them on for a profit. To make a living, a horse dealer had to have an instinctive feel for a horse, and Gerry had inherited this quality from his father.

Golden Miller and Gerry Wilson carried all before them, winning two more Cheltenham Gold Cups as well as the Aintree Grand National, but within eighteen months of his appointment Wilson became embroiled in a controversy that was to haunt him for the rest of his life. The incident that sullied Wilson's honourable and successful career occurred during the running of the 1935 Grand National, for which *Golden Miller* was a popular fancy. A public hero by this stage, the horse already had four Gold Cups and a Grand National to its name and looked very likely to go on and win a second, successive Grand National. It had been heavily backed to do so in the ante-post market, but it was also a popular second leg of the Spring Double, a long-odds double in which the backer had to pick the winner of the Lincolnshire Handicap on the flat as well as the winner of the Grand National. Thousands of punters aimed at this elusive double annually, but on this occasion the Lincolnshire, the first leg of the double, had been won by *Flamenco*, ridden by Eph Smith, which was a heavily supported 8-to-1 favourite. This put the cat among the pigeons because most of the surviving doubles were running on to *Golden Miller* in the Grand National, the best-backed horse in the ante-post market and certain to be the best-backed horse on the day of the race.

The press was full of the bookmakers' plight. *The Sporting Life*'s headline predicted '*Golden Miller* Heading for 6-to-4', anticipating a substantial cut in the horse's price in an attempt to put punters off backing it. Strangely, *Golden Miller*'s price continued to be offered at 5-to-2, with certain bookmakers appearing to be particularly keen to take bets on the horse, which was surprising given that it looked sure to be a shorter price on the day. Matters took a sinister turn when a leading bookmaker warned Basil Briscoe that certain people were determined that *Golden Miller* would not win the Grand National, and an attempt would be made to nobble the horse. The trainer took the warning seriously, employing two detectives to watch over *Golden Miller* day and night and to ensure no unauthorised persons got near it.

Golden Miller reached Aintree safe and sound, surrounded by the detectives. In the parade ring before the big race, the horse walked round covered in a large blanket and a hood, well inside the path away from the rails, with the two detectives between the horse and the crowd to prevent an acid attack. Set to carry 12 stone 7 lb—just 5 lb more than when successful the previous year— *Golden Miller* looked a certainty, bar a spectacular nobbling incident on the way to the start. Nonetheless, it was still freely available at 2-to-1 in the betting market.

In a marked change of tactics from those that had proven so successful the previous year, Gerry Wilson took up a position on the inside, close to the running rail. This was a surprise because although it was the shortest route, there was a higher risk of interference and the drop on the landing side of the fences was markedly steeper at the part of the fence nearest the rail. Running prominently, *Golden Miller* managed to avoid interference and was travelling nicely in third place as they jumped Valentine's Brook, but disaster struck at the next fence, the eleventh, which was an open ditch. In those days there was no racecourse commentary, the stand at Aintree being a long way from the action, so spectators had to read the race themselves through their binoculars. Most observers saw nothing happen, but all of a sudden Miss Paget's blue and yellow colours could not be seen. Where was the favourite? As the field swept past the stands, with a circuit to go, *Golden Miller* was not among them.

The film of the race shows the incident clearly: *Golden Miller* faltered coming to the fence, but Wilson seemed to make no effort to rouse his mount, who leaped high and bold, easily clearing the 6 ft ditch and the fence beyond, but jumping to the left as he did so. The jockey was pitched up onto the horse's ears but regained his seat in the saddle, only to slide off, feet first, many yards beyond the fence, close by the rail.

The race was won by *Reynoldstown*, owned and trained by Major Noel Furlong of Cork and ridden by his son, Frank, an amateur. As the Furlong family celebrated their unexpected victory, the stunned crowd watched Gerry Wilson calmly riding *Golden Miller* back to the unsaddling enclosure, the horse apparently sound and none the worse from the incident. The jockey reported that *Golden Miller* was never moving well, had gone lame approaching the fence, had blundered and unseated him; Dorothy Paget blamed Basil Briscoe for galloping the horse too hard in training; Briscoe was blaming everybody. The argument continued in Miss Paget's private box, where she rebuked her trainer so harshly that in his defence he blurted out that Wilson had stopped *Golden Miller* by jumping off. Briscoe went on to point out that he had been warned by a bookmaker before the race that the horse was going to be stopped and stopped it was—by Wilson. The battle of words developed into a full-blooded row, their loud, heated exchange being clearly audible through the wooden wall of the box. Miss Paget could be heard defending the jockey as she continued to place the entire blame on Briscoe because he did not report the warning to her and had not taken proper heed of it—if indeed there had been a warning at all. Red mist descended on poor Basil Briscoe: he completely lost his temper and told the ranting owner to take *Golden Miller* out of his yard as quickly as possible.

The split between Miss Paget and her trainer ended the row in the box, but it did not settle the matter because *Golden Miller* was engaged in the Champion Chase the following day. A decision had to be made as to whether the horse was fit to run in that race. Briscoe, still the official trainer and responsible for the horse, had *Golden Miller* examined by several vets, none of whom could find anything wrong. Wilson was adamant that the horse was lame, so *Golden Miller* was then ridden up and down on the course by a variety of riders, including a mounted policeman, while the owner, trainer and a host of spectators watched its movements carefully. All agreed that the horse appeared to be sound. Briscoe advised the owner that the horse should run, but Miss Paget dithered. The row flared up again when it was suggested that another jockey should replace Wilson, but eventually it was decided to defer any decision until the following morning.

The next day *Golden Miller*, with Wilson up, was given an early morning gallop, after which the horse underwent an intensive veterinary examination and was declared sound and ready to race. The conditions of the Champion Chase suited *Golden Miller* much better than the Grand National because the race was not a handicap. All the runners carried the same weight, instead of *Golden Miller* having to concede weight all round. *Golden Miller* should have been a long odds-on shot, but was available at even money because of all the controversy of the previous day. With rumours circulating about the Grand National fiasco, reports of the squabbling connections and allegations about the horse being stopped, the attendance was wary of backing *Golden Miller* on this occasion. How right they were! *Golden Miller* only got as far as the first fence. The horse hit the fence, but managed to clear it, but Gerry Wilson was unseated and the horse ran off riderless. When *Golden Miller* was retrieved and was coming in, ridden by its lad, Mick Boston, the sight of the beaten favourite led to a spontaneous chorus of boos from the crowd. Boston responded by pointing in the direction of Wilson, as if to say, 'that is who you should be booing', a gesture that heaped even more suspicion on the jockey. Always reluctant to discuss the episode, which did not help his case, Gerry Wilson never managed to completely shake off the suspicion that he had stopped *Golden Miller* from winning a second Grand National.

During the inquests that took place in pubs throughout the land, the case against Wilson revolved around the remote part of the course where the incident had occurred, his failure to ride the horse into the fence and his strange fall from the saddle. An accomplished horseman and a formidable jockey, Wilson appeared to have survived his mount's awkward jump and regained his seat, only to come off all too easily well beyond the fence itself. The appearance of 'stepping off' the horse and the direction of the fall gave the impression that it was done deliberately: if the horse's jump to the left was the cause of the unseating, the jockey would have been pitched off to the right, into the centre of the course. In that event, Wilson would have been thrown into the path of the oncoming horses, but he had conveniently slipped off to the left, where he was able to duck under the rail and out of harm's way. Most observers were sceptical about Wilson's claim that *Golden Miller* was never going well—the horse had been jumping well, holding a prominent position readily—and the assertion that the horse was lame was simply unbelievable. The horse showed no sign of lameness and if the jockey really did think that it was lame, why did he remount and ride it home rather than leading it in? Most damning of all, the vets had been unable to find any sign of injury or lameness, and the connections considered it fit to race the following day. Would a jockey really be keen to ride a lame horse in a steeplechase?

Wilson also faced an allegation about his riding of *Golden Miller* in the Champion Chase, when he was unseated at the first fence. Some race-readers were of the opinion that the jockey did not give his mount a proper view of the fence as he galloped behind the leaders, suggesting that Wilson may not have wanted to win that race either. On the other hand, it must be said that the stewards were apparently satisfied with both rides and Wilson was never officially charged with any wrongdoing in connection with these races. Hurt by the controversy and suspected by the public, Wilson soldiered on at the head of his profession but lost the mount on *Golden Miller*, which was transferred to the stable of Owen Anthony and would be ridden by his stable jockey in future.

In the Judge's Chair

Racing judges often got finishes wrong, just as those so-called experts who judge finishes in order to bet on the outcome sometimes get them wrong. One of the most controversial incidents in the history of Irish racing occurred at the Phoenix Park in August 1941, when the judge, a Mr F.F. Tuthill, declared *Fair Crystal* the winner of the Phoenix Plate, a valuable two-year-old race popularly known as 'The Fifteen Hundred'. To most observers, however, *Avon Port* appeared to have beaten *Fair Crystal* by at least half-a-length, but the judge gave the verdict the other way by a neck. In those pre-photo-finish days, the judge's decision was final and once declared could not be changed—not by him, and not by the stewards. Mr Tuthill could have made an honest mistake, or he could also have been right and all the observers who thought *Avon Port* had won by half-a-length could have been wrong. But the general consensus was that *Fair Crystal* was a fortunate winner and a terrible mistake allowed David Frame from Bray, Co. Wicklow, his trainer W.J. 'Rasher' Byrne and jockey T.P. Burns to collect a valuable prize when their horse had actually been beaten. The losers, Frederick Myerscough, owner and trainer of *Avon Port*, and jockey Joe Taylor had no choice but to take the knock on the chin: there was nothing that could be done.

The result of the race enabled the conspiracy theorists to construct a tale of villainy involving Frank Tuthill, whom they alleged had a possible motive for his decision in the fact that he owned the stallion, *Fairhaven*. This horse, which was the sire of *Fair Crystal*, stood at Mr Tuthill's Owenstown Stud in Maynooth. As the theory went, having sired a winner of such importance, *Fairhaven* would be more sought after by breeders, leading to an increased stud fee and patronage—all to the judge's financial benefit. It is easy to accuse a person of deliberate wrongdoing, but in this case it has not been proved conclusively that the judge made a mistake in the first place. Mr Tuthill was in a box right on the finishing line and was better placed to make a decision than his critics. The problem was that Mr Tuthill was open to the charge that he was the beneficiary of his decision, which the majority of the racegoers believed was clearly wrong. The Turf Club was naïve, to say the least, to allow a person who might be perceived as an interested party to act as judge. We will never know whether the decision was right or wrong, but it must be said that Mr Tuthill never lost the confidence of racehorse owners, who make up the members of the Turf Club. He continued to be licenced to act as a judge until his retirement in 1956, when he was sixty-seven years of age.

Ghost Riders

One of the enduring myths of the Aintree Grand National involved the Irish-trained *Caughoo*, winner of the great steeplechase in 1947. *Caughoo* was owned by John McDowell, the famous Dublin jeweller and owner of the Happy Ring House on O'Connell Street (which will be remembered by several generations because of its advertisements, which were an integral part of the show at the city's cinemas for many years). Trained by his brother, Herbert, a veterinary surgeon, *Caughoo* won successive Ulster Grand Nationals at Downpatrick in 1945 and 1946, but came to Aintree the following year as an unquoted 100-to-1 no-hoper. The talented jockey Aubrey Brabazon, who had ridden *Caughoo* to victory in the previous year's Ulster equivalent, was offered the ride but turned it down in favour of *Luan Casca*, third favourite to win the race but still a 22-to-1 chance. The McDowells then engaged jockey Eddie Dempsey, who made his first ever trip to England for the race.

A record field of fifty-seven runners went to post, which was run in a dense fog. The combination of the big field and the weather conditions turned the commentary into a shambles: nobody in the stands could see a thing and the radio commentators were all at sea, flummoxed by the sheer number of runners, which appeared only as silhouettes. *Luan Casca* fell at Becher's Brook on the first circuit, giving Aubrey Brabazon a bad fall in which he broke a couple of ribs, one puncturing his lung. He told me that this painful injury was one of the most sickening he had ever experienced, but he felt twice as sick when he eventually heard what had won the race! *Lough Conn*, ridden by Daniel McCann, led the field past the stands and out into the country for the final time and reached Becher's Brook with a clear lead of at least ten lengths. By the time the horses came back into the view of those in the enclosures, *Caughoo* emerged from the fog with a huge lead over *Lough Conn*, then there was a break to *Kami* and *Prince Regent*. Never looking likely to lose from that point and in spite of a terrible blunder at the final fence, *Caughoo* romped home by twenty lengths to record an easy victory.

A few years later Eddie Dempsey and Daniel McCann got into an argument that led to fisticuffs and ultimately ended up in court. The evidence revealed that the fight broke out when McCann accused Dempsey of cheating him out of a Grand National win. McCann alleged that Dempsey had pulled up *Caughoo* on the first circuit. While he was hacking home he heard the roar of the crowd, seeing him emerge from the fog, and decided to rejoin the race and jump the last two fences. McCann was adamant that he was leading on *Lough Conn* and nothing had passed him, and he could not believe his eyes when he saw *Caughoo* in front at the second-last fence. Dempsey strenuously rejected the allegation, which was not resolved one way or the other in the courts. The public preferred McCann's version of events, and the incident became another legend of the Grand National.

McCann had alleged that Dempsey's reaction was on the spur of the moment when he heard the crowd cheering his mount. Through various tellings and retellings the story later had it that Dempsey had deliberately hidden out in the country, waiting for the field to come round again, at which point he rejoined the race. Was the allegation true? It certainly could have happened because rain and a dense fog obscured the field from the officials, commentators and the public alike and there was utter confusion because no less than thirty-six horses either fell or were pulled up, while many others became hopelessly tailed off. In other words, there were horses everywhere.

I looked up the Running Commentary on the 1947 race in *The Grand National—An Illustrated History of the Greatest Steeplechase in the World*, written by Clive Graham and Bill Curling, which was published by Barrie & Jenkins of London in 1972. Photograph 184 shows *Lough Conn* leading the field over Becher's Brook on the first circuit, and I can clearly identify *Caughoo* in the middle of the field, towards the centre of the course. Although it is a black-and-white photograph, the colours of *Caughoo* show up well because they were royal blue & emerald green halved, white sleeves and cap. The white sleeves and cap, together with the white noseband, stand out clearly. Just to be sure these were the colours actually carried, I also looked up a black-and-white photograph of *Caughoo* passing the winning post, which confirms the colours and the white noseband.

Photograph 185 shows *Lough Conn* leading over Becher's Brook on the second circuit, surrounded by four loose horses, and the commentary states: 'Then came the winner *Caughoo* (nose band—on left of picture), *Bricett* (vertical stripes), *Musical Lad* (nose band—on right) and the grey *Kilnaglory*. *Prince Regent* is in the next group. *Lough Conn* failed to stay, and, in the end, *Caughoo* won easily.'

Unfortunately, the horse identified as *Caughoo* is not clearly visible in the photograph: only the white noseband and the white left sleeve of the jockey can be seen. Bill Curling asserts that the horse is *Caughoo*, which would put paid to Daniel McCann's accusation, but conspiracy diehards might just have the teeny-weeniest of doubts, which would enable the myth—and the controversy—to live on.

A Horseshoe for Luck?

In my experience, good horses enjoy any good luck that is going while the inferior horse often fails to get the rub of the green. The same can be said of jockeys, trainers and even owners. Luck goes with winners because generally one makes one's own luck, with obvious freak exceptions. A typical example of an unlucky horse was the enigmatic *Captain Christy*, a brilliant hurdler on its day, as evidenced by its runaway victory in the 1972 Irish Sweeps Hurdle when it slaughtered the reigning Champion Hurdler, *Bula*. Unfortunately, the horse could not reproduce that form in the following year's Champion Hurdle, finishing third behind *Comedy of Errors*, but it did win the Scottish Champion Hurdle. Sent chasing the following season, *Captain Christy* turned out to be a spectacular jumper at speed, but developed a habit of falling, which frustrated punters. Having thrilled the Irish contingent by winning the Gold Cup, despite a bad blunder at the last fence, with the veteran jockey and reformed alcoholic Bobby Beasley in the saddle, *Captain Christy* fell in the Irish Grand National but came out and won the valuable Power Gold Cup the following day.

Captain Christy was a punters' nightmare: brilliant one day, lacklustre the next, jumping fence after fence like a stag only to lose concentration and fall when it was least expected. Many punters found they were backing the horse every time it got beaten and had nothing on it when it won: a clear case of sod's law! The punters' love/hate relationship with *Captain Christy* began early in its career. Making its racing debut in 1971, when owned by Tom Nicholson, *Captain Christy* was a winning favourite in the last race at the Galway and at the Listowel festival meetings and was marked down as an exciting future prospect. Evidently Major Joe Pidcock thought so too because he purchased the horse for £10,000 and it made its hurdling debut in his 'straw, black cap' at the Limerick Christmas meeting. An enthusiastic sportsman, the Major owned, trained and rode the horse himself, but his inexperience did not deter the punters. They backed *Captain Christy* as if defeat were out of the question and made the horse favourite, but the race became a fiasco when some of the runners took the wrong course and the sporting Major followed them.

Some punters alleged that the Major was tricked by the professional jockeys, whom they accused of resenting the amateur riders. The charge, which was not substantiated, was not without some justification because competition from amateur riders was a topical issue at the time. Fearing for their livelihoods, the professionals openly objected to the number of rides that the amateur Bill McLernon was being given in races open to professionals and refused to ride against him. McLernon stood down in order to avert a strike, but the issue was only resolved when the stewards agreed to limit the number of races in which an amateur rider could ride against professionals. Major Pidcock made amends when partnering *Captain Christy* in the first maiden hurdle of the New Year at Baldoyle, but the punters had deserted him in favour of Barney Moss's *The Met*, trained by Paddy Mullins. The sporting Major soon deserted the unlucky *Captain Christy,* too, selling him to Jane Samuel later that year.

Doping to Win, Doping to Lose

The earliest form of doping was called 'nobbling' and involved administering medicine to the horse to prevent it winning a race. The nobbler usually worked, directly or indirectly, on behalf of a bookmaker with a large liability on a race due to ante-post bets, which were taken on the basis of 'all in, run or not', so it was really a case of ensuring the horse did not run. Any poison would do: the horse's welfare was not in the least bit important, and if other horses were killed in the process, well, that was too bad.

In May 1811 a number of horses suddenly became ill, at least one of them later died, after drinking water from one particular water trough on Newmarket Heath. A similar crime had occurred two years earlier when the water at the stables of trainers J. Stevens and Richard Prince was contaminated with arsenic; several horses died and others were permanently damaged. The re-occurrence of attacks on horses in training was regarded as so serious that the Jockey Club offered an award of 500 guineas for information that would lead to the conviction of the culprit. This huge award tempted those with the relevant information, and led to the name of Daniel Dawson being linked to the crime. Dawson was eventually arrested and charged with numerous offences of poisoning horses between 1809 and 1811, but was convicted on only one charge. His accomplice, who had provided the poison, was a man named Cecil Bishop and Cecil now decided to give evidence against Dawson. He told a shocking story of a man determined to put a horse out of action, without regard for any other animals in the vicinity. Bishop testified that he had supplied a cocktail designed to make horses sick, but Dawson complained that the horses could smell it and would not drink the water. Dawson demanded a stronger potion because the people he was working for did not want any possibility that the horse might be able to run—nor did he care how many horses had to be killed or injured in order for him to complete his mission successfully. Bishop then supplied a solution of arsenic, which did not have a strong smell, and admitted that, on the instructions of Dan Dawson, it was he who contaminated the water trough of Richard Prince, the Newmarket trainer, by means of a syringe.

In his defence, Dawson claimed that what he did was not a crime unless the prosecution could prove malice against the owner of the horses affected. He argued that his intention was not to kill the horses, only to injure them sufficiently, therefore his only crime was that of trespass. This did not impress the court, however. Dan Dawson was found guilty and sentenced to death. He was hanged at Cambridge on 8 August 1812.

The unsupervised races of steeplechasing provided fertile ground for corruption and cheating. In 1854 a big gamble developed in the market on the Grand National when a horse named *Miss Mowbray*, formerly trained by J.F. Mason but now under the care of George Dockeray, was backed to win a fortune. Successful in 1852 and second to one of the *Peter Simple*s the following year, *Miss Mowbray* was on the tip of everyone's tongue and its price kept tumbling as the public piled money on the horse. Rumours had it that the former crack jockey Jem Mason would be coming out of retirement to ride the mare, which further encouraged the public gamble, and *Miss Mowbray* was made the hot favourite. On the day of the race it was a different story as the bookmakers on the course scrambled to lay *Miss Mowbray*, topping each other's price in their eagerness to take in money and causing the mare's price to drift ominously. The suspicious movement in *Miss Mowbray*'s price indicated that something was amiss, and indeed it was: the horse developed a sore leg and was withdrawn. The large crowd cried 'foul', showering the owner and trainer with jeering abuse. They in turn protested their innocence, claiming they themselves had backed *Miss Mowbray* and stood to win a large sum. Dockeray was adamant that *Miss Mowbray* was fit and well on arrival at Aintree, but some unknown person had applied a 'blister' to the mare's leg without his knowledge. The mare had been nobbled, and the bookies were the prime suspects.

As the nobblers got more experienced, veterinary science fought a losing battle to keep up with the advances in drug development and vets simply could not tell whether a horse was ill, or had been given something to make it ill. A case in point involved the race-horse *Orme*, favourite for the Two Thousand Guineas in 1892, which took ill a couple of days before the race. The horse's trainer,

John Porter, suspected it had been poisoned, but the vets thought a bad tooth might be the culprit.

Doping to make a horse lose a race, or be too ill to run, was comparatively easy, but doping a horse to make it run fast enough to win a race was another matter entirely. At the turn of the twentieth century doping horses was such an inexact science that the stewards did not believe it posed a threat to the integrity of racing. Consequently, the Rules of Racing did not prohibit the use of drugs in order to increase a horse's stamina, or to make it run faster. All that changed after an influx of American owners, trainers and jockeys, forced to seek pastures new when the State of New York closed down its racetracks, which introduced the very undesirables whose villainous ways had brought about the closure into European racing circles.

Back home the Americans had been using a cocaine-based drug, called a 'speedball', to make horses run faster and this was now unleashed into European racing, sending bookies running for cover. Backed by the drug, the Americans plunged into the betting ring, helping themselves to the bookies' money and making hay while the sun still shone, all the while destroying public confidence in the integrity of racing. Forced to act, the authorities included an anti-doping rule in the 1903 Rules of Racing, which would become a major headache for trainers in future years. The stewards ruled that the trainer was entirely responsible for a horse under his care. It was his job to protect his horses from dopers and if he failed in this duty, he was in breach of the Rules and the penalty was the withdrawal of his licence. The stewards were not interested in finding out *who* actually administered the illegal substance. If a horse ran in a race with a prohibited drug in its system, the trainer was responsible and that was that. This tough rule did help to stamp out the wilful use of medication in order to make a horse win a race, but it also resulted in glaring injustices and led to the stewards being called before the courts.

The Abject Failure of the Anti-doping Rules
In 1930 trainer Charles Chapman lost his licence because his charge, *Don Pat*, failed a dope test, the facts of the case being

reported in the *Racing Calendar* and repeated in *The Times*. Chapman sued for libel on the grounds that the statement published gave the impression that he had lost his licence for doping a horse, rather than for failing to ensure it was not doped by a third party. The jury awarded Chapman damages of £13,000, but the Appeal Court set it aside on the grounds that the *Racing Calendar* was a privileged publication and protected by law.

During the Second World War English racing continued without interruption, albeit centralised and limited and with no jumping-races being run. However, all the Classic races were held during those years, enabling the breeding industry to continue unscathed. It was a very different situation in France, where racing was closed down, some of the best stallions were pinched by the Germans and the breeders were left with no races and no market for their stock. One would therefore expect that the French breeding business would be in the doldrums and British breeders, who enjoyed continuous racing throughout the war, would be ruling the roost in the post-war years, but in fact the opposite happened. French horses dominated all the big British races after the war, winning nine of the twenty English Classic races run between 1947 and 1950. Nothing was said about this at the time, but some years later there were persistent rumours of the use of medication in French training stables, fuelled by comments made by a leading trainer there and by the inability of these big French winners to make a successful mark at stud. If anyone believed that only the French were 'at it', they had their heads in the sand: it was likely that some trainers in Ireland and England were employing medication, too. Indeed, anyone who bothers to look back on the careers of trainers will notice that some of them suddenly found it much more difficult to train winners after proper dope-testing procedures were put in place.

As the stewards attempted to confront the particular problem of doping to win, the integrity of racing was threatened by an outbreak of 'nobbling', which was aimed at preventing well-backed horses from running in big races, a practice that became prevalent in the late 1950s and early 1960s. The crude attempts to attack horses by spraying acid on them as they paraded before a race forced the authorities to tighten up security at racecourses. This in turn forced the nobblers to change tack, and they now carried out their dirty deeds in the less secure stable yards. The attacks were outrageously audacious: the nobblers simply walked into the training stable, mostly at night, entered the box of the target horse and administered the dope. At first trainers did not realise what was happening, suspecting natural causes for the illness of the horse, but when a pattern began to emerge it was obvious that a gang was targeting big-race favourites and hitting them in their own boxes, under the trainer's nose.

In 1958 *Alcide*, the ante-post favourite to win the Derby, was found distressed in its box and had to be withdrawn from the race. It transpired that the horse had broken a rib, which its trainer thought was the result of an accident rather than the deliberate blow that almost certainly caused the injury. Three years later the 'talking horse' *Pinturischio*, favourite to win the Derby before he had even run in a race, suddenly went down with a mystery illness and dope was found to be the cause. Two months later the sprinter *Sing Sing* fell ill on the morning of the July Cup and was unable to run. *Sing Sing*'s illness might have been put down to a bug, but with the *Pinturischio* case fresh in the memory, a sample of *Sing Sing*'s saliva was sent for analysis and it was discovered that the horse had been drugged. In 1964 the Irish-trained *Tragedy*, owned by Anne Biddle, was strongly fancied to win the One Thousand Guineas but trailed in last, running so badly that the stewards ordered it to be tested. It was found that the horse had been doped. In light of this litany of evidence trainers were forced to tighten stable security, employees had to be security cleared and stable yards could never again be left unattended.

Vincent O'Brien Falls Foul of the Rule
Meanwhile, in Ireland, the inflexibility of the rules would come to haunt the stewards and lead to a radical overhaul of the rules relating to doping. It all began on Wednesday, 20 April 1960, the day after the Fairyhouse Easter meeting, when Mr Walter Burmann's *Chamour*, trained by Vincent O'Brien and ridden by his Australian stable jockey, Garnie Bougoure, won a modest

maiden at the Curragh, a race confined to horses that had never won a race. There was no gamble, although *Chamour* was the odds-on favourite, which was to be expected of a Vincent O'Brien-trained maiden holding a Derby engagement, and nothing untoward happened that afternoon to give a clue to the sensation that was to follow. All winning horses were routinely given a dope test after the race, whereby samples of the horse's saliva and sweat were taken for analysis. The samples taken from *Chamour* were found to contain traces of a drug or stimulant, which led to the stewards holding an enquiry on Friday, 13 May.

Unlucky for some, in this case Vincent O'Brien, the enquiry found that a drug or stimulant had been administered to *Chamour* for the purpose of affecting its speed and/or stamina in the race, and the horse was disqualified. The stewards informed O'Brien that his licence was being withdrawn for a period of eighteen months and that none of the horses under his care could fulfil their engagements unless and until they had been transferred to another licenced trainer. Shocked by the severity of the sentence, O'Brien could only say, 'I did not drug this, or any other, horse and I trust my staff. My personal gain from *Chamour*'s victory was twenty pounds—10 per cent of the stake.' Walter Burmann offered a £5,000 reward for information that would lead to the conviction of the person who administered the drug. *Chamour* was not banned from racing, but one of the most powerful and successful racing stables in Europe would have to be disbanded and Vincent O'Brien, one of the most famous trainers in Ireland and Britain, was no longer allowed to set foot on a racecourse. The stewards later relented on one point only: that the Ballydoyle stable could remain intact under the supervision of Vincent's brother, Phonsie, but Vincent himself could not enter the property while disqualified.

There was a drug problem in Irish racing at the time. The use of 'medication' in training, either as a painkiller or to mask other drugs, was too sophisticated for the post-race dope test, which was failing to detect such usage. The dopers were getting away with it in a blatant fashion. So, when a positive sample did come to light the stewards decided to make an example of the most famous trainer in Ireland in a botched attempt to make the dopers mend their ways. The O'Brien case implied that the trainer was doping a horse, a horse that was likely to be among the best in Ireland, in order to win a lowly maiden race, which did not make any sense. Furthermore, there was not a shred of evidence that the trainer had administered the banned substance and it was clear that neither the owner nor the trainer benefited from the doping of the horse. The case against O'Brien was made to look ridiculous when *Chamour* easily won the Gallinule Stakes, a valuable Classic trial, before going on to win the Irish Derby. The public gave its verdict on the Curragh on that Derby day in June, cheering loudly and chanting, 'We want Vincent'. The trainer had been vindicated in the eyes of the people.

Stung by the harshness of the sentence and determined to clear his name, Vincent O'Brien began court proceedings against the stewards, stressing that he was not seeking damages, only a declaration that he did not dope *Chamour*. As the case smouldered on, the stewards finally relented: O'Brien's suspension was reduced to a year and he was permitted to return to live in Ballydoyle, his residence attached to his stable. *Chamour*, on the other hand, was destined never to race again. The race on hard ground in the Irish Derby caused splints to form on its legs, which prevented it from running again that year, but it was decided to keep *Chamour* in training as a four-year-old. The horse hit the headlines again the following February when it died suddenly in its box, reviving the debate on racecourses and in pubs.

When O'Brien's action came to court the stewards clarified the findings and apologised to the trainer, stating that they never intended to suggest he had doped *Chamour*. They stated that although a drug or stimulant had been administered to *Chamour*, they did not find that Vincent O'Brien had administered the drug or stimulant, or knew of its administration.

The Relko *Case Leads to a Rule Change*

It was widely accepted that the rule holding the trainer entirely responsible, even if no evidence could be produced against him, would have to be changed, but the *Relko* saga made it clear that the

traditional method of taking sweat and saliva samples was antiquated. *Relko*, trained in France by Francois Mathet, ran out a six-
length winner of the Epsom Derby and came to the Curragh in an
attempt to confirm his greatness by winning the Irish Derby as
well—a feat accomplished only once before. Odds-on to win the
race, *Relko* behaved badly during the parade in front of the stands,
but got to the start all right, only to suddenly go lame and be
sensationally withdrawn. A fortnight later the bombshell came
from the Jockey Club: the samples taken from *Relko* at Epsom
proved positive and the stake was being withheld pending an
enquiry. It then transpired that the urine sample had proved
positive, but the saliva sample was negative. The case against *Relko*
was further weakened when the samples taken from the horse at
the Curragh were found to be negative.

After five months the Jockey Club exonerated *Relko*'s trainer,
but this effectively meant that the horse could not be disqualified
because of the way the relevant rule was written: 'Any horse which
has been the subject of fraudulent practice may, at the discretion
of the stewards, be disqualified.' Because the stewards did not find
the trainer guilty of fraudulent practice, *Relko* could not be disqualified and was allowed to keep the race. The fact that a drug
was found in its system after the Derby, together with the fiasco at
the start of the Irish Derby, tarnished *Relko*'s reputation, which
was sullied even more by its woeful career at stud, and nowadays
the horse is remembered, rightly or wrongly, as the Derby winner
that 'got away with it'.

The confused and outdated drug rules were again put under
scrutiny by the *Hill House* affair. At Newbury on 18 February 1967,
the Ryan Price-trained *Hill House* took the Schweppes Gold
Trophy Handicap Hurdle, winning effortlessly by twelve lengths to
a chorus of boos, catcalls and whistles from the crowd in the
stand. This rare display of public unease began as soon it was
apparent that *Hill House* was going to win. It was a spontaneous
bout of anger from punters, many of whom had had their fingers
burned when the horse had never been seen with a winning
chance in a race just one week earlier. An enquiry into the horse's
improved form turned into a doping enquiry when *Hill House*

failed the post-race dope test. An angry public was demanding action, but Ryan Price was fiercely denying he had done anything wrong, leaving the stewards in a very uncomfortable place between these polarised positions. The enquiry lasted six months, during which time the controversy raged in the media, and eventually concluding that *Hill House* had doped itself! The stewards' decision was that *Hill House*'s improved form between 11 and 18 February was due to the fact that the horse had manufactured its own cortisol.

In the eyes of the public it was a ridiculous conclusion. The stewards were effectively saying that here was a horse that had doped itself when the money was down, never having doped itself before. It also never succeeded in doing so again. Bought by the bookmaker John Banks, *Hill House* never won another race. Even the stewards may have doubted their own conclusions, if the punters of the time are to be believed. Afterwards ordinary punters had a rule of thumb to hedge their bets if a Ryan Price horse was involved in a stewards' enquiry—the benefit of the doubt would always go the other way!

In the light of the *Relko* case, the stewards changed the rule so that 'fraudulent practice' did not have to be proved: if traces of a prohibited substance were found in the sample, the horse was liable to disqualification. Unfortunately, the rewritten rule caused considerable controversy when the Ascot Gold Cup winner of 1971 fell foul of it, completely by accident, and was summarily disqualified. Peter Walwyn, *Rock Roi*'s trainer, informed the stewards that a week before the Ascot race his vet had prescribed a drug to alleviate some stiffness in the horse. The manufacturers of the drug advised that the course of treatment should stop seventy-two hours before a race, and the trainer testified that *Rock Roi*'s treatment ceased 118 hours before the race—plenty of time to allow the drug to clear from the horse's system. For some reason this horse retained minute traces of the drug in its system longer than the average horse. Nobody could foresee this and the amount was so small it could not possibly have assisted the horse in the race, but under the rule *Rock Roi* had to be disqualified. The stewards accepted the trainer's explanation and exonerated him.

This decision led to one of the biggest debates of the year regarding the question of whether the stewards were right or wrong. Those who held the view that they were wrong pointed to the fact that the drug in question, butazolidin, was permitted to be given to racehorses in certain states in America. However, the British had introduced a 'zero-tolerance' policy as far as drugs were concerned. The American system allows horses to run on certain medication, painkillers and anti-bleeding drugs, provided they are declared, and is based on the belief that the modern horse would be unable to stay sound racing on dirt tracks without such medical assistance. In Europe, on the other hand, where the racing industry is very much in the hands of breeders, the prevalent opinion is that the use of medication in racing could be detrimental to the normal selection of suitable breeding stock. After the *Rock Roi* case drug manufacturers and vets revised the clearance times for drugs to ensure that a similar incident would not happen again.

The ability of the laboratory to detect tiny traces of a recognised drug or stimulant can be measured by the *No Bombs* case, with occurred in August 1979. Trained by Peter Easterby, *No Bombs* won a hurdle race at Worcester, was routinely dope tested and its sample was found to contain traces of a banned substance. At the subsequent enquiry, Peter Easterby could not explain how the illegal drug was administered, but recalled that the horse had taken a bite of his lad's Mars Bar shortly before the race: he wondered if that might have been the cause of the failure? Further tests were conducted and the scientists proved that the small traces of caffeine and theobromine found in the sample taken from *No Bombs* was consistent with the amount of chocolate and cocoa in a large bite of that popular chocolate bar. The discovery of the source of the banned substance did not help the connections of the horse as *No Bombs* lost the race, although Easterby was exonerated.

The following year the testing procedures came under scrutiny again when two of the six Irish-trained winners at the Cheltenham festival, Gold Cup winner *Tied Cottage* and winner of the Queen Mother Champion Chase, *Chinrullah*, both failed the post-race dope test. Like *No Bombs*, the banned drug theobromine was detected in the horses' systems and was traced to the feed, which was found to have been accidentally contaminated and was administered unknowingly. Both horses were disqualified, which was a particular disappointment for the connections of *Tied Cottage*, which had finished second in 1977 and had fallen at the last fence the following year when looking the likely winner. This particular problem involved a number of different feed manufacturers and led to a spate of disqualifications in Ireland, which caused some resentment because the races were awarded to the horse that finished second, and in most cases that horse had not been tested at all!

In the light of these cases, some people believed the modern dope test was too sophisticated and there should be a threshold level. The stewards stated that they would never tolerate a 'threshold', so the debate switched instead to 'a minimum level of detection'. This campaign was led by the Aga Khan, whose filly *Aliysa* was disqualified after winning the Oaks, the premier fillies' Classic race, because traces of the prohibited substance camphor were discovered in the post-race sample. The Aga Khan contested the result of the test on the grounds that his own scientists had proved that camphor could occur naturally and further that the camphor-containing product could not be identified and could have come from hay, carrots, or wood-shavings. The case went on and on before the stewards dismissed the Aga Khan's defence and *Aliysa* was disqualified—528 days after the race had been run! Unable to accept the decision, the Aga Khan removed his ninety horses from their British stables to John Oxx's Curragh stable, stating that until the British drug-testing procedures were changed dramatically, 'No horse of mine will be trained here and no horses of mine will race here.'

Faced with all these controversies, the Jockey Club was forced to act. It ordered an examination of the drug theobromine and its natural presence in vegetable ingredients, and accepted the overwhelming evidence. It did not accept a threshold level—an imaginary point at which a drug will enhance a horse's performance—but did set a level of tolerance for theobromine, set well below the threshold, which it termed 'a minimum limit of detection', or a 'reporting level'. While it did not help *Tied Cottage*, the new procedures did save many horses from disqualification and eliminated a problem neither the feed merchants nor the trainers could solve.

Doping by Natural Diet

Although the governing bodies of horse-racing in Ireland, Great Britain, France, Germany and Italy work together on all aspects of the sport, progress on any one issue can be painfully slow and changes are not necessarily implemented in all these countries at the same time. During the winter of 2002, thirty-five horses in Britain—including the Irish-trained *Be My Royal*, winner of the Hennessy Gold Cup—and nine in Ireland all failed the dope test because traces of morphine were found in their samples. The substance responsible was traced back to the feed supplied by Connolly's Red Mills, Goresbridge, Co. Kilkenny, a long-established supplier of specialist horse feeds to the racing industry. One by one the horses were disqualified. Red Mills voluntarily compensated the connections, while the company challenged the testing procedures with the Jockey Club in England and the Turf Club in Ireland. The case is still going on, but Noel Brennan of Red Mills told me that his company uses no drugs or other medicinal additives in any of its feed; furthermore it is the only firm in Ireland or Britain that has an on-site testing facility to ensure that its products conform to the Rules of Racing. Records of the batch of nuts fed to *Be My Royal* and the other affected horses reveal that the company's tests showed that the level of morphine was below the limit of detection, and that the traces were so low they could not possibly affect a horse's performance one way or the other.

Everybody is aware of the red 'morphine' poppy that is grown illegally in the Third World, but few people realise that the Irish red poppy, which is commonly found in fields, also contains morphine, only in much smaller amounts. When ingested, as against injected, nearly 80 per cent of the drug is rendered inactive and will have no affect on a horse whatsoever. (The same is true of arsenic, which is also naturally present in some types of grass and, if they were looking for it, would crop up frequently during the routine dope tests.) The point is that if a horse eats some hay that contains an ordinary Irish poppy plant, it can show up as morphine in the dope test and cause its disqualification. There are others too, hordenine, for example, which occurs naturally in barley, and atropine, found in plant life, both of which will result in a horse's disqualification if detected in a post-race sample.

It appears that the Jockey Club's drug policy is already moving in the same direction as it did with theobromine. In 2003 the dope test samples of seventeen horses were found to contain traces of morphine in small amounts. Not only were the horses not disqualified, the connections were not even notified and no enquiry was held into any of the cases. The Jockey Club seems to have accepted that in the case of morphine there should be a minimum level of detection. Of course, this is not much use to the connections of *Be My Royal* and the other forty-three horses, but as far as Noel Brennan is concerned it is a step in the right direction. While the process of law grinds on, a consensus seems to be growing that the established feed companies have been exposed to a threat from a naturally occurring incidence in their raw material, from which they have no means of defence. These companies are proactively working with scientists in America to build a case to convince racing's governing bodies to modernise their doping rules to take account of this phenomenon.

The problem for racing is that rumours persist that some trainers have a 'bottle' that contains a drug the laboratories have not been looking for, enabling them to dope horses under their care and get away with it. The stewards reject this, however, arguing that the absence of cases involving deliberate doping indicates that it is not a problem in racing. In the absence of any evidence it is reasonable to accept the stewards' version, but it is essential that owners and trainers accept that the testing procedures are fair. And the industry is working towards making it even more effective. In January 2005, for example, the Jockey Club stewards decided to copy a practice that is now standard in athletics and freeze the samples taken from horses. This means they can be re-examined in future years for drugs that are unknown at the moment.

Is all the hassle and expense of trying to stamp out the use of drugs in racing worth it? The answer is almost certainly 'yes' although, as one Irishman put it to me, 'Sure, if all the runners are doped, then the best horse will win.' You can't say fairer than that!

The Real Dopers stay a Step Ahead

Dopers, or 'climbers' as they are called in Northern Ireland because of their agility climbing fences, continued to lurk in the background, taking advantage of the confusion concerning the rules and definitions of medication, artificial doping and natural doping. Occasionally, albeit very occasionally, the dopers were caught redhanded and when they were they were dealt with severely. One particularly well-known Belfast bookmaker, who died around the turn of the century, was convicted of doping a greyhound named *Tanyard Chef* in the 1960s and was sent to jail for the crime. The conviction ended his bookmaking career because he was never again granted a betting licence, but it also proved a deterrent to others—at least for a time. But a decade on this ex-bookie was at it again.

In those days to get a horse from Southern to Northern Ireland meant crossing a frontier, with Customs to pass through, which meant paperwork had to be completed. Horseboxes from the South bringing runners to the Maze and Downpatrick racecourses would have to stop at the border-post and bring the relevant forms into the office in order to get clearance to cross. One particular raceday at the Maze in the mid-1970s, the ex-bookie lay in wait at the Customs Post, loitering unsuspiciously among the lorries and the men passing through, watching the horseboxes coming north. He took a special interest when the box belonging to one of the big Curragh stables pulled in, the staff alighted, locking the cab as usual, as they proceeded to the office for clearance to cross. The stable staff did not bother locking the small side door of the box, it led only to the horse stalls where there was nothing to steal and the door was too small for a horse to get out. This was just what the ex-bookie had previously observed by accident and he was ready with his syringe. As the stable staff walked off, in he went and injected three fancied, short priced runners racing that evening. The job was done in minutes and the dopers were well away before the stable staff returned, completely oblivious to what had happened.

The three horses ran abominably that evening and were well beaten but nobody noticed that they had been doped. The stewards ordered each to be examined because of its poor showing, all three showed signs of distress, which the vet put down to a virus. The following day the leading Curragh trainer, whose three horses had been doped, announced that he was closing down his stable for three weeks because of the virus that had struck his yard. Often described as the invisible menace, the virus usually only comes to light during heavy exertion, by which time a horse can be permanently damaged. The ex-bookie openly boasted with delight that his evil deed was being blamed on the virus and how he had fooled several vets and a leading trainer!

As recently as the 1970s and 1980s a doping duo named Terry and Tom operated at greyhound tracks, notably Dungannon and Newbridge. They specialised in sprint races, where the traps were situated on the far side of the track and worked at stadiums that turned off the lights, as a money saving measure, between races. Terry backed the favourite, while Tom lurked in the grass before emerging to spray a dope solution in the traps of the other five dogs. The traps had to be sprayed less than ten minutes before a race because the drug would lose its effect after that time and the pair got away with it for years. They were never caught because they never doped a favourite, always the outsiders, and people backing a favourite never arouse suspicion.

In 1991 a 'man with a can' was identified stalking favourites at minor Irish racecourses and point-to-points, spraying the horses with some drug to make them listless. He should have taken note of Terry and Tom's successful doping spree but he could not resist the 'get rich quick' system of doping short priced favourites and getting greedy bookmakers to lay them on his behalf. He had been operating on and off long enough for the authorities to identify that there was a problem, but officialdom now knew who he was, as well as the bookmakers off whom he was feeding. Caught red-handed in the racecourse stable yard, the 'man with the can' was mistakenly released, which meant that he could not be prosecuted without a realistic prospect of conviction. He got away with it, and still lurks in racing circles, but at least the incident frightened him off as well as the cesspool of hangers-on and the problem went away. Or did it? One thing is certain, the problem with drugs is that nobody, except the dopers themselves, has any idea of the scale of the problem, or if indeed there is a problem.

Equus Interruptus

Although the Rules of Racing uncompromisingly state that 'no person shall alone or jointly with any other person or persons deter or prevent or conspire to or attempt to deter or prevent a horse from winning a race or from running to its maximum ability', in practical terms it is not a rule at all, merely an aspiration. For as long as I have been going racing there has been an unwritten rider to the rule, which allows a horse not to run to its maximum ability if by doing so it would damage its long-term prospects. I call these particular unofficial exemptions to the rule 'institutional non-triers', and everyone in racing accepts them as part and parcel of the game. Institutional non-triers are debutants, horses coming back after a lay-off and those which have yet to receive a handicap mark.

However, there are two understood exceptions to this flexible interpretation of the rule. The first applies when a horse is the favourite, or has been well backed by the public, in which case it must be ridden on its merits; the second is 'Thou shalt not get caught!' In other words, a non-trier must always appear to be trying, at least to the eyes of the average spectator, and any blatant attempts by a rider to stop a horse will be severely punished. The job must be done properly; the integrity of racing cannot be compromised, so every horse must appear to be doing its best, even when it is not! In effect, this means that long shots can be handled in this manner. Should a long shot unexpectedly become a fancied horse, it must be run on its merits.

Stewards have always been prepared to turn a blind eye to a young horse being given an easy introduction to racing as a hard race early in a horse's career, when it is weak and not fully fit, can ruin it. Similarly, trainers are never brought to book when a horse in their charge requires two or three runs in order to reach racing fitness. But by far the most common, and controversial, breach of the rule is allowing horses run behind the field with no intention of winning the race, the sole purpose being to get a handicap mark. This practice is particularly noticeable in two-year-old races and in maiden hurdles.

When horse-racing was in its infancy, riders rode at 'catch weights', meaning no weights were specified. When it became clear that a horse ran faster with a lighter jockey in the saddle, owners began to poach an advantage by employing lighter riders, or by arranging crash diets. The whole point of racing horses was slowly lost because the lightest rider was winning the race rather than the fastest horse, which led to the recording of weights and a weighing-out and a weighing-in procedure for all jockeys. The next step was to alter the weights carried in order to make a one-sided race competitive, thus the handicap was invented.

As far back as 1750, *Ponds Racing Calendar* records a handicap match, but it is unlikely that the term 'handicap' originated from horse-racing. It was probably borrowed from a card game called Handicap, a betting game not unlike Loo, in which players win and lose money to each other at the end of each round, but also must contribute to the pool for the following round. The pool was called the 'cap' and each player had to work out how much he had to 'hand i' the cap', or give in to the pool. On 18 September 1660 Samuel Pepys recorded in his diary: 'To the Mitre Tavern in Wood Street, a house of the greatest note in London. Here some of us fell to handicap, a sport I never knew before, which was very good.'

Actually, the practice of handicapping has been long established in the game of Chess, with the better player giving up a piece before the start of a game. In horse-racing, horses are handicapped by weight: the better the horse, the heavier the weight it is set to carry, which gives every horse some chance of winning. With bookmakers readily prepared to stand one in a handicap, confident that the race will be competitive and that virtually every runner will attract some level of bets, huge bets can be struck, giving the punter an opportunity to win a big sum for a relatively small stake. Of course, this large betting market and the big prize money on offer encourages connections to attempt to get their horse leniently handicapped, which many do by perfectly legitimate means, such as not running it at all, or by running it over a wrong distance, or on ground unsuited to its gait.

There are many adages that racing folk quote regarding handicaps, such as 'always back top weight in a handicap', which, like all generalisations, contains a grain of truth, but in my experience the surest way for a horse to get well handicapped is not to run. The handicapper gives a rating to every horse he handicaps, which is a figure expressed in pounds weight and given to a horse according to its position *vis-à-vis* other horses it races against and the distances between them. Each time a horse runs, its rating is reviewed, but a quirk of the system means that during a season the ratings rise gradually. This means the ratings of horses that have raced regularly during the season will find their level of rating rising as compared with those of horses that have not raced.

A good example of this was *Five Nations*, owned by Phonsie O'Brien, and trained by his daughter, Gillian. With British champion jockey Willie Carson in the saddle, *Five Nations* won the Irish Cesarewitch Handicap on the Curragh in 1982, carrying 8 stone 2 lb. It returned the following year, having been unraced in the meantime, and was set to carry 5 lb less! Now a blot on the handicap, *Five Nations* was a popular fancy, being backed down to 6-to-4—a particularly short price in a handicap—and duly hacked up. Bookies fumed, scratched their heads and wondered how the horse had managed to drop in the weights, considering that it had won the race the previous year. Gillian O'Brien had used a legitimate tactic to get her horse more favourably handicapped, that was her job and no bookmaker or punter had any reason to protest.

Unfortunately, human nature being what it is, many people bend the rules until they crack. In order to get their horses leniently handicapped they run them over the wrong distance, or stop them from performing. A favourite trick is to stop the horse on the flat while trying over jumps, or to stop a horse over hurdles while running it fairly over fences; modern handicappers apparently take no notice of a horse's form under another code! Another illegal trick used by trainers is to stop a horse from winning too many consecutive handicaps. One usually finds at least one disappointing run in the middle of a winning sequence, just to encourage the handicapper to think he has at last found the horse's true mark. The point I am making is that non-trying goes on and virtually everybody does it to some extent, and every punter worth his salt will be able to separate the likely winners from the deadwood.

One of the most notorious races ever run in Ireland was the T.J. Cross Maiden Hurdle (Division 1) at the 1982 Listowel festival meeting. The race was a complete farce because none of the runners was seriously trying to win. Some were being given a quiet race, others were being schooled on the racecourse, two were waiting for another day and the remainder were worse than useless and their jockeys never even dreamed of winning the race on them. The race was run at a snail's pace in the early stages, as nobody would make the running. All the jockeys had been instructed to settle their mounts at the rear of the field, to get them jumping properly out of the way of those that were racing seriously. As jockeys restrained their mounts, *Pagan Love*, a rank outsider ridden by an unknown rider, pulled its way to front and began to go further and further ahead. None of the other eighteen runners made any attempt to chase the leader, who was never challenged at any stage, eventually winning the race in a hack canter, being 'whistled' home by the bemused crowd. The reaction of the crowd forced the stewards to take action, despite their natural sympathy for the trainers and riders. After an enquiry, they cautioned all the trainers with horses in the race, with the exception of P.J.P. Doyle, the trainer of the winner. The stewards singled out two of the runners for not being allowed to run on their merits, the favourite and the second favourite (surprise, surprise), and penalised their trainers and jockeys with a modest fine.

The Listowel festival again hit the headlines for the wrong reasons a decade later when a favourite drifted alarmingly in the betting. Word spread like wildfire that the favourite would not win on this occasion, the betting ring was buzzing with rumours and the Ring Inspector reported the facts to the stewards before the race started. Armed with the information that, as far as the bookmakers were concerned, the horse was not going to win, the stewards watched the race very closely. During the race the favourite was going so well, hitting the front with a mile to race, it looked a certainty. One professional punter, who had refused to back the favourite before the race because he had heard that it was 'dead', changed his mind and backed it in running because so well was the horse going that he just could not see how the jockey could stop it from winning. No sooner had he struck the bet, he was squealing with the rest of the punters because the jockey promptly pulled the horse up.

There was an outcry after the race, from disgruntled punters and from the press, and everyone was genuinely shocked by the blatant stopping of a favourite. The stewards held an enquiry, but it soon transpired that proving the horse had been stopped was not as simple a proposition as it sounds. The jockey claimed the horse had gone lame and he therefore had no option but to pull it up. He denied point-blank that he had been asked to stop the horse and cited in evidence that he was leading the field and look-ing the likely winner when his mount suddenly got injured. The Turf Club's own vet seemed to support the jockey's evidence that the horse was lame and the case was dropped. Unfortunately for one newspaper, in its coverage of the meeting it carelessly made an allegation that the favourite did not try to win the race, was promptly sued by the connections and had to pay out substantial damages. Once again the lesson is clear: it is much easier to make allegations than it is to prove them.

A jockey's life is a hard one. It is made harder still by the owners and trainers who employ him because convention demands that a jockey must always obey his orders. Indeed, when the stewards hold an enquiry they will always ask the jockey what his instructions were and will fine him if they were disobeyed. Owners and trainers are not supposed to instruct a jockey not to win a race, but they often do and a jockey must obey, otherwise he will be boycotted. Yet time and time again when the stewards decide that a horse has not been ridden on its merits, it is the rider who bears the brunt of the punishment dished out, usually receiving a suspension.

The late John Harty found himself in this difficult position at Limerick Junction races, near Tipperary town, some years ago. His original instructions were to win the race because a big gamble had been organised, but the coup went wrong in the betting ring.

Unfortunately, those backing it for the connections were not familiar with that course's betting ring, where the big bookmakers are not in the same position as they tend to be on most other courses. When the bookmakers on the rails priced their boards, they put this horse in at 20-to-1 and the 'boys' rushed to get on, not realising these were the small bookmakers who were opening the market and would not be prepared to lay a big bet. The backers should have been suspicious because the big bookmakers of the time never got up early to bet, but in their eagerness to get the money on that thought never occurred to them. The upshot was that the horse's price tumbled from 20-to-1 to 2-to-1, they had only got a couple of hundred pounds on and of that only buttons was at prices over 10-to-1. To the dismay of those trying to back the horse, when the big bookmakers did get up to bet they took the price from the small layers, chalking up the horse at 2-to-1. Now confirmed as the 2-to-1 favourite, the decision was made to abandon the coup and stop the horse.

By this time the horses had left the parade ring and were on their way to the start, so the trainer had to run as fast as he could to the start, which was directly in front of the stands, to inform the jockey. Waving his hands furiously, he caught the attention of John Harty, who was giving his mount a look at the first hurdle, and the jockey trotted the horse over to the rail where the trainer was standing. Between pants and gasps, the trainer informed Harty that the money was not on, the gamble was off and the horse must not play any part in the finish. Just like poor Horace Pink some fifty years before, John Harty realised that not trying on a favourite was a very different matter from not trying on an outsider, so he considered his options. Knowing that his head would be on the block if the stewards held an enquiry into the horse's running, Harty was anxious to give himself some kind of alibi. With this in mind he informed the Starter that he was not feeling too well, having been wasting to do the weight, hoping that this would explain any weakness on his part in the closing stages of the race. In a rare display of initiative, the Starter used his powers to prevent the horse from taking part and announced that it had been withdrawn!

It would have been much better for the connections if the horse had been well beaten rather than withdrawn because the book-makers would now be wary of it next time out. Still, they got some consolation because the horse won its next race at Navan and they got 4-to-1 for their money. Not as good as 20-to-1, but then a 4-to-1 winner is better than a 20-to-1 loser!

It must be said at this point that very rarely will a top jockey be asked to 'pull' a horse—that task is invariably left to the lesser lights, who must obey orders and are in no position to call the tune. However, I do know of a leading flat jockey who was booked to ride a horse at Naas that he knew little about, except that it was fancied to win. On his arrival in the parade ring, the jockey noticed that the trainer was agitated, the owner's countenance was as black as thunder and the mood was sombre. Furtive and obviously embarrassed, the trainer stammered to the jockey that the market had been taken on the owner, who was not prepared to trade at the short odds now on offer and they were very sorry but they did not want the horse to win. The jockey replied, 'I can get beaten a short head any time you want me to, but please don't ask me to win a short head.' True to his word, he successfully got the horse beaten—by a short head!

Pacemakers, Stayers and Spoilers

Nothing annoys punters more than when their selection is beaten by a second string, in other words by a less fancied horse from the same stable. Once upon a time the Rules of Racing allowed an owner who had two or more horses running in the same race to declare to win with one of them, which permitted his other horse, or horses, to be prevented from beating it. While this rule only allowed the second string to be prevented from beating the first string, the horse would still have to run on its merits against the other runners. Fearing that the rule was damaging public con-fidence in racing, the stewards scrapped it and nowadays every horse must be run on its merits. In some other racing countries, notably in France, horses in the same ownership are coupled for betting purposes, but not so in Ireland. It must be said that the vast majority of second strings are, in my opinion, not run on their merits, either being slowly away or never being put into the race until too late. They are often used as a pacemaker, blazing away at a cut-throat gallop that is impossible to sustain, and even if it is, then the jockey on the pacemaker will pull his mount wide entering the straight in order to allow the more fancied runner a clear run up the running rail. It is common practice, but it can hardly be said that the second string is being ridden to obtain the best possible placing, as the rules insist. Occasionally one gets away and wins, to the chagrin of punters who tend to rule out second strings from their calculations and then, in their frustration, blame the trainer: 'He doesn't know what day of the week it is.' The issue of pacemakers is not covered properly in the rules and the current rules requiring a horse to be ridden to obtain its best possible placing are simply a farce. I fully accept that you cannot expect an owner to see a betting coup foiled by an over-achieving pace-maker, but rather than turn a blind eye to clear breaches of the Rules in this regard, the stewards should draw up rules to deal with human nature.

One of the most sensational incidents regarding a pacemaker took place in 1954 and involved *Premonition*, trained at Newmarket by Irishman Cecil Boyd-Rochfort, who was the trainer to HM The Queen. *Premonition*, owned by Brigadier W.P. Wyatt, had been involved in controversy before, having been disqualified and placed last after beating *Chamier* in the Irish Derby. It had subse-quently won the St Leger and a Cup race campaign was planned for the 1954 season. Cup races are valuable long-distance events, such as the Ascot Gold Cup, for which a horse requires stamina in abundance. However, these races sometimes found it difficult to attract many runners, making a false pace in the early stages more likely, which would favour the horse with a bit of finishing speed rather than the conventional stayer. The trainer suggested that Brigadier Wyatt purchase a pacemaker for *Premonition* and they secured *Osborne* to do the job, a middle-distance handicapper with a bit of pace.

As a reward, *Premonition*'s lad, thirty-year-old Roy Burrows, was allowed to ride *Osborne* in its pacemaking role, which he did successfully in the Yorkshire Cup. A fortnight later *Premonition* reappeared to contest the Winston Churchill Stakes at the now defunct Hurst Park in London, for which he started the red-hot favourite at odds of 8-to-1 ON. As instructed, Roy Burrows made the running on *Osborne*, while the stable jockey, Harry Carr, settled *Premonition* in third place. All was well until Carr began to niggle at his mount approaching the straight as he tried to close up on his pacemaker. Niggling turned to an all-out assault as Carr urged *Premonition* forward, but his mount was making little impression on *Osborne*, who was bowling along merrily in the lead. With the winning post looming, Burrows began to wonder where *Premonition* was, so he looked back to see his beloved charge toiling in his wake. The bewildered stable lad clearly reined his mount in while repeatedly looking back to see how *Premonition* was going. With Burrows making no effort to ride a finish on *Osborne*, *Premonition* inched closer and closer and flat to the boards managed to get up in the very last stride to win by a short head.

Amid the inevitable outcry that followed, the Hurst Park stewards decided not to deal with the case, referring it instead to the Jockey Club, a move that was criticised by the racing community. But it was hard to see how the local stewards could do anything else: *Osborne* was clearly prevented from winning the race, the Royal trainer was involved and if he were treated differently from others, it would have brought racing into disrepute. The Jockey Club held its enquiry, behind closed doors as usual, and Captain Boyd-Rochford gave evidence that his instructions to Burrows before the race were, 'Be second if you possibly can'. The stewards of the Governing Body found that *Osborne* had not been ridden on its merits, fined Captain Boyd-Rochfort £100, the maximum fine open to them, for giving Roy Burrows inadequate riding instructions and suspended the jockey for three weeks.

Deeply upset by the verdict, Captain Boyd-Rochfort sought comfort from his owners, the vast majority of which expressed the opinion that he had done nothing wrong and had been harshly treated by the stewards. Yet surely the trainer could have expected nothing else, his pacemaker having been deliberately pulled up before thousands of spectators, right in front of the stands? The

stewards could not turn a blind eye! It subsequently turned out
that *Osborne* was a decent stayer indeed, winning both the
Goodwood and Doncaster Cups, races it was supposed to help
Premonition to win. Unknown to its connections, *Premonition* had
been set a mammoth task to try to beat the seven-year-old while
giving him 7 lb in weight. The hard race broke *Premonition*'s heart,
it lost its form completely and never won another race.

Premonition was the best horse owned by Brigadier Wilfred
Wyatt, but it certainly caused him considerable grief. Although the
horse won eight races, including the St Leger, it ran disappointingly in the Epsom Derby, for which it started joint favourite, and
then was disqualified when it won the Irish equivalent.
Premonition may also had been indirectly responsible for Captain
Boyd-Rochford throwing Brigadier Wyatt out of his yard, which
he did the following year when the owner was abruptly told to
remove his horses. The incident occurred when the Brigadier
turned up unexpectedly to see his horses work one morning,
something he often did, but on this occasion the trainer saw red,
abused his owner and ended an association that had lasted over
twenty years. It was at Brigadier Wyatt's insistence that Roy
Burrows ride *Premonition*'s pacemaker, and perhaps Boyd-
Rochfort secretly blamed him for the debacle. In any case, it was a
shocking way to treat a loyal and generous owner.

The problem with pacemakers, or second strings, has cropped
up regularly down the years, but nothing has ever been done about
it. In 1949 two wonderful stayers, *Alycidon* and *Black Tarquin*,
clashed in the Ascot Gold Cup and there was considerable controversy when Lord Derby, the owner of *Alycidon*, decided to run two
other horses, *Stockbridge* and *Benny Lynch*, to make the pace.
Stockbridge led until the halfway point, when *Benny Lynch* took
over, and in the end *Alycidon* prevailed. The horse on the wrong
end that day, *Black Tarquin*, was owned by the American William
Woodward and trained by Captain Boyd-Rochfort, and many
observers, including HM King George VI, felt that Lord Derby had
acted in an unsporting manner. These reservations seem to have
been overcome with the passing of the years, however, and today
the running of a pacemaker is usual practice.

The Cheltenham Gold Cup of 1992 proved controversial when trainer Jenny Pitman, who had won the race the previous year with *Garrison Savanagh*, was accused of running a spoiler, *Golden Freeze*, a decent two-miler that was most unlikely to stay the distance of this three-mile race. *Carvill's Hill* dominated the race, while Jenny's hopes rested with *Toby Tobias*. *Carvill's Hill* was installed the even-money favourite, its principal rival being the French-trained *The Fellow*, beaten a short head in the race the previous year. *Carvill's Hill*, acclaimed by many as one of the best steeplechasers of recent times, was a very useful horse in Ireland when trained by Jim Dreaper, winning many big races before being sold to Paul Green, who sent the horse to the leading English trainer Martin Pipe. *Carvill's Hill* had won the Welsh Grand National in awesome style by twenty lengths before returning to its native land to win the valuable Hennessy Gold Cup at Leopardstown, where the winning margin was fifteen lengths. Now it was expected to seal its place amongst the great chasers by winning the big Cheltenham race: the Gold Cup.

Ridden by Martin Pipe's stable jockey, Peter Scudamore, the champion jockey who had ridden his 1,500th winner less than a fortnight earlier, *Carvill's Hill* set off in front and was immediately taken on by *Golden Freeze*, ridden by Michael Bowlby. That did not particularly worry Peter Scudamore because *Aquilifer* had tried to do just that in the Welsh Grand National and he would have been content to settle his mount in second place. *Golden Freeze*, as expected, took on *Carvill's Hill* going to the first fence, unsettling the favourite, who made a terrible mistake and was fortunate not to have fallen. *Carvill's Hill*'s jumping error left *Golden Freeze* in a clear lead, which suited Scudamore, and he attempted to settle his mount in behind the leader. This is where the race became controversial because at this point Michael Bowlby reined back *Golden Freeze* in order to be upsides the favourite jumping the second fence. The theory was that having another horse in close proximity when jumping would unsettle *Carvill's Hill* and force it into jumping errors—which is precisely what happened. Although the non-staying *Golden Freeze* ran out of steam and was pulled up, leaving *Carvill's Hill* with a clear lead, the numerous

jumping errors had taken their toll and the horse tired. Headed by
the eventual winner, *Cool Ground*, at the second last, *Carvill's Hill*
eventually finished last of the five finishers. The winner, *Cool
Ground*, was given an exceptional ride by Adrian Maguire to beat
The Fellow by a short head, the French horse suffering back-to-
back short head defeats in the race.

Afterwards the stewards held an enquiry into *Carvill's Hill*'s and
Golden Freeze's running, which exonerated Michael Bowlby of the
charge that he had not ridden *Golden Freeze* on its merits. Jenny
Pitman confirmed that *Golden Freeze* was a genuine pacemaker
and not a spoiler, but the racing public was divided on the subject.
The connections of *Carvill's Hill*, although annoyed by the tactics
and rejecting that *Golden Freeze* was run as a genuine pacemaker,
did not put their horse's failure down to the antics of Michael
Bowlby. *Carvill's Hill* was later found to have pulled muscles in its
chest as well as aggravating an old tendon injury, and this was the
probable cause of its poor jumping in the race. Indeed, the leg
injury sustained in that race ended *Carvill's Hill*'s racing career
and the horse, which never ran again, was officially retired two
years later.

Pipped at the Post

One of the most memorable controversies of recent years was the
King's Lake/To-Agori-Mou saga of 1981. The English-trained *To-
Agori-Mou* came to the Curragh hoping to emulate *Right Tack* and
become only the second horse to win both the English and Irish
Two Thousand Guineas. In the absence of *Storm Bird*, its main
rival was *King's Lake*, trained by Vincent O'Brien and ridden by his
new stable jockey, Pat Eddery, who had just taken over from Lester
Piggott. At the time relations between Vincent O'Brien and the
press had deteriorated to such an extent that the trainer refused to
release any information about his horses and the races in which
they were likely to run. The row started after O'Brien withdrew
the ante-post favourite and stable star *Storm Bird* from the Two
Thousand Guineas. The late withdrawal, on the grounds that the
horse was coughing, irritated the press because the stable had
apparently told a reporter a couple of hours earlier that *Storm Bird*

had worked well and was a definite runner. Batting for the punters, the newspapers made a series of allegations against the trainer, who retaliated by refusing to speak to journalists at all.

To-Agori-Mou, with Greville Starkey up, started favourite at slight odds-on, with *King's Lake* a 5-to-1 chance, and the pair fought out the finish. In the closing stages *King's Lake* veered towards his rival, although the pair did not collide, but Starkey responded dramatically by standing up in the saddle. Despite losing ground because of the swerve, *King's Lake* won a thrilling race by a neck. The stewards immediately called an enquiry.

The Curragh Acting Stewards, Major Victor McCalmont, Lt-Col Sir John Silcock, Cyril Myerscough and Edmund Loder, assisted by the Stipendiary Steward Peter Martin, held their enquiry into the finish of the race. They decided that *King's Lake* had accidentally caused interference to *To-Agori-Mou*, concluded that the interference had enabled it to improve its placing, and reversed the placings of the two horses. The stewards' decision to award the race to the favourite did not go down well with the bookmakers, who had expected *King's Lake* to keep the race, and of course they had an interest in the outcome. Influential and impartial race readers were divided on the subject, however. Timeform believed that *King's Lake* should have kept the race because the interference was minimal and Starkey had made the most of it. However, the veteran commentator Peter O'Sullevan and the colourful know-all John McCririck held the opposite view—that *To-Agori-Mou* would have won the race with a clear run if *King's Lake* had not swerved. Understandably, Vincent O'Brien appealed the decision to the stewards of the Turf Club.

The appeal came before Christopher Gaisford St Lawrence, Lord Killanin and John Byrne and the hearing lasted over six hours. Unlike the original enquiry, lawyers were permitted to represent the parties and three senior councils were present. The video of the race was watched over and over again as the lawyers argued about the admissibility of oral evidence given to the local stewards by jockeys Wally Swinburn and Stephen Craine. But the crux of the issue was whether *King's Lake* had improved its placing by interfering with *To-Agori-Mou*. This was a matter of opinion. One set of stewards held that it had, but in the end the Turf Club stewards decided on the opposite view. They allowed the appeal, overturned the decision of the acting stewards and gave the race back to *King's Lake*.

The decision to reinstate *King's Lake* took most observers by surprise and was greeted with hostility by the British press. Geoff Lester of *The Sporting Life* called the decision 'nothing short of scandalous'. Naturally the connections of *To-Agori-Mou* were unhappy, Guy Harwood describing the reversal as 'diabolical', but so too were the acting stewards who had made the original decision and who now felt let down by their colleagues. The Chairman of the panel, Major Victor McCalmont was so upset that he publicly announced his resignation from the Turf Club as a result of the reversal. In a statement he said: 'I feel that my authority has been completely undermined and the racing public would not have any confidence in my judgement any longer.'

After all the uproar had died down somewhat, the two horses met again on the first day of the Royal Ascot meeting, with *King's Lake* 6-to-4 favourite to confirm his superiority, while *To-Agori-Mou* was priced at 2-to-1. In another exciting finish the two game horses flashed past the post together, the photo finish deciding that on this occasion *To-Agori-Mou* had won by a neck. In his moment of joy and vindication Greville Starkey rather inadvisedly aimed a 'V' sign at Pat Eddery right under the nose of the Queen, which action was greeted with cheers from his supporters and with shocked surprise from the ladies in the Royal Enclosure. The jockey was fortunate indeed that the stewards took no action against him—perhaps indicating they felt he had a point.

The two horses raced against each other twice more. *King's Lake* triumphed at Goodwood by a neck and *To-Agori-Mou* came out on top by a nose at Deauville, where the pair finished second and third behind *Northjet*. There was little or nothing between the two horses: both were strong, courageous and competitive and roused the passions and loyalties of their respective supporters. No wonder the affair was so divisive and controversial!

Was *Shergar* Stolen to Land a Betting Coup?

On a Wednesday afternoon on the Epsom Downs, in June 1981, a powerful bay horse with a prominent white blaze on his face and four white socks on his legs, being ridden by baby-faced, nineteen-year-old jockey Walter Swinburn, clad in the 'green jacket, red epaulettes' of the Aga Khan, stormed up the hill to win the Derby by ten lengths. Starting a slight odds-on favourite, the horse was *Shergar*, named after a Himalayan village, and its brilliant performance was underlined by the ease of the victory—the ten-length margin being the greatest in the history of the 170-year-old race. The racing public had seen an awesome performance and hailed the arrival of a new, formidable champion.

Shergar's trainer, Michael Stoute, made it clear that the horse's next target was the Irish Derby, run at the Curragh, close to its birthplace, where it would endeavour to become only the eighth horse to do the Epsom/Curragh Derby double. In the three weeks between the two races there was a real scare, the type that always keeps the connections of good horses on tenterhooks. One morning *Shergar* dislodged his lad on the gallops and sped off, riderless, over the horizon towards the village of Kentford, leaving panic and turmoil in his wake. As lads scattered in pursuit of the almost priceless animal, a local fireman driving down a main road noticed a loose horse galloping up the road towards him. Acting on instinct, the fireman stopped his car across the road, blocking it, and jumped out and grabbed the horse as it pulled up approaching the obstacle. Having no idea what horse it was, or where it had come from, the fireman led it to the safety of a nearby stable. His quick-thinking had avoided a disaster, for *Shergar* would either have collided with a vehicle or his legs would have been destroyed from galloping on the jarring surface of the road. The fireman had saved the Derby winner, and must have been jolly surprised when he found out its identity. Much to Michael Stoute's relief, *Shergar* was sound and fears that the horse might have sustained a hidden injury were dispelled when he worked impressively on the gallops.

Hot on the heels of that scare came another setback: *Shergar*'s regular jockey got into trouble riding at Royal Ascot. Walter Swinburn was riding a horse named *Centurius*, a half-brother to

Grundy, who had been the fourth horse to win both the English and Irish Derbies, and was cruising to victory—or so he thought! Out of the blue Willie Carson produced *Bustomi* with a challenge, forcing Walter Swinburn to go for his whip to rouse his mount. Unfortunately, his whip was in his right hand and *Centurius* began to drift off the rails away from it, carrying *Bustomi* out into the centre of the course. With the horses neck and neck, a flustered Swinburn did not realise that his mount was hanging, made no attempt to switch his whip to his left hand to try and straighten up *Centurius* and, despite consistently hampering *Bustomi*, the latter took the race by a neck. The stewards held an enquiry. They found the young jockey guilty of careless riding and disqualified *Centurius*, placing it last, and suspended Swinburn for seven days. With the suspension due to begin on Irish Derby day, Swinburn was now unable to ride *Shergar* at the Curragh and 'that man' Lester Piggott was booked to ride in his place. That was bitter news for the Swinburn household because only a month previously Walter's father, Wally, who was stable jockey to Dermot Weld and regular rider of *Blue Wind*, had been 'jocked off' and replaced by Piggott in the Epsom Oaks. *Blue Wind* went on to win the Oaks by seven lengths and the incident deprived the Swinburn family of a big Epsom Classic double with *Shergar* and *Blue Wind*.

Installed a hot-favourite at 3-to-1 ON, *Shergar* had won its three previous races by ten, twelve and ten lengths and the huge crowd that came to the Curragh to see the champion run in the Irish Derby speculated and bet on whether the horse could maintain this impressive two-figure sequence. So there was general disappointment when Piggott eased *Shergar* down when the horse shot clear of the field and dawdled past the post four lengths to the good. Piggott explained afterwards that he did not wish to push the horse out on the firm ground.

Reunited with Walter Swinburn, *Shergar* proved superior to the older horses by winning the King George VI and the Queen Elizabeth Stakes by four lengths before going to Doncaster for the St Leger. Starting 9-to-4 ON, *Shergar* performed poorly, finishing a disappointing fourth behind *Cut Above*. Michael Stoute declared he had made a mistake in running the horse, confessing that he had second thoughts on the day, but by that time he felt it was too late and would have been unfair on the public to withdraw *Shergar*. Swinburn explained to television viewers that the lapse proved that *Shergar* was 'only human'! Plans to run *Shergar* in the Prix de l'Arc de Triomphe were abandoned for purely commercial reasons—the fear that a defeat would devalue the horse—and it was retired to the Aga Khan's Ballymany Stud on the Curragh to take up stallion duties.

On the eve of his second covering season, at about 8.40pm on Tuesday, 8 February 1983, a gang of armed men burst into the Ballymany Stud. Using walkie-talkies to keep in contact with each other, the gang members—one of whom was dressed as a policeman—held the wife and children of the stud groom at gunpoint, while the groom, James Fitzgerald, was forced to take them to *Shergar's* box. The stallion was loaded into a horsebox, which was pulled by an old brown car, and driven off into the night. *Shergar*, gang, car and horsebox were never seen again!

Meanwhile, Mr Fitzgerald was kidnapped, driven off in a van, threatened and warned not to call the police, before being presented with a ransom demand for £2 million and dumped on a lonely road, twenty miles away. There were at least six members in the gang, three of whom were armed, and their abuse and threats had shocked and frightened the stud staff to such an extent that chaos followed their departure. Afraid to defy them and call the police, the staff frantically tried to contact the Stud Manager, Ghislain Drion, as well as the Aga Khan, who was in Switzerland. Seven hours elapsed before anything was done. At 4.00am Mr Drion phoned Alan Dukes, Ireland's Minister of Finance, and told him what had happened; the Minister informed the Gardaí.

In due course the kidnappers made contact, sending a photograph of a horse, said to be *Shergar*, with a copy of *The Irish News*, a Belfast newspaper, of 11 February in the foreground. A gang member spoke on the telephone with Ghislain Drion, a Frenchman whose English was not perfect. They could not, or would not, understand him and failed to get him to understand them. The result was a fiasco: the Stud had no idea who was holding *Shergar*, the police openly admitted that they 'hadn't a clue', and rumours befuddled the situation further. Matters were confused even more by a number of hoax ransom demands, including false contacts and code words. The only reasonable or logical demand understood by the Stud, and it could not be sure whether it was a hoax or not, was a contact phone number in Paris.

In an attempt to bring some semblance of order to the chaos, the Aga Khan appointed Sir Jakie Astor, a shareholder in the stallion, to negotiate with the kidnappers. Unfortunately, Sir Jakie needed time—there being thirty-two members of the *Shergar* syndicate to be consulted—but too much time had been lost already. The members of the *Shergar* syndicate included Robert Sangster, Vincent O'Brien, Lord Derby, the Maktoum brothers, Paul Mellon, Stavros Niarchos and Walter Haefner—people who were scattered in different countries, making regular contact difficult. He soon discovered that the syndicate was divided: some were willing to pay a ransom, others refused point-blank to have anything to do with it.

In retrospect it seems that the crucial call was received on the evening of the Saturday after the kidnap, 12 February, which followed up the photographs sent as proof that *Shergar* was alive and well. Forced to play for time, Sir Jakie said that the Stud Manager was not satisfied with the proof presented and that concrete evidence was needed that the horse was alive before they could start negotiations. The caller replied, 'If you're not satisfied, that's it', hung up and it is believed that the real kidnappers never called again. Reports were occasionally received that *Shergar*'s head could be found in a certain place, resulting in every ghoul in the country rushing to that place to see the gruesome sight. Each time they were, thankfully, disappointed.

During the next few months rumours, hoax calls, theories, claims and leads flooded the media and the Irish breeding community. One day Stan Cosgrove, *Shergar*'s vet, received a call from a man named Denis Minogue, a Co. Clare horse dealer, telling him that he had been taken to a place, blindfolded, and had seen *Shergar*. Although this was in August, six months after the stallion disappeared, Cosgrove received answers to his questions that convinced him *Shergar* might still be alive, and when told that

£40,000 would secure its release, he sent on the money. Mr Minogue returned the money because he failed to establish contact with the kidnappers, but later he managed to do so and went back to Cosgrove, stating that the ransom was now set at £80,000. Cosgrove agreed to the demand, gave the money to Denis Minogue, who would make the drop as directed by the kidnappers. Ordered to meet the kidnappers at a secret *rendezvous*, Minogue parked his car, left the £80,000 in the boot and walked to the meeting place; the kidnappers never showed. When he trudged back to his car, Minogue found the boot had been jemmied open and the money was gone. Assuming that the kidnappers had helped themselves, Minogue waited for *Shergar* to be released, but the horse never appeared. It was now obvious that it would never been seen alive again.

There had been speculation that the IRA might have taken *Shergar* in order to get paid a ransom as the organisation was active in the kidnap of prominent people at the time. It seemed logical that the kidnap unit might go for a softer target, a valuable horse, and particularly one owned by a group of wealthy foreigners; but the police have no evidence or intelligence that the IRA was involved. It was easy to blame it on the IRA—the kidnap had the appearance of a paramilitary style operation and few other gangs would have had the capacity to make the horse disappear without trace.

The IRA theory thus became the most popular, but it certainly was not the only theory: many abounded, some logical, others ridiculous, but all earnestly put forward by lovers of a juicy conspiracy. The most popular non-IRA theory was that *Shergar* might have been stolen by a person who had a grudge against the Aga Khan, a kidnap inspired by spite rather than one with a financial motive. The flimsy basis for this theory was a legal battle ongoing in France between an American racehorse owner, Wayne Murty, and the liquidator of the Marcel Boussac industrial empire, which had gone bust. Having made his fortune from textiles, Boussac entered racehorse ownership just after the Great War and his stud and stable dominated French racing for almost forty years. By the late 1970s his textile business was on the verge of bankruptcy,

Boussac found himself short of money and sold his bloodstock to Wayne Murty, lock, stock and barrel, for cash. After the American had parted with his money, but before he had taken possession of the horses, Boussac was declared bankrupt and the liquidator moved in, collected the horses as assets and sold them all to the Aga Khan on behalf of the creditors. Mr Murty had paid his money directly to Boussac, and was now left without the horses, just another unsecured creditor of Marcel Boussac and a victim of the collapse. Although this incident had nothing to do with the Aga Khan, it did not stop a whispering campaign alleging that Mr Murty might have had a motive for stealing *Shergar*. It was non-sense, of course, but it does illustrate the type of wild allegations that were doing the rounds at the time.

Many, many other ridiculous theories were in circulation about the kidnap. One of them pinned the blame on the New Orleans Mafia no less! The event that linked the disappearance of *Shergar* with the Mafia was the death of the French bloodstock agent Michel Gambet in December 1982. Gambet was found dead in a burning car in Kentucky, with a gunshot wound to his head. Apparently he owed money to the Mafia. Gambet was said to have borrowed the money in order to purchase a horse named *Vayrann* from the Aga Khan, but he never bought the horse and failed to repay the loan. Although Gambet paid the ultimate price for his default, that still left the Mafia out of pocket and, as the theory goes, the gangsters reckoned that the Aga Khan owed them a horse.

Other theories in the 'ridiculous' category speculated that *Shergar* had been stolen by a jealous stud owner who was anxious to eliminate a rival stallion—which ignored the fact that *Shergar* was being used by its owners for their mares and was not competing with the average stallion at stud on the open market. This was then amended to infer that *another* stud master had stolen *Shergar* to replace *another* stallion, which is impossible because all thorough-breds are blood-typed to prove parentage. Some people raised the sinister words 'inside job', suggesting the owners had staged the kidnap so that they could collect insurance, but most of the owners had no cover for kidnap or theft and were never paid a penny.

The 'mad Sheikh' theory suggested that *Shergar* was successfully smuggled out of Ireland by an eccentric Arab millionaire to his stud in the desert. There the horse could cover the mad Sheikh's own mares, out of reach of blood tests, papers and other annoying regulations that tend to destroy a good theory. The most romantic theory was that *Shergar* was taken to land a betting coup in a bumper race. A bumper is a flat race for amateur riders, confined to horses that had not raced at three years, and is used to introduce inexperienced jockeys and horses to racing. All runners in bumpers tend to be prospective jumpers, so *Shergar* would definitely have the class to win any bumper easily—that is, of course, if it could have run unrecognised.

The reason why so many theories abounded was that the kidnap of *Shergar* was never solved and many questions have been left unanswered. The only credible theory on the affair could not be verified because the police never got one decent lead and the general confusion made it a perfect case for a conspiracy. The unanswered questions do leave a slight doubt about whether the IRA was involved at all, although a rogue element may well have been the culprit. How come nobody saw the brown car pulling a horsebox that Saturday evening? This might indicate that the kidnappers did not take *Shergar* a great distance from the Curragh. If it had taken the horse on a long journey, it must surely have been seen because someone, somewhere in a car would have been impatiently trying to pass, having got stuck behind an old, slow-moving box on a narrow road. If the IRA had taken *Shergar*, why did it not admit it? That organisation frequently apologises when things go wrong and has never been afraid to claim responsibility for sickening atrocities, besides which the stealing of a horse would be very mild indeed.

It is likely that sometime during the operation something went wrong, perhaps the stallion became unmanageable, or got badly injured and had to be shot. This would explain why the gang gave up trying to extort a ransom, but if that was the case, where is the body of *Shergar*? Is it credible that the IRA would transport a dead horse halfway across Ireland just to bury it? How was it buried? Did the gang dig the grave themselves, or use a JCB? Surely the kidnappers would have dumped the dead horse by the side of some by-road and disappeared as quickly as they could? The only indication that it was an IRA operation comes from private statements from men who claimed to be in that organisation. Not one scrap of evidence has been produced to prove this case and certainly *Shergar*'s burial place has never been identified. It might have been an IRA splinter group, or a criminal gang, but the same questions apply and they are not easily answered.

A decade after *Shergar*'s disappearance that question was still being asked: was the horse killed? The absence of a body posed a major problem for some members of the *Shergar* syndicate, who had not insured the horse specifically against theft. The Norwich Union Insurance Company paid the Aga Khan, but refused to pay on Stan Cosgrove's policy, which did not have a theft clause in it, because there was no proof that *Shergar* had been killed. Cosgrove, a vet who manages the Moyglare Stud in Maynooth, eventually produced a sworn affidavit by a former IRA man stating that the stallion went berserk shortly after his abduction and had to be destroyed. The affidavit stated that the kidnappers were taking the horse to Co. Leitrim, near the border with Northern Ireland, but had to stop several times on the way to try and calm *Shergar*. After they shot the horse, they buried it in a bog in Aughnasheelan, on the Leitrim–Fermanagh border. The Norwich Union was not satisfied that this was proof of death, however, informing Cosgrove that he would have to produce *Shergar*'s bones if he wanted payment.

In the summer of 1993 Stan Cosgrove was contacted by someone claiming to be able to solve his problem. This time it was a woman who made contact, calling herself 'Marli' and demanding £40,000 in return for the bones of *Shergar*. Once bitten, twice shy! Stan Cosgrove was not going to part with his money without some proof that the caller was genuine, but 'Marli' was not very co-operative. With no proof forthcoming, it was decided to offer 'Marli' 10 per cent of the eventual insurance settlement in return for information that led to *Shergar*'s remains. The offer was declined as 'Marli' wanted cash up front!

That was not quite the end of the saga because in 1996 an Irish

TV programme pursued a claim that *Shergar*'s bones had been found in Co. Donegal. The source of the claim was a Northern horse dealer who, acting from a tip-off by the IRA, had dug up some of the bones of *Shergar* the previous year and contacted Stan Cosgrove. Stan did not believe the story and was not interested, but later the story was taken up by RTÉ and received a lot of publicity. There was talk of the bones being sent away for DNA testing, but the horse dealer's credibility was called into question when it was revealed that he had been convicted in a Belfast court in 1989 for falsely declaring that a horse was dead. When questioned about that conviction the horse dealer destroyed any credibility he had left by stating that he refused to recognise the court, claiming the charges were politically motivated and were the work of freemasons and the Orange Order!

Shergar vanished into thin air. Perhaps the champion did make it back to the track, running anonymously in place of an inferior horse, landing a gamble before being hastily disposed of to the nearest pack of foxhounds. Its distinguishing white blaze and socks could easily have been painted out and a well-planned switch enacted, allowing the great *Shergar* to anonymously relive another moment of glory before a cruel end. The true *Shergar* story has not yet come out, but perhaps some day it will and a future book on betting coups may tell of the exploits of the lost winner of two Derbies, returning in triumph to the winner's enclosure of an unfamiliar racecourse, unrecognised and unappreciated. On the other hand, if those who landed this mythical coup with *Shergar* are real professionals, nobody will ever hear about it.

The Game of the Name

This is the old chestnut of naming horses, and naming horses confusingly! There are instances of different horses racing under the same name in the Grand National. Two horses named *Pioneer*, one a previous winner of the race, ran in 1848, for example. This must have been the tip of the iceberg, if all the steeplechases run during the course of a year were taken into account. Whatever its extent, the naming fiasco caused confusion and invited blatant abuse.

When a body was established to oversee jump-racing, a proper register of names was set up, and this went a long way to ending the many abuses inherent in the system. However, a new problem was soon to emerge.

As different racing nations began keeping a *Thoroughbred Stud Book* and instituting naming systems independent of the *General Stud Book*, from which all thoroughbred horses descend, a potential loophole was exposed when foreign-bred horses first began to race in Britain and Ireland. Occasionally two horses of the same name appeared around the same time, one bred here and the other abroad, although it was a rare occurrence because of the perils of transporting horses. But, of course, as time passed, this began to change and there was increased traffic of horses across the English Channel and the Irish Sea.

After the Second World War French trainers began aiming their charges at the top English and Irish races. The influx of these foreign-bred and foreign-named racehorses convinced the stewards that these must be easily identifiable to prevent confusion over horses' names. Accordingly, the stewards decided that all foreign-bred and foreign-named horses would carry the suffix 'II' when racing here. The most famous of these horses were *Fraise de Bois II* and *Tambourine II*, winners of the Irish Derby, and *Sea Bird II*, winner of the Epsom Derby.

By the late 1960s agreement had been reached among the leading racing nations that a standard suffix would be used internationally. The country of birth of a horse—which is not necessarily the country of its breeding—would be appended to its name in an abbreviated form, e.g. GB, IRE, FR, USA, GER, etc. The first Irish Classic winner to carry the new suffix was *Prince Regent FR*, winner of the 1969 Irish Derby. The benefits of the new system were immediately apparent with regard to the two stallions called *Bold Lad*, one of which was Irish-bred and standing at stud in Ireland, the other being the American-bred *Bold Lad*, at stud in France. They were now easily distinguished as *Bold Lad IRE* and *Bold Lad USA*. According to the rules of the system, when a horse ran in its country of birth, no suffix was necessary, therefore, for example, in Ireland *Bold Lad IRE* raced simply as *Bold Lad*.

The system had been in place for twenty-five years and was working perfectly, but a simple error opened up the opportunity for a betting coup that gave the bookmakers a right cleaning. In 1995 trainer Roland O'Sullivan, based in Bognor Regis, had a seven-year-old sprinter in his stable named *Crystal Heights FR*, which had ability and had shown useful form in the past. Under trainer W.A. O'Gorman, *Crystal Heights FR* had won on the 'all-weather' track at Southwell and at a minor event at Brighton at three years, earning a Timeform rating of eighty-five. In 1992 it was sold to Mr Joseph for 5,000 guineas. Coming back after an absence, *Crystal Heights FR* was entered to run at the 'all-weather' tracks, which accommodate the lowest class of racehorse, and Roland O'Sullivan was confident it could pick up a race or two. When making the entry O'Sullivan omitted the suffix 'FR', which suggested the horse was *Crystal Heights GB* and the suffix had been dropped because he was racing in his homeland. *Crystal Heights GB*, by *Wolver Heights*, was a nine-year-old that had begun its career with Ron Sheather, winning a claiming race at Leicester in August 1988 before losing interest in racing. Accurately described by Timeform, as a rogue and rated at sixty-six, *Crystal Heights GB* was sold to go hurdling in 1988 and by 1995 was a very moderate hunter, running in point-to-points.

When it was declared to run on the all-weather at Lingfield Park, the pundits and tipsters dismissed the chances of *Crystal Heights*, the 'point-to-pointer'. As did the bookmakers, who put it in as a 33-to-1 no-hoper, blissfully ignorant of the fact that it was not that horse at all but the infinitely superior *Crystal Heights FR*. Needless to say, the connections did not tell the bookmakers that they were making a mistake, that this horse was not, in fact, the nine-year-old rogue that was now point-to-pointing unsuccessfully but rather the seven-year-old sprinter with winning form. They had no obligation to tell them. No, they did what most people would do—helped themselves! They feasted with relish on the fancy prices of 33-to-1, 25-to-1 and 20-to-1, then sated themselves completely by backing the horse at all prices down to 2-to-1 favourite. The on-course bookies were hit, so too were the shops, but it was only when the horse won that the bookmakers realised it was *Crystal Heights FR*!

During the recriminations that followed Roland O'Sullivan blamed Weatherbys, the body that took the entry and issued the details to the press; Weatherbys blamed the trainer, pointing out that he was responsible for ensuring that the 'FR' was marked clearly on the entry form. O'Sullivan retaliated that the horse's passport had been lodged, as required, and that it stated clearly that the horse was *Crystal Heights* FR. The blame went round and round, but the bookmakers still had to pay up and did so most unwillingly. They did threaten to sue Weatherbys for compensation, alleging that the firm had been negligent in failing to identify the horse correctly and that the horse ought not have been allowed to run if described incorrectly on the race card. It all came to nothing, of course. The bookies had been well and truly caught and the row soon died down as the bookies knuckled down to the business of getting their money back! Regardless of error and blame, the bookies should have smelled a rat when a point-to-pointer, and a useless one at that, was being backed to win a sprint, even a low-class sprint on the 'all-weather'. So, what's in a name? Everything!

Charles Byrnes tames the Ring

Charles Byrnes, who trains at Ballingarry, Co. Limerick, runs the hottest betting stable in Ireland at present and is probably the best gambling trainer since Barney Curley hit the bookies for six back in the mid-1980s. A gambling stable is one that lays horses out to land a gamble in a particular race, so it tends to attract betting owners whose greatest wish is to clean out the bookies. Formerly a big punter, and a bookmaker for a very brief period, Charles Byrnes understands betting, has proven that he can get a horse fit and has a knack of finding weakly contested races for his charges to win. He has also shown that his horses do more than simply land gambles: *Cloudy Bays* has proved a quality steeplechaser, has won valuable races and is now competing with the best. All gambling trainers run into trouble with the stewards sooner or later, and Charles Byrnes' first serious brush with authority happened recently when the lesser fancied of his two runners was cited by the stewards on the grounds that it was not ridden on its merits.

The incident occurred in a race at Mallow (now annoyingly called Cork Racecourse), in which *Laetitia* looked the likely winner of the race but managed to get beaten, having got an inadequate ride. A crowd, mostly comprised of bookmakers, vented their anger on the course, but off-course TV viewers also phoned up in some numbers to complain. RTÉ and Sky News featured the race on their news programmes and the incident was described by Gordon Holmes, Chairman of the Turf Club's Appeals & Referrals Committee, as 'the worst case of this type we've had to deal with.'

The incident occurred on Sunday, 24 April 2005 when Charles Byrnes ran two horses from his stable in the Coolmore Brian Boru National Hunt Flat Race over a distance of two-and-a-quarter miles. The better fancied of the pair was *Alpha Royale*, owned by the Anywhere But Home syndicate, which started at 7-to-1 having been well supported in the market, and the outsider of the two, an unsupported 14-to-1 shot, Mrs Mary M. Hayes' *Laetitia*, ridden by an inexperienced amateur rider, twenty-eight-year-old Limerick auctioneer Michael Purcell. The race was due to start at 4.55pm, but the Starter let the field off one minute early, which in times gone by would have made the race void.

Had *Laetitia* simply hacked round at the tail of the field, nothing would have been said by anyone, but the hapless Mr M.G. Purcell found himself in a challenging position in the straight, going ominously well. His discomfort was increased because the horse he was challenging was the better-fancied stable companion, which nobody, except the bookmakers, wanted him to beat. There followed an inept performance from the rider, which was interpreted by many who watched the race on the course and on television, rightly or wrongly, as a reluctance to beat his stable companion. In the midst of the post-race furore the beleaguered rider explained, 'I'm totally unfit, to be honest, and got unbalanced in the closing stages. I'm an office man and only ride about once a fortnight. Even when I gave my mount a slap, I actually missed. I just wasn't up to it.'

At the subsequent stewards' enquiry, which lasted seventy-five minutes, Charles Byrnes stated in his evidence that he was dissatisfied with Mr Purcell's riding and agreed it was not satisfactory.

The stewards noted the trainer's comments and took no action against him. However, Michael Purcell was dealt with most severely, being fined €2,000 and receiving a fifty-day suspension for breaching Rule 212: 'Every horse which runs in a race shall be run on its merits whether its owner runs another in the race or not.' This would appear to suggest that the stewards did not accept that the jockey was incapable of riding a finish, whether due to tiredness or incompetence. In any case that would be no justification, as even an inexperienced amateur rider should at least be fit enough to do the job if he accepts a mount.

It was the complaints from TV viewers that attracted the attention of the news media, with the result that pictures of the finish were broadcast to a wider audience. Annoyed at the publicity, which was damaging to racing, particularly when the taxpayer was giving a grant of over £50 million annually to the sport, the Irish Sports Minister John O'Donoghue got involved. He publicly expressed his concern at the impact of such incidents on Irish racing and called on the Turf Club to look again at the incident to see if there were any further breaches of the rules. The Minister had been present at the races that afternoon, where he would have been confronted by complaining bookmakers and members of the public, but his intervention was unprecedented nevertheless. His comments may also be an indication of an uneasy alliance between the two factions that make up the governing body of Irish racing, the private Turf Club, which traditionally controlled the sport but now is only responsible for the integrity of racing, and the semi-State Horse Racing Ireland, which finances the sport and does the administration work. The Minister stated that:

I was disappointed to see the contentious riding display and I'm concerned that incidents like this will negatively influence people's views of Irish racing and will seriously undermine Horse Racing Ireland's efforts to promote Irish racing and encourage the general public to come racing … Incidents such as the one witnessed at Cork only serve to hinder the positive promotion of Irish racing both at home and abroad.

Mary Hayes, the owner of *Laetitia*, appealed against the horse's suspension, but Michael Purcell did not appeal his sentence. This allowed the horse to contest a bumper at Kilbeggan a fortnight later, which it duly won, and then to enjoy the suspension, if it were confirmed, out on grass. Insensitive to the criticism, Charles Byrnes appeared to give the two fingers, *à la* Harvey Smith, to the stewards by availing of the appeal procedure, which had no earthly chance of succeeding, allowing *Laetitia* to run at Kilbeggan and effectively rendering as meaningless the suspension given to the horse. That said, most punters would have a natural sympathy with Charles Byrnes as everyone knew *Laetitia* was a second string and would have been virtually unbacked with the bookies. Even the bookmakers understood the trainer's dilemma. John Dineen, who struck a number of biggish bets about *Alpha Royal*, declared: 'You cannot blame connections for not trying with a second string. Everyone would do the same in their place and punters hate losing out in such a manner.' He also was of the opinion that the incident did not affect the integrity of Irish racing in any way, which is true as far as punters are concerned. However, nobody can deny that it was very bad PR for racing as far as the wider racing public was concerned.

The appeal by Mary Hayes against *Laetitia*'s sixty-day suspension came before the Turf Club's Appeals & Referrals Committee, chaired by the Limerick solicitor Gordon Holmes, on Wednesday, 11 May. Mrs Hayes stated in evidence that neither she nor her husband were to blame, that they had been out of the country on the day of the race and only got back the following day, and that she believed she ought not be saddled with a penalty which, if put into effect, will cause her considerable financial loss. Having heard the evidence the Committee dismissed the appeal, but also stated that it was not satisfied with Charles Byrnes, expressed dissatisfaction with the accuracy of his evidence and cautioned him regarding the accuracy of his evidence in future. Mrs Hayes was ordered to forfeit her €380 deposit and also to pay €500 towards the cost of the appeal hearing. The Committee used precedence set by the *David's Lad* case, which had gone to the High Court, and ruled that any disqualification of a horse was not a punishment on the owner, but a consequence of the actions of a jockey or trainer.

Most successful gambling stables encounter bad publicity from time to time as they endeavour to stay one step ahead of the book-maker and the handicapper. While this sometimes means sailing quite close to the wind as far as the Rules of Racing are concerned, generally it is the handicapper, the bookmaker and the punter who have to be misled, not the stewards. Most of the time this can be done within the rules of racing, but it always irritates punters when a stable lands a gamble with a horse that, on the face of its form, does not look a likely winner. Consequently, gambling trainers would not be popular among betting-shop regulars, who amusingly point out that with certain trainers a horse with a string of duck eggs before its name is actually the form horse! Most gambling stables have a short shelf life because they eventu-ally run out of bookmakers willing to take their bets. When that happens, those owners who had flocked to the honey pot move on just as quickly when the honey is gone.

Gambling owners are also risky; being flush with money one day and clean broke the next, which can make life difficult for those who train for them as they chase up unpaid accounts. Gambling owners come and go like summer showers, a fact of life all gambling trainers must face up to and which forces them to seek a more secure type of owner who has a big, regular income and can afford to have a horse in training. The more substantial owner, who might admire the skills of the gambling trainer, tends not to like being associated with excessive betting and is embarrassed by brushes with the stewards. Therefore, gambling must be a stepping-stone in a trainer's career, a period in which the trainer will accumulate some money and establish his name before moving on to a more traditional trainer's role. Charles Byrnes has the ability to make the grade at a higher level and should now have enough money to take on the best jumping trainers. Expect him to train more winners and to land fewer and fewer gambles.

PART 6
THE COURSES AND THE RACES

'The Turf, and long may we be above it.'

JORROCK'S TOAST

THE COURSES

ASCOT (BERKSHIRE). LONDON 25M; READING 14M.
Royal racecourse founded by Queen Anne in 1711, featuring the midsummer Royal meeting, famous for its hats and top-class racing. Ascot introduced the parade of runners in front of the stands before each race.

BELLEWSTOWN (CO. MEATH)
There are records of racing at Bellewstown as far back as 1726, making it, after the Curragh and Down Royal, the third oldest course in Ireland. In 1844 the course received sponsorship from the Railway Company, one of the first to do so. Its jumping course was laid out in 1871, but thirty years ago steeplechasing was discontinued. This sharp country course on Crockafotha (Hill of the Fairies) still has an outside betting enclosure and a traditional funfair.

BOYERSTOWN (CO. MEATH)
A steeplechase meeting that raced under the Meath Hunt and Navan title over a course about a mile from Navan town until it closed in 1933. Racing had been held there for over 180 years. For a period of twelve years, 1921–1933, Navan had two racecourses, the other being Proudstown Park, which races nowadays as Navan.

BRIGHTON (SUSSEX). LONDON 52M.
A U-shaped racecourse, two miles from the town, with a steep hill that resembles Epsom. The Grand Stand, which is 400 ft above sea level, offers a good view of the racing. Brighton races only on the flat and is a minor meeting.

CARTMEL (LANCASHIRE). GRANGE 2M; BARROW-IN-FURNESS 15M.
Minor, little used hilly jumping course in England's Lake District featuring the longest run-in in Britain. Attracts a holiday crowd rather than seasoned punters and is overlooked by an old priory.

CHELTENHAM (GLOUCESTERSHIRE). BIRMINGHAM 46M; BRISTOL 44M.

Jumping course that moved to its present site in 1902. The famous National Hunt festival is run here annually in March, which attracts the top jumpers and is particularly popular with Irish owners and racegoers.

CHESTER (CHESHIRE). LIVERPOOL 18M.

Racing has been held on the Roodee since 1540, making Chester the oldest meeting in Britain to be held on its original location. Only flat races are run on this tight course and racing can be seen from the old walls of the city. For over 200 years the runners had to be walked through the streets of the city from the racecourse stables to the racecourse, but this practice ended in 2005. The new racecourse stables adjacent to the course are in use from May 2006.

CLONMEL (CO. TIPPERARY)

There has been racing in Clonmel since 1845, but the Powerstown course was not enclosed until Villiers Morton Jackson established Powerstown Park in April 1913. He decided to confine the bookmakers to a permanent betting ring rather than allowing them to roam the enclosures, an innovation that was immediately copied by other courses. Jackson sold the property to the Irish Coursing Club in 1932 but continued to live in the big house, now demolished, until his death.

CURRAGH (CO. KILDARE)

Owned by the Turf Club and the headquarters of Irish racing, the Curragh is the home of all five Irish Classic races. As far back as 1673 King Charles II donated two Plates to be run for on the Curragh and it is the oldest racecourse in Ireland. The Curragh is a major training centre.

DONCASTER (YORKSHIRE). LEEDS 28M.

Racing is held on the Town Moor close by the town and is home to the oldest Classic race—the St Leger—first run in 1777. The meeting was moved from Cantley Common to the Town Moor in 1778. Flat- and jump-racing are held here.

DOWNPATRICK (CO. DOWN)

A small, hilly course near the place where St Patrick is buried, which is the venue of the Ulster Grand National and one of only two courses in Northern Ireland. This course dates from 1867, but the old course had been used since 1685.

DOWN ROYAL (CO. DOWN)

The Maze course is the second oldest in Ireland, after the Curragh, with records showing that King James II gave money for a race to be run here in 1684 for the purpose of encouraging the sport of horse-racing. The Down Royal Corporation of Horsebreeders, founded by Royal Charter in 1685, moved its base here from Downpatrick in 1789. The course survived a crisis in 1983 when it looked as if it would have to close down, but it was saved by the intervention of the prominent Northern owner Kelso Stewart.

EPSOM (SURREY). LONDON 15M.

The Epsom races were mentioned by Samuel Pepys in his famous diary of 1663 and Epsom is home to two Classic races—the Derby and the Oaks. It features the famous Tattenham Corner and boasts records of racing here dating as far back as 1648.

FOLKESTONE (KENT). DOVER 7M; LONDON 70M.

The course, the only one left in Kent since the closure of Wye in 1974, is at Westernhanger, eight miles from Folkestone, and opened in 1898. A small-time course, on the flat and over the jumps, Folkestone was earmarked for closure in 1963 but managed to survive.

GALWAY (BALLYBRIT, CO. GALWAY)

Progressive, popular festival course with a stiff, uphill finish and a ruined castle. The course opened in 1869 and features the Galway Steeplechase Plate and the Galway Hurdle, which was a two-day meeting until a third day was added in 1961. Nowadays the festival extends over seven days and the racecourse management is the best in Ireland.

GOODWOOD (SUSSEX). LONDON 58M; CHICHESTER 5M.

'Glorious Goodwood' dates from 1802 but was established as a first-class racing venue due to the efforts of Lord George Bentinck (1802–1848). Features rich, springy downland turf with steep undulations and Trundle Hill offers a unique head-on view of the racing.

GOWRAN PARK (CO. KILKENNY)

Opened as Goresbridge Races in 1914, Gowran Park was the first racecourse to offer a commentary to its patrons when the late Michael O'Hehir called the horses in March 1952. Its principal race, the Thyestes Chase, is run in January.

HAYDOCK PARK (MERSEYSIDE). MANCHESTER 18M.

The old Newton Races were transferred to this course in 1899. Offers top-class flat- and national hunt racing over an excellent track and offers patrons a good view of the proceedings.

HURST PARK (HAMPTON COURT). LONDON 15M.

Raced on Molesey Hurst, near Hampton Court, on the Surrey bank of the River Thames until it closed down in 1962. This was the old Hampton course enclosed, which re-opened as Hurst Park in 1890. Only a mile from Kempton Park, its big races, the Triumph Hurdle and the Victoria Cup, were transferred to Cheltenham and Ascot respectively.

KILBEGGAN (CO. WESTMEATH)

The meeting dates from 1843 but lapsed until revived on the Loughnagore course in 1901. The only racecourse in Ireland that races exclusively under National Hunt Rules, Kilbeggan manages to provide competitive racing from moderate horses.

KILKENNY (DANESFORT)

A Kilkenny racemeeting was run between 1762 and 1869 over the Dunmore course. The meeting was revived in 1874 and run at Danesfort, on the main Kilkenny–Waterford road. It catered for flat- and jump-racing and its flat course could cater for five and six furlongs sprint. It ran a spring and an autumn two-day meeting and featured a valuable two-mile steeplechase called the Citizens' Plate and the Ormonde Plate for two-year-olds. The Killkenny meeting finally closed in 1899.

LEOPARDSTOWN (FOXROCK, CO. DUBLIN)

Modelled on Sandown Park, Leopardstown opened in 1888 and is the best viewing racecourse in Ireland. Fred Clarke, whose family was associated with the course for many years and who lived in a house in the grounds, sold the racecourse to the Racing Board at a price way below the market value in order that it be preserved for racing. It is now the only racecourse in Dublin.

LEWES (EAST SUSSEX)

Exposed racecourse high up on the South Downs where Fred Archer had his last rides before his premature death in 1886. The Grand National winning horse of 1921, *Shaun Spadah,* is buried here and Lewes prison is nearby. It was also an established training centre, Jack 'Towser' Gosden being the most famous before he moved to Newmarket. The racecourse closed in 1964.

LIVERPOOL

The Aintree course has been the home of the Grand National since 1837 and features big fences like Becher's Brook, the Canal Turn, Valentine's and the Chair. The Grand National course, which is used only a few times a year nowadays, involves the runners crossing the Melling Road and heading out into the country before returning back to the racecourse proper.

NAAS (CO. KILDARE)

Opened in 1924, Naas at one time was known as the 'punters' graveyard' because the ground used to get very heavy, which was responsible for some shock results. It was drained many years ago and is now a fine course, but it lacks a really important fixture. Future champion trainer Paddy Prendergast trained his first winner at this track, as did Anne Biddle with *Flying Tiger* in 1966, the latter being the first woman to officially train a winner in Ireland.

Navan (Co. Meath)

Opened in 1921 as Proudstown Park to avoid confusion with the Meath Hunt and Navan races, which were run over the Boyerstown course, situated one mile from Navan town, which was extant at the time. *Arkle* won his first race here, his dam *Bright Cherry* having won three times on the course previously, as did jockey Willie Robinson, later associated with *Arkle's* big rival *Mill House*. A fine jumping course with wide bends and a steep, uphill finish, Navan was the place where a woman rider beat the men over jumps for the first time, when Anne Ferris won a hurdle race in June 1975.

Newmarket (Suffolk). London 62m; Cambridge 13m.

This great heath on the Suffolk–Cambridgeshire border is owned by the Jockey Club and is the main training centre in England. It has two distinct racecourses, the Rowley Mile course and the July Course (originally used only in July but now used from June to August), as well as extensive training gallops and facilities. The imposition of Newmarket Rules 250 years ago was so successful in driving the crooks and the riff-raff out of racing that the Rules were subsequently adopted by virtually every racecourse in Britain.

Phoenix Park (Dublin)

Established in 1902, the Phoenix Park ran the first ever evening meeting on Saturday, 13 July 1929, when the off time of the first race was 6.30pm. This charming racecourse, situated at the Ashtown Gate of the Park, was modelled on Hurst Park and was redeveloped in 1982, but that did not save it. The course closed down in 1990.

Roscommon

Racing on the Lenabane course was revived in May 1948 having been closed for twelve years. A country course popular with race-goers, it is situated halfway between Galway and Sligo and runs summer flat and jumping meetings.

SANDOWN PARK (ESHER, SURREY). LONDON 15M; EPSOM 7M.

The first enclosed or park course in Britain was opened in 1875. Its feature race, the Eclipse Stakes, is run on the flat but Sandown has a superb jump course, with its well-known 'Pond' fence. It abolished its Silver Ring in 1973, the first English racecourse to do so.

THE RACES

ANGLESEY STAKES, CURRAGH: TWO-YEAR-OLDS; 6 FURLONGS (GROUP 3)

First run in 1829, it is the oldest race in Ireland run over its original distance. Named after Henry Paget, First Marquis of Anglesey, Lord Lieutenant of Ireland, it was once one of the most important two-year-old events in the calendar, but its prestige has waned and it is now a Group 3 race.

ASCOT GOLD CUP, ROYAL ASCOT: 20 FURLONGS (GROUP 1)

The premier race for stayers has been run every June since 1807. Once one of the most important races in the calendar, in recent years its prestige has waned because breeders tend to shy away from breeding from stayers, fearing that they get slow horses. Now open to geldings, the race goes on amid a clamour to have its distance reduced to two miles.

BALDOYLE DERBY, BALDOYLE

Run between 1874 and 1914, this race was usually confined to three-year-old colts and fillies and initially it was more valuable than the Irish Derby. For some reason the race was dropped in 1902 and although revived a couple of years later, it never recovered its former glory, despite the success of *Orby*, who two weeks later became the first Irish-trained horse to win the Derby.

BERESFORD STAKES, CURRAGH: TWO-YEAR-OLDS; 8 FURLONGS (GROUP 3)

Dating from 1857, this race is run over one of the stiffest mile courses in the British Isles. Originally designated a Group 2 race, it was down-graded to Group 3 in 1992.

Champion Hurdle, Cheltenham: 2 miles
Introduced into the Cheltenham meeting in 1927 as a hurdle equivalent to the Gold Cup. Among the great winners of this race are *Brown Jack* and the three-time winners *Hatton's Grace*, *Sir Ken*, *Persian War*, *See You Then* and *Istabraq*.

Cheltenham Gold Cup, steeplechase: 3 miles, 2 furlongs
Framed to allow the best horses compete on equal terms, rather than the traditional handicap, the Gold Cup was first run in 1924. The famous *Golden Miller* won the race a record five times in succession; *Arkle* won it three times; but *Prince Regent*, marooned in Ireland in his prime because of the war, won it only once.

Churchill (Winston) Stakes, Hurst Park: 14 furlongs
First run in 1946 as a handicap, the race was won twice by Winston Churchill—with his grey horse *Colonist II* in 1951 and again ten years later with *High Hat*. When Hurst Park closed the race died, probably because Ascot ran a race named the Churchill Stakes on the Saturday after the Royal meeting.

Classic Race
There are five Classic races each year: the Two Thousand Guineas, One Thousand Guineas, Derby, Oaks and St Leger. All are open to fillies, but colts cannot run in the One Thousand Guineas and the Oaks, so a filly can win all five Classics while the most a colt can win is three. Having said that, it is almost impossible for a filly to carry off all the Classics because it involves running in two big races in a few days, twice within a period of one month. The brilliant racemare *Sceptre* nearly managed it in 1902, when she won four Classics and finished fourth in the Derby, for which she started the hot favourite. Previously *Formosa* won four Classics in 1868, but one was a dead heat in the Two Thousand Guineas. *Formosa* did not run in the Derby.

Classic Race (Irish)
Ireland's racing pattern is modelled on the British, but the Irish Triple Crown has only been in place since 1922 and has been won

just twice: *Museum*, with the veteran Steve Donoghue up, in 1935 and Joe McGrath's *Windsor Slipper*, ridden by Morny Wing, in 1942. No filly has managed to win more than two Irish Classic races.

CORONATION CUP, EPSOM: 12 FURLONGS (GROUP 1)

First run in 1902 to celebrate the coronation of King Edward VII. It is essentially a Derby for older horses run over the same course and distance.

DERBY STAKES, EPSOM: THREE-YEAR-OLD COLTS & FILLIES; 12 FURLONGS (GROUP 1)

The greatest horse-race in the world, the Blue Ribbon of the Turf was founded in 1780 by Lord Derby and Sir Charles Bunbury, who tossed a coin to determine whose name the race would carry. Sir Charles lost the toss, but he won the first running of the Derby with *Diomed*. Run in early June, the Derby is the second leg of the colt's Triple Crown.

DERBY (IRISH), CURRAGH: THREE-YEAR-OLD COLTS & FILLIES; 12 FURLONGS (GROUP 1)

A Classic first run in 1866, it is now Ireland's premier flat race. Run at the end of June, the Irish Derby is one of the most valuable races in the Irish calendar. It was sponsored by the Irish Hospitals' Sweepstakes from 1962, the first Classic race to be commercially sponsored.

ECLIPSE STAKES, SANDOWN PARK: 10 FURLONGS

Founded in 1886, the race is popular because it is run in midsummer over the fashionable ten-furlong distance. Always popular with owners, the most famous running of the race was in 1903 when John Gubbins' Derby winner of the previous year, *Ard Patrick*, beat the brilliant filly *Sceptre* and that year's Derby winner *Rock Sand* in a memorable race.

GALWAY HURDLE, HANDICAP: 2 MILES

Run at the Galway festival in late July, the Galway Hurdle was first run in 1913. *Blancona* won the race in 1925 and went on to win the Galway Plate the following year.

GALWAY PLATE, HANDICAP STEEPLECHASE: 2¹/₂ MILES

First run in 1869, *The Liberator* (1875) and *Drogheda* (1897) went on to win the Grand National at Aintree. *Tipperary Boy* won the race three times in a row—the only horse to do so.

GROUP RACE

A system of Pattern Races was agreed between the major Turf authorities in Europe to provide a balanced programme of top, non-handicap races, covering all age groups and run over various distances. Group 1 includes the Classics and the Championship races; Group 2 is for horses just below the top standard, and the races may allow some weight penalties and allowances; Group 3 comprises races that are introductory races to the higher Groups. From 1972 all the Pattern Races were identified with a Group and, depending on the quality of the fields attracted, a race may go up, or drop down a Group when reviewed by the Pattern Committee.

JULY CUP, NEWMARKET: 6 FURLONGS (GROUP 1)

One of the top sprint races in the calendar, it was first run in 1876 and has been won by a number of the top sprinters down the years. However, few are as romantic as *Sundridge*, the only horse to win the race three times, who, despite having a wind problem, rose from Selling Plates, the lowest standard of race, to become a champion. He did the same at stud, starting out at a low fee of nine guineas he became a champion sire and his son, *Sunreigh*, made a mark on the American Turf.

KERRY NATIONAL, LISTOWEL: HANDICAP CHASE; 3 MILES

First run in 1945, the Kerry National is the feature race of the Listowel festival, run annually towards the end of September. The best horse to win the race was the 1997 winner *Doran's Pride*.

KING GEORGE VI & THE QUEEN ELIZABETH STAKES, ASCOT: 12 FURLONGS (GROUP 1)

Dating from 1951, the 'King George' is a tough race for a three-year-old, having to take on older horses after running a number of hard Classic races. Has had its fair share of exciting finishes, but may be a race in decline.

LEOPARDSTOWN CHASE, HANDICAP: 3 MILES

At one time one of the most important steeplechases in the calendar but its February date means it is squeezed between the big races at Leopardstown at Christmas and Cheltenham. *Arkle* won this race three times in the 1960s and each year went on to win the Cheltenham Gold Cup.

NATIONAL STAKES, CURRAGH: TWO-YEAR-OLDS; 7 FURLONGS (GROUP 1)

National Produce Stakes was founded in 1849 and has consistently been one of Ireland's top two-year-old races. The 'Produce' was dropped from the race title in 1960. Designated as a Group 2 race in 1971, it was upgraded to a Group 1 in 1985.

OAKS STAKES, EPSOM: THREE-YEAR-OLD FILLIES; 12 FURLONGS (GROUP 1)

First run in 1779 and named after Lord Derby's Epsom house, the Oaks is really the Derby for fillies and is run at the same meeting in early June.

OAKS (IRISH), CURRAGH: THREE-YEAR-OLD FILLIES; 12 FURLONGS (GROUP 1)

A Classic first run in 1895, it is run in July and is Ireland's most important race for fillies. In 1963 Guinness began a sponsorship that would last twenty-one years, greatly adding to the race's prestige.

ONE THOUSAND GUINEAS, NEWMARKET: THREE-YEAR-OLD FILLIES; 8 FURLONGS (GROUP 1)

Introduced in 1814 as a fillies' version of the Two Thousand Guineas, the first winner was *Charlotte*, whose connections had also won the first running of the Two Thousand Guineas. Like that race and the Derby, the One Thousand Guineas was framed by Sir Charles Bunbury, a steward of the Jockey Club who was deprived of immortality by the fall of a coin at Epsom.

ONE THOUSAND GUINEAS (IRISH), CURRAGH: THREE-YEAR-OLD FILLIES; 8 FURLONGS (GROUP 1)

A Classic run in May, dating from 1922, this race has been gaining in prestige in recent years because the much improved prize money is drawing top-class fillies to the race.

PHOENIX STAKES, CURRAGH: 6 FURLONGS (GROUP 1)

For many years the 'Fifteen Hundred', as it was popularly called, was run over five furlongs at the Phoenix Park. When that course closed in 1990 the race was transferred to Leopardstown, but when the new M50 motorway ended racing over five and a straight six furlongs, the race was moved again, this time to the Curragh.

RAILWAY STAKES, CURRAGH: TWO-YEAR-OLDS; 6 FURLONGS (GROUP 3)

Sponsored by the Great Southern & Western Railway, this race was first run in 1851 and for many years was one of the most valuable races in Ireland. Like its sister race, the Anglesey Stakes, its prestige has waned in recent years and it is now a Group 3 event.

ST LEGER STAKES, DONCASTER: THREE-YEAR-OLD COLTS & FILLIES; 14 FURLONGS (GROUP 1)

The oldest Classic is run in September and was first run in 1776 when a field of six, none of them named, lined up for the Starter. The subsequently named *Allabaculia*, owned by the Marquis of Rockingham, won the race, which was the first ever run for three-year-olds at Doncaster. It was one of the last races run on Cantley Common; the meeting was moved to the Town Moor the following year. During a celebration dinner given by the Marquis of Rockingham at the Red Lion Inn it was decided to name the race in honour of Lt-Gen Anthony St Leger, a popular sportsman of the time, whose filly by *Trusty* had finished second to *Allabaculia*. Anthony St Leger actually pronounced his name 'Sellinger' and lived in Park Hill, a mansion situated near Cantley Common, but the race has always been called the Saint Leger.

ST LEGER (IRISH), CURRAGH: THREE-YEAR-OLD & UP COLTS & FILLIES; 14 FURLONGS (GROUP 1)

Run in September, strictly speaking this race is not a Classic anymore having been opened to older horses since 1983. Dating from 1915, *Royal Lancer* (1922) and *Trigo* (1929) were the only horses to have won both the English and Irish St Legers. *Vinnie Roe* won this race three times in succession in 2001–2004.

STEWARDS CUP, GOODWOOD; HANDICAP: 6 FURLONGS

From 1834 the Senior Acting Steward of the Goodwood meeting presented a Cup valued £100 for a race of their choosing, consequently the distances varied from year to year. When it transpired that the race over six furlongs was the most successful, the Cup was allotted to the six-furlong handicap from 1840.

TRIPLE CROWN

An honorary title bestowed on horses that win three Classic races. Fifteen colts have won the Triple Crown of the Two Thousand Guineas, Derby and St Leger, the last being *Nijinsky* in 1970. Nine fillies have won the Triple Crown consisting of the One Thousand Guineas, Oaks and St Leger, *Oh So Sharp* (1985) being the last to have done so.

TWO THOUSAND GUINEAS, NEWMARKET: THREE-YEAR-OLD COLTS & FILLIES; 8 FURLONGS (GROUP 1)

Sir Charles Bunbury, a steward of the Jockey Club, introduced this race to complement the prestigious Derby and St Leger. First run in 1809, the prize fund was guaranteed at 2,000 guineas (£2,100), which was how it got its name. Run in April, the inaugural winner was *Wizard*, owned by Christopher 'Kit' Wilson from Tadcaster, Yorkshire, trained by T. Perren and ridden by Bill Clift. By coincidence, the three also won the inaugural running of the One Thousand Guineas five years later with *Charlotte*.

TWO THOUSAND GUINEAS (IRISH), CURRAGH: THREE-YEAR-OLD COLTS & FILLIES; 8 FURLONGS (GROUP 1)

This Classic race was inaugurated in 1921 and is run in May each year.

INDEX